AA never coherent

1965 EO — LBJ
1974 EO — RmN

outreach VS. pref (172)

p.164 →

W9-AUS-975

TURNING BACK

TURNING BACK

The Retreat from Racial Justice
in American Thought and Policy

STEPHEN STEINBERG

BEACON PRESS

BOSTON

Beacon Press
25 Beacon Street
Boston, Massachusetts 02108-2892

Beacon Press books
are published under the auspices of
the Unitarian Universalist Association of Congregations.

99 98 97 96 95   8 7 6 5 4 3 2 1

Text design by Christine Taylor
Composition by Wilsted & Taylor

Library of Congress Cataloging-in-Publication Data

Steinberg, Stephen.
    Turning back : the retreat from racial justice in American
thought and policy / Stephen Steinberg.
        p.   cm.
    Includes bibliographical references and index.
    ISBN 0-8070-4110-6
    1. United States—Race relations.   2. Race
discrimination—Government policy—United States.
3. Affirmative action programs—United States.
I. Title.
E185.615.S744   1995
305.8'00973—dc20   95-23053
                                                               CIP

*Dedicated to Danny and Joanna
with hope that their generation can fulfill
Martin Luther King's celebrated dream.*

Contents

Preface

> Look around. Can't you see the tensions in Watts?
> Can't you feel the fear in Scarsdale?
> Can't you sense the alienation in Simi Valley?
> The despair in the South Bronx?
> The rage in Brooklyn?
> We cannot play ostrich. Democracy cannot flourish amid
> fear. Liberty cannot bloom amid hate. Justice cannot
> take root amid rage. We must go against the prevailing wind.
>
> Justice Thurgood Marshall, July 4, 1992

Through most of its history the United States *has* "played ostrich," failing to address, much less remedy, the racial divisions and inequalities that are the legacy of slavery. Much the same thing can be said of social science, despite the vast body of scholarship and writing that purport to deal with issues of race and racism. The triumph of liberal social science—the source of much self-congratulation (at least until the 1994 publication of *The Bell Curve*)—was its invalidation of the biological theories that once provided spurious scientific legitimation for the caste system. As is commonly acknowledged, however, social science failed to anticipate the eruption of racial conflict in the 1950s and 1960s, arguably the most important domestic event of the post–World War II era. Less often acknowledged is the failure of social science to identify civil rights as an issue until forced to do so by the rise of black insurgency.

The racial crisis, however, jolted social scientists out of their complacency and demanded new models that could shed light on the forces that were tearing American society apart. Not only did social science break with past assumptions, but it also opened the canon to

ix

minority and radical voices that had previously been marginalized. The result was a "scholarship of confrontation" that fulfilled Richard Wright's exhortation to present the Negro problem "in all of its hideous fullness, in all of the totality of its meaning."

This intellectual renaissance was short-lived, however—truncated before it could fully develop an alternative paradigm to the one that had prevailed prior to the civil rights upheaval. Instead we have witnessed a reversion to earlier models and assumptions, fueled by an escalating racial backlash in the society at large. This book attempts to develop a critique of "the scholarship of backlash," and to recover some of the wisdom that emanated from the protest movement. Thus, this book is propelled by Thurgood Marshall's admonition to go against the prevailing wind. It is not a negative debunking, however. Rather it is an attempt to contribute to the revitalization of social science as an agent of the principles that Marshall alluded to: democracy, liberty, and justice.

Going against the prevailing wind, in the spirit that Thurgood Marshall meant it, is both challenging and mentally exhausting. It is easier, as every airborne creature knows, to have the wind at your back. It can also be lonely. I was spared the perils of intellectual isolation by colleagues at Queens College who embody critical thinking at its best. I also received much support from Phyllis and Julius Jacobson, the editors of *New Politics*, a journal that thrives on challenging the prevailing orthodoxies.

My intellectual debt to Bob Blauner is evident throughout this book. As a graduate student at Berkeley, I was influenced not only by his teaching, but also by the critical spirit that he brought to the intellectual enterprise. He also provided me with valuable criticism on chapters of this book, as did other colleagues and friends: Gertrude Ezorsky, Raymond Franklin, Gordon Lafer, Hylan Lewis, Soloman Resnick, John Rex, Adolph Reed, Benjamin Ringer, Ron Scapp, and Emanuel Tobier.

Over the years I have benefited from a stimulating intellectual dialogue with students in the Ph.D. Program in Sociology at the CUNY

Graduate Center, especially Janet Amerasinghe, Vallentino Ellis, Bruce Haynes, Youngmi Lim, Donal Malone, and Neil Mc-Laughlin. As this roster of names suggests, I have profited immensely from the diversity that is the hallmark of the City University of New York. How else does one get outside the interior provinces of one's mind?

The life of the mind is inextricably bound with life itself, and I want to acknowledge my debt to my family: to my mother who imbued me with a liberal ethos; to my father who fought against the prevailing winds in his life; to Sharon who has been my intellectual soulmate; and to Danny and Joanna, who challenged me to look to the future.

Finally, my thanks to Deb Chasman, my editor at Beacon Press, for her scrupulous editing and good judgment, and to Nancy Evans of Wilsted & Taylor who copyedited the manuscript with surgical precision.

My Education as a Teacher of Race Relations

> He has understood the system so well because
> he felt it first as his own contradiction.
>
> Jean-Paul Sartre, Introduction to Albert Memmi's
> *The Colonizer and the Colonized*, 1965

Nineteen seventy-one was the best of times and the worst of times in American higher education. For somebody about ready to fall out of the academic cradle—that is, to receive a Ph.D.—jobs were plentiful, indeed more so than at any time since. In my case, I had completed a nine-year stint in the Sociology Department of the University of California at Berkeley, and decided to forsake all of the seductive pleasures of the West Coast and reclaim my Eastern roots. My California friends winced in disbelief when they heard that I was moving to New York City, which at the time was experiencing a crime wave that spilled over into middle-class neighborhoods. Expatriates from New York—the survivors—would assault me with unsolicited horror stories about muggings, burglaries, and other atrocities. I remember lying awake the first night frozen with fear because the door to my apartment was not yet fortified with a second lock and the other mechanical and electronic devices that, my friends warned me, might slow down but would never stop a determined intruder. My office at the Graduate Center of the City University of New York was on 42nd Street, only a block away from the infamous strip of sleazy cinemas and porno shops—a far cry from the spacious beauty surrounding the Berkeley campus. My job also involved teaching a course on race relations at the uptown campus of the City College of New York, which had just undergone two years of strife leading to an open admissions policy that would permanently transform the racial and ethnic make-up of the student body.

Although jobs were plentiful, the discipline itself was in disarray. The early 1970s marked the midpoint of an intellectual revolution that began in the 1960s, but had yet to reach full blossom. This amounted to what Thomas Kuhn calls "a paradigm shift."[1] Established theory and models came under critical scrutiny, and orthodoxies and assumptions that had long pervaded mainstream sociology were aggressively challenged. Nowhere was this more the case than in the field of race relations. Objections were raised even to this nomenclature, which, its critics insisted, was anything but value-free. "Race relations," it was held, diverted attention away from the *systemic* sources of racism, and instead treated racial conflict as involving little more than troubled "relations" between groups, presumably rooted in ignorance and fear. "The political economy of race" was the denotation preferred by the new breed of scholars, since this language stressed the structural linkages between racial and ethnic trends and larger political and economic institutions.

As a graduate student at Berkeley, I experienced the reverberations associated with this paradigm shift on a deeply personal level. Third World activists on the Berkeley campus advanced viewpoints that were sharply at odds with the gruel that filled sociological texts on race relations. These uncertified theorists, building on ideas and rhetoric associated with anticolonial revolts in the Third World, contended that America's ghettos, reservations, and barrios were "internal colonies," the result of a process of domination and exploitation similar to that which defined the relationship between European colonizers and their overseas colonies. Years later, scholars would engage in hairsplitting debates about the relevance of the "colonial analogy." What was most important about the colonial analogy, however, was not its specific empirical claims, but its focus on the political and economic dimensions of race that had been studiously neglected by the race relations school.

Implicitly, the colonial model challenged the tendency among social scientists to abstract racist ideologies from the political and economic context that engendered and sustained those ideologies. In the colonial model, racism was not merely a property of discrete individuals, to be measured by batteries of psychological and attitude tests, but an attribute of a society that produced and tolerated systematic inequalities along racial lines. This is what the activists on the front lines meant when they denounced the United States as "a racist society." Eventually this idea was translated into respectable academic jargon with the term "institutionalized racism," which was introduced into the sociological lexicon with the publication of *Black Power*.[2] This book was a collaborative work by Stokely Carmichael, a front-line activist, and Charles Hamilton, a black political scientist. It is a prime example of how an idea spawned by a grassroots political movement made its way into academic discourse.

Although I was not personally involved in political groups or activities during my years at Berkeley, I was certainly affected by the powerful intellectual and political currents swirling around the campus, all the more powerful because of their proximity and the small but often important ways that they impinged on the personal sphere of life. However, my more important connection to the shifting world of race relations was through Robert Blauner, who taught seminars on race and ethnicity in the Department of Sociology and, unlike me, had developed personal ties with student activists associated with the Third World movement. Blauner's disenchantment with the race relations model and his own evolving perspective resulted in a series of essays that were eventually published in his book *Racial Oppression in America*.[3]

In retrospect, it would have been a big help, when I presented myself to my first class at City College in September 1971, to have had *Racial Oppression in America* on my list of required readings, but it was another year before the book was in print. In periods of great intellectual ferment, like the 1960s, there is an inevitable lag between the germination of new ideas and the publication of books, especially texts for college students, that reflect these new ideas.

Instead, I assigned my class *Beyond the Melting Pot*, written by Nathan Glazer and Daniel Patrick Moynihan. Originally published in 1963, the paperback had gone through seven printings and an expanded second edition had just been published. The book seemed tailor-made for my students at City College, inasmuch as it dealt with the five largest minority groups in New York City: blacks, Puerto Ricans, Jews, Italians, and Irish. Free of excessive jargon, the book, I believed then, would certainly engage the interest of students. I must confess, also, that when I first read the book in 1963, I found little to take issue with in Glazer and Moynihan's treatment of race and ethnicity. I can say this with certainty because I still have my copy of the original 1963 edition, and it is filled mostly with respectful highlighting and notations in the margins. However, the 1970 edition that has served me over the last quarter-century is blotched with X's, question marks, exclamation points, and expletives, all signifying critical responses ranging from disbelief to outrage. What passed as unimpeachable social science in 1963 appeared as tendentious drivel by the 1970s. Such are the perils of a paradigm shift![4]

Despite my reservations, it was difficult to resist a book that dealt with the five largest minority groups in New York City in a single volume. Thus, *Beyond the Melting Pot* was part of the intellectual baggage I carried with me, literally, on my journey to City College. This began on the Upper West Side where the subway car was predominantly white. By 96th Street the car was racially mixed, probably more so than any other place in New York City. After 115th Street, where Columbia University is located, I was conspicuously in the minority. Finally, at 137th Street, the stop for City College, Glazer, Moynihan, and I entered a world populated almost entirely by people of color.

It was with no small degree of apprehension that I walked the metaphoric plank between the subway and the CCNY campus. This hill—with its perils, both real and imagined—was the symbolic stumbling block to the sociological imagination. To get beyond the conventional assumptions regarding race and class, so egregiously represented in *Beyond the Melting Pot*, I would have to gain control

over the apprehensions that this neighborhood aroused in me. In saying this, I do not mean that I had to undergo some kind of ritualistic
mastery of fear. Although I made at least sixty expeditions that year
to the college on the hill without incident, a colleague, also from
Berkeley, had the sobering experience of being mugged at knife-
point. As a streetwise New Yorker, I have learned not to engage in romantic denial of the dangers lurking behind the poverty line. But as a
politically conscious person, a product of the sixties, I have also
learned not to allow fear and self-interest to dictate my politics and
my sensibilities.

The challenge that the hill represented was less to emotion than to
intellect. What sociological inferences were to be drawn about this
ghetto neighborhood: the shabby tenements, littered streets, aban-
doned houses and cars, groups of young men hanging out on stoops
and corners, and dealers brazenly peddling drugs? All of the props
were in place for a retelling of the stock morality tale that pervades *Beyond the Melting Pot* and most sociological texts. In the master narrative of this tale, civic virtue, moral principle, and social ideals are
all imperiled by an array of (literally) dark and sinister forces. Different storytellers have produced variations of this tale, focusing on different aspects of the Black Nemesis: of chronic social disorganization
and a tangle of pathology; of a breakdown of the norms that govern
middle-class society; of a deviant subculture that tolerates and even
sanctions criminal behavior; of a welfare dependency that destroys
initiative and rewards sloth; of broken families and fragmented communities that eviscerate the social bond; and of a self-perpetuating
culture of poverty that, in the bald language of the 1965 Moynihan
report on the black family, "is capable of perpetuating itself without
assistance from the white world."[5] There is much evidence, at least
of a superficial nature, to support all of these inferences, since the
very poor—those who constitute the underclass—do not comport
themselves according to the norms that are assumed, often incor-
rectly, to prevail among the middle and upper classes. The statistics,
like those compiled for the Moynihan report, present a bleak picture
of broken families, of children born out-of-wedlock, of welfare de-

pendency, of school dropouts and delinquency, and so on. The question is not whether such facts exist or whether they should be discussed, but rather how they should be *interpreted*: whether these observations are accepted at face value, or whether they are placed within a larger historical and social context; whether as social scientists we indulge in gratuitous moral judgments, or whether we *explain* the behavior that violates prevailing codes of morality; that is, whether we label this behavior as antisocial and treat it as self-explaining, or whether we establish the *linkages* between the behavior we can observe and the more distant and less visible social forces that are ultimately responsible for the production and reproduction of the ghetto and all its notorious ills. Paradoxically, these more remote forces are more easily discerned, not at close range, but from the ivory tower at the top of the hill.

Over twenty years have passed since I taught that first class at CCNY, and I do not recall in specific detail how my students responded to *Beyond the Melting Pot*. I do remember, though, that my black students were deeply affronted by passages in the text. What they displayed was not anger so much as disbelief. Like most students, my students at CCNY started out with a naive faith in "higher" education, and did not expect to encounter the base distortions and misrepresentations that they had come to expect in the society at large. When they encountered racism, even with an academic gloss, it left them with a feeling of bitter disappointment. Their frustration was often vented on white students who found in the text sanction for their own prejudices, and this occasionally led to acrimonious exchanges. As the instructor, I reveled in the fact that these classes were lively, but probably was not sufficiently mindful of the hidden injuries of race and the impact that these "lively" exchanges had on minority students. One day I noticed that a student was dawdling in the corridor for the entire class. Afterwards I chided her for not coming in, whereupon she revealed that she had deliberately kept some distance from the nerve-racking tension inside the classroom.

On another occasion I was lecturing on the origins of racism. Citing Winthrop Jordan's study *White Over Black*, I observed that even before Europeans discovered Africa, a host of negative attributes were associated with the color black, including darkness, death, and the diabolical. A black hand was promptly raised in the back of the classroom, and the student informed me, with undisguised irony, that "we knew it was there all along." In a flash I realized that his comment had far-reaching implications that I had not fully comprehended. If Europeans did not "discover" Africa, then how much more of the field of race relations had been constructed from an unconsciously white perspective? Icons came smashing down. The "discovery" of America, the "conquest" of the West, the "emancipation" of slaves, the "immigrant odyssey"—indeed, all aspects of our national history—including the idea of nation itself—needed to be reexamined taking minority perspectives into account.

I do not mean to imply that I relied on such encounters with students to develop a critical perspective on the field of race relations. Often students do not have the sophistication or the self-confidence to openly challenge a professor or the author of a hallowed text. Although some students, like the one just cited, did make insightful comments that influenced my own evolving perspective, a more subtle mechanism was at work. I had brought *Beyond the Melting Pot* deep into the heart of Harlem, through that impoverished neighborhood, to a class where blacks had more than a token presence. These students became the prism through which the text was refracted. I read it as I imagined they did, or, to be more precise, as I would have if I were they. In effect, I came to identify with "the other" in a way that would scarcely have been possible in a class where the students were, like me, white and middle-class. Thus, the mere fact of having an interracial class helped me to get critical distance, not only from the canon, but also from my own assumptions.

In saying this, I am not advancing a racial epistemology that privileges insiders—in this case, blacks—with greater knowledge of themselves than outsiders can attain.[6] Just because my black students were offended by certain of Glazer's claims does not mean that they are right and Glazer is wrong.[7] Indeed, insiders easily develop group loyalties and sensitivities that might lead them to reject facts and interpretations that are unpleasant or compromising. Nor am I suggesting that there is a black point of view shared, more or less, by all African Americans. Nor am I unmindful that some black scholars endorse Glazer's theories of race; indeed, they are spouting up with increasing frequency these days (often with laudatory blurbs by Glazer on the dust jackets of their books!). Granted, there is no equation between race and truth. The point, however, is that, prior to the mid-sixties, virtually no minority voices and perspectives were represented within social science. In the case of *Beyond the Melting Pot*, the editors, reviewers, and audience were predominantly white, and there were few black students in Glazer's classes who might have offered him that invaluable prism on his own ideas.[8]

Like all writers, Glazer's perspective and sensibilities were molded out of his life experiences. One wonders if he would have written a different book if he had had more intimate knowledge of or association with black America. At least the following gaffe in his chapter on "Negroes" would scarcely have been possible: "It is not possible for Negroes to view themselves as other ethnic groups viewed themselves because—and this is the key to much in the Negro world—the Negro is only an American, and nothing else. He has no values and culture to guard and protect. He insists that the white world deal with his problems, because . . . he is so much the product of America." In the introduction to the 1970 edition, Glazer discloses that this passage has caused him "considerable pain," presumably because of criticism that he received from black scholars. Having had time to reconsider, he offers the following revision: "It is not possible for Negroes to view themselves as other ethnic groups did because the Negro is so much an American, the distinctive product of America. He bears no foreign values and culture that he feels the need to guard from the surrounding environment. He insists that the white world deal with his problems because, since he is so much the product of America, they are not *his* problems, but everyone's."[9] Glazer has not recanted very much. He fails utterly to see that African Americans have evolved a distinctive cultural system out of their unique experience on American soil. This oversight is all the more astonishing since Glazer and Moynihan make this very point with respect to white ethnic groups. [10]

No amount of equivocation or mincing of words can excuse Glazer's failure to recognize that, no less than other "hyphenated" Americans, African Americans possess all the essential elements of a viable ethnicity: a common ancestry and history; a sense of peoplehood; a multiplicity of social, religious, and cultural institutions; and a distinctive culture clearly evident in language, art, music, literature, and every other creative and aesthetic form. What are we to make of the fact that Glazer virtually negates Puerto Rican culture as well? After waxing poetic about the importance of culture and family as countervailing forces to poverty, he writes:

> In both these aspects Puerto Rico was sadly defective. It was weak in folk arts, unsure of its cultural traditions, without a powerful faith. . . . Nor was there much strength in the Puerto Rican family. . . . Children were loved in Puerto Rico—this was fortunate since there were so many. And yet many observers believed that their mothers often loved them to the point of overprotection to make up for neglect by their husbands. [11]

Glazer's disparagement of black and Puerto Rican culture is all the more striking against the background of the sentimental and almost adulatory treatment that he and Moynihan accord to Jewish and Irish culture. The crowning irony is that in reviewing the 1963 edition of *Beyond the Melting Pot* for the *New York Times Book Review*, Oscar Handlin opined that "the two chapters on the Negroes and the Puerto Ricans are excellent," but found the chapters on Jews, Italians, and Irish "less satisfactory." [12]

With the scholar's voice of reason and objectivity, conveyed through his polished prose, Glazer elevated the "conventional wisdom" to the level of social theory, thus imparting it with scientific legitimacy. Below are five other passages that amount to little more than a pseudoscientific iteration of ordinary stereotypes:

Perhaps another way in which Negroes differed from European immigrant groups was that they did not develop the same kind of clannishness, they did not have the same close family ties, that in other groups created little pools for ethnic businessmen and professionals to tap.[13]

In the end, the most important factor [in explaining the lack of Negro businesses] is probably the failure of Negroes to develop a pattern of saving. The poor may have nothing to save, but even those better off tend to turn earnings immediately into consumption.[14]

The array of jobs potentially available for Negro men and boys in New York raises special problems. There is a great clothing industry, but although the Jewish male found work at sewing machines no threat to his manliness, other males have not been so adaptable. Neither the Negro nor the Puerto Rican man seems to find the garment industry attractive.[15]

The Negro middle class contributes very little, in money, organization, or involvement, to the solution of Negro social problems.[16]

And yet one cannot help asking: why were schools that were indifferent to the problems of the children of other groups, forty and fifty years ago, adequate enough for them, but seem nevertheless inadequate for the present wave of children? . . . There is little question where the major part of the answer must be found: in the home and family and community—not in its overt values, which . . . are positive in relation to education, but in its conditions and circumstances. It is there that the heritage of two hundred years of slavery and a hundred years of discrimination is concentrated; and it is there that we find the serious obstacles to the ability to make use of a free educational system to advance into higher occupations and to eliminate the massive problems that afflict colored Americans and the city.[17]

The subtext to Glazer's disquisition on Negroes seems to be that Negroes are not Jews! According to the myth that Glazer helped to spin, Jews escaped poverty through their exemplary value system. Jews had cohesive families and communities. Jewish immigrants scrimped, saved, and sacrificed to claw their way out of poverty. Jewish men worked at sewing machines without fretting about their manhood. Uptown Jews extended philanthropy to their downtown cousins. And a distinctive passion for education provided immigrant Jews with a crucial strategy for escaping poverty. According to Glazer, blacks languished in poverty not because of any innate inferiority, but because centuries of racism had ravaged their culture, leaving them without the strengths of family, neighborhood, and community that sustained Jews in their pursuit of the American dream.

That *Beyond the Melting Pot* was the recipient in 1963 of the *Saturday Review of Literature*'s Anisfeld-Wolf Award for its contribution to improved intergroup relations might be dismissed as an ironic comment on the times. However, the book's influence on the field cannot be so easily dismissed. Here in this acclaimed book was the framework for an updated sociology that accepted blame for the *origins* of America's race problem, but that deviously shifted the responsibility for present-day racial inequalities onto blacks themselves. As Glazer wrote in the concluding sentence of his chapter—his final affront to my students: "whatever the origins of the burden, on whose shoulders does it fall, and how can it best be overcome?"[18]

That New York City's one million blacks were consigned to live in several huge ghettos; that their neighborhoods, schools, housing, and living conditions were all far below the standard of the surrounding white community; and that they suffered pervasive discrimination in the job markets that denied them the possibility of escaping these impoverished ghettos—none of this receives more than passing mention in *Beyond the Melting Pot*. Consistent with this shifting of blame, Glazer ends the chapter with a call for greater self-examination and self-help on the part of blacks, who must overcome not racism, but their own cultural impediments. Such was Nathan Glazer's contribution to the field of race relations in 1963, as the civil rights movement approached its historic climax.

After two years at CCNY, I accepted an invitation to teach at Queens College, which was acclaimed as "the jewel" of the City University, and offered a campus life relatively free of the tensions that were so palpable at CCNY. However, I more often found myself at intellectual loggerheads with my students at Queens College. I came to define my pedagogical mission as one of disabusing them of their misconceptions with respect to race, ethnicity, and class. In a sense, I sought to bring them on the same intellectual journey that I had taken in my professional life.

My Queens College students have presented a formidable challenge to my powers of persuasion. Most come from families who have themselves struggled to pull themselves out of poverty. Many are of recent immigrant background, believe in the American Dream, and look unfavorably on groups whom they passed on their journey to the middle class. In a sense, my students have personified the divisions of race and class that were the subject of the course. I sought to provide them with a perspective that was different, and in ways fundamentally opposed, to the one they brought into the classroom. I welcomed their tenacity in defending their beliefs, even as I struggled with equal tenacity to subject these beliefs to critical examination. It was a tug-of-war over contested intellectual terrain, with my authority as a teacher counterbalanced by their sheer numbers.

Teaching and research do not have the clear division for me that they have for most professors, because I have come to realize that my students' ideas about race, ethnicity, and class are only less sophisticated variants of ideas that pervade mainstream social science. Social scientists, after all, are deeply immersed in the societies that they study, and despite their best efforts to be "objective," this turns out, for many good reasons, to be an elusive goal. Inevitably, and often unconsciously, social scientists make inferences or advance interpretations based on limited, personal experience, reflecting their personal values and convictions. At their best, social scientists transcend the personal domain, with the help of a disciplined body of theory and research, and advance fresh new ideas. At their worst, however, social scientists merely take ordinary beliefs and translate them into respectable academic jargon, a pseudoscientific language that camouflages value as fact, and stereotypes as social truth.

Given this overlap between popular mythology and social science, I especially welcomed the challenge that my students represented. By taking on their half-baked and often crude notions about race and class, I found myself rethinking my own presuppositions and honing my arguments against ideas that were firmly ensconced in the profession as well.

When it comes to my colleagues, I feel no compunction in being combative, but I am not so disposed when it comes to my students. Scholars should know better, and ought to be held accountable when they, however unwittingly, act as compradors for a racist system. However, it is hard to blame students for misconceptions that are almost universally held in our society.

The overriding purpose of my course is to explain racial and ethnic hierarchy. My point of departure is the question echoed by my students: "We made it, why haven't they?" There is nothing wrong with this question, I tell my students, so long as it is not asked rhetorically—that is, to foreclose discussion by suggesting that the facts speak for themselves. There *is* something wrong, however, in the presupposition that "we" have qualities that "they" are lacking. The qualities that my students have in mind are precisely the ones that Glazer cites in explaining why Jews, Irish, Italians, and others have been successful, more or less, in comparison to blacks. Chief among these—or so it is claimed—is strength "in the home and family and community," the institutional breeding ground for high aspirations and values that are presumed to lead to success. My position does not deny the obvious: groups *do* differ in their aspirations and values, and in ways that may well affect their prospects for mobility. My point, however, is that these cultural differences, when they exist, properly mark the beginning, not the end, of sociological inquiry. That is to say, cultural differences must be *explained* in terms of their historical and material sources. It is only when culture is taken at face value and treated as self-explaining that we fall into the trap of imputing cultural superiority to groups on the top and cultural inferiority to groups on the bottom.

I well remember one student who stubbornly resisted my arguments as we waded through a number of historical and sociological works. She was from an Italian-American background where "home and family and community" were strong forces in her life, and she was impatient with my seeming disregard or negation of "culture." We scuffled from time to time during the semester, neither of us yielding any ground. Then one day she announced—music to a teacher's ears—that "I think I see what you mean," and proceeded to tell the class the following story:

A woman invited some guests to dinner. As she prepared the dinner roast, her guests noticed that she lopped off a chunk of meat and threw it away. Puzzled by this apparently gratuitous and wasteful act, they asked her why she did that. The question caught her by surprise—she could only say that her mother had always done that. Now, her curiosity aroused, she asked her mother the same question, and got the same answer: *her* mother had always done that. Determined to solve the mystery, she finally put the question to her immigrant grandmother—an old-world matriarch—who shrugged and said: "The pot was too small."

Indeed, this charming story makes my point—that culture must be understood in terms of its material sources and functions. Just as this woman lopped off the side of her beef because the pot was too small, others tailor their aspirations and adapt their strategies for survival when opportunity is restricted. Conversely, individuals and groups who encounter a favorable structure of opportunity respond accordingly, and exhibit high motivation, zeal for work, and the other virtues that we associate with success. Again, my point is not to deny that individuals and groups differ in their values, but rather to *link* their disparate values to different historical situations and external structures. It is a small point, but one that saves us from fatal error.

Aside from serving as energetic sparring partners for my intellectual pugilism, my students at Queens College have also nudged me into new areas of exploration. One memorable example began with a discussion of Richard Gambino's *Blood of My Blood*, a book about the Italian-American experience. In a passage that probably raised few hackles outside my classroom, Gambino observes that, even as immigrants, Italian women rarely worked as domestics. To quote Gambino: "No matter how poor, the Italian-American woman to this day does not work as a domestic. For to work in the house of another family (sometimes an absolute economic necessity in the old land) is seen as a usurpation of family loyalty by her family *and by her*. And if one loses one's place in la via vecchia, there is no self-respect."[19] In this instance it was an Irish hand that went up, and my student, a detective in the New York City Police Department, was on the attack. What is Gambino saying about the Irish? That they *liked* working as domestics? That they *lacked* family pride? That Irish men were any *less* protective of their wives and daughters? His own mother had worked as a domestic, and he rejected the unstated (and therefore untested) assumptions of Gambino's self-congratulatory treatment of Italians.

Yet it was a matter of historical fact that few Italians and surprisingly large numbers of Irish worked as domestics. How was this to be explained? The books I consulted also lapsed into cultural reductionism, suggesting that Irish had a "cultural tolerance" for domestic work that was absent among other groups. Like my student, I rejected the notion that cleaning somebody else's toilets could ever be a matter of "occupational choice." I resolved to research the question myself, and this eventually resulted in a chapter in my book *The Ethnic Myth* entitled "Why Irish Became Domestics and Italians and Jews Did Not." The answer was unusually clear-cut. Because of a collapse of Ireland's agricultural economy, the family system was shattered and large numbers of Irish women immigrated on their own. This was rarely the case for Italian or Jewish women. Because they were fleeing persecution, most Jews immigrated as families. In the case of Italians, it was typical for the male breadwinner to make the journey first and, once he had established an economic foothold, to send for his wife and children. For Irish women who lacked a male provider, the prospect of working as a live-in domestic offered them a roof over their head and a modest income. It was only a temporary expedient, however, and their daughters exhibited no greater proclivity for domestic work than did the daughters of Italian and Jewish immigrants.

A year or two later, when I presented this analysis to a class of adult students, I encountered adamant resistance from an older Irish student whose mother also had worked as a domestic. She insisted that her mother did exhibit a "cultural tolerance" for domestic work, that she regarded it as a worthy vocation, that she had genuine affection for her employers, and that she had no regrets about her life. It is easy to write, as I did in *The Ethnic Myth*, that "to affirm class is not to deny culture," but it is not easy to convince people of this proposition when it *seems* to be at odds with their life experience. As I tried to explain to my student, individuals and groups always rationalize what *is*, especially when they have little choice in the matter. If no other avenues of opportunity exist, if domestic work is your best "shot," if it assures your economic survival, if your employers are decent, then it is not surprising that individuals and groups will find ways to rationalize their situation. As they tell themselves, "you have to make the best of it." The key point, however, is that this attitude is essentially a compromise with reality, not a cultural "value" that exists independently of these contingencies. The proof is that whatever accommodation her mother made to her situation, my student was not raised to be a domestic, nor would she have accepted this as her lot in life.

Currently, blacks comprise only 8 percent of the student body at Queens College, a far smaller percentage than at CCNY. They differ in their social background as well. Some are children of immigrants from the Caribbean who arrived with education and skills. Many of the African-American students also come from middle-class families, and their social outlook is shaped as much by class as by race. For example, one black student enrolled in my class on urban poverty sheepishly told me that she grew up believing that welfare was for poor blacks. At other times, however, race manifested itself in unanticipated ways. After a black woman was crowned Miss America for the first time, I asked my students what they thought. The white students were cynical: it was just window dressing; it would not change anything; it was a totally insignificant event that would soon be forgotten. My black students, on the other hand, regarded the crowning of a black Miss America as a momentous event. To them, it was a validation of black beauty, and therefore of themselves. At first I thought they were buying into the inanity of the Miss America contest, but then I recalled Malcolm X's graphic description in his autobiography of conking his hair with lye ("this was my first really big step toward self-degradation").[20] Against this background, "the first black Miss America" was indeed a momentous event.

If there is truth in the saying that the view from the top is different from the view from the bottom, this applies with equal force to the horizontal view across the racial divide. I do not mean to suggest that my black and white students were always at odds with one another, for this was not the case. Even when they were in essential agreement, however, they often had a subtle difference in perspective. For example, one semester our class undertook an experiment to test for racial discrimination in housing. Two students, one black and one white, were sent to the same realtors, ostensibly to rent an apartment. Invariably, the black student was either "cooled out" or steered to inferior properties in "black neighborhoods." This experience evoked different emotions in the two students. The white student was shocked and outraged at this display of naked racism. The black student, however, had a déjà vu attitude, which seemed to temper his sense of outrage. He told the class that he felt sorry for the white realtors as they squirmed and dissembled. He was embarrassed for them as well as for himself. His overriding emotion was not anger so much as it was disdain, verging on contempt. Indeed, it is probably easier for white America to comprehend the anger of its racial victims than it is to imagine that blacks might actually regard their oppressors with disdain.

It bears repeating that I do not claim that there is a single "black perspective" or that because an argument is advanced by a black person, it is necessarily more plausible or valid. On the other hand, it can hardly be denied that blacks are bound to approach discussions of race from a different vantage point. Nor can it be denied that black perspectives have rarely been represented in mainstream social science. Perhaps it is their doctrinaire faith in "the scientific method" that allows social scientists to write about groups that they barely know first-hand. Writers of fiction almost never take this license despite the fact that, unlike social scientists, they are not bound by rules of evidence. Would Philip Roth, even in his wildest imagination, contemplate writing *Native Son*? Would Richard Wright presume to write *Goodbye Columbus*? Can "facts" ever be interpreted outside any context of experience? Perhaps this is why so much social science perpetuates myth, while novelists so often penetrate societal fictions about the racial experience.

There is yet another reason to heed the insider's point of view.

Whites, at least collectively, have incentive to distort racial reality. They do so in order to gloss over unpleasant truths that evoke guilt, that undermine their faith in American institutions, or that necessitate remedial action that is not in their self-interest. For opposite reasons, blacks are less prone to an uncritical acceptance of the collective rationalizations and myths that justify or excuse racial hierarchy.

Perhaps the paramount lesson that I have learned as a teacher of race relations in a polyglot university has to do with the inescapable subjectivity of ideas. There is not one truth, but many truths, and they must be balanced against each other. Like a kaleidoscope, the fragments of social "data" assume dramatically different configurations and meanings depending upon one's vantage point. Does this mean that we are trapped in a hopeless subjectivity, that one interpretation is as good as the next? Not necessarily. In the first place, we can use this epistemological cynicism to see through the knowledge claims that merely serve established institutions. Then, once we give up our innocence—which for me, involved the realization that Glazer and Moynihan's acclaimed book was riddled with bias and error—we are free to explore alternative perspectives and interpretations. Herein lies the paradox that vitalizes the intellectual enterprise. By forsaking the idea that there is a single truth to be discovered, we overcome a major barrier to the discovery of new and unexpected truths.

1

RACIAL LIBERALISM
The Rise and Fall of a Paradigm

1

An American Dilemma
A New Liberal Orthodoxy on Race

> Myrdal does not bring to light the social determinants
> of this well-known dilemma; he merely
> recognizes it and rails against its existence.
>
> Oliver C. Cox, *Caste, Class, and Race,* 1948

Monumental" is the modifier most commonly attached to Gunnar
Myrdal's study *An American Dilemma*. Ever since its publication in
1944, critics and scholars routinely refer to "that monumental study
of race relations in the United States," conducted by the Swedish
economist Gunnar Myrdal.[1] How does a book—especially a book on
so fraught a subject as race in America—become a "monument"?
Who makes this judgment? On what criteria? And what, exactly, is
being celebrated? Is it the wisdom compiled between the covers? Is it
that Myrdal unearthed facts previously unknown or shed new light on
familiar facts? Or rather is it that, like beauty, "monumental" is in the
eye of the beholder?

Obviously, the critics, not the author, determine whether a book is
relegated to that dreaded trashbin of history, or whether it is acclaimed and elevated to the pantheon of "classics." What begs for explanation is *why* Myrdal's opus was embraced as the definitive and
authoritative work on race in America. This distinction lasted for
nearly two decades, but it would not endure forever. As the nation
was thrust into a full-blown racial crisis in the early 1960s, it became
clear not only that Myrdal had failed to anticipate black insurgency
and the civil rights upheaval, but that his acclaimed theoretical

framework was of little value in making sense of these unanticipated events. As will be seen, the same factors that explain Myrdal's reign of popularity for two decades also explain his ultimate fall from intellectual grace. "Truth," one might say, had been vitiated by history.

Of course, there was something monumental in the sheer dimensions of *An American Dilemma*. The book consisted of forty-five chapters and, together with its ten appendixes and two hundred fifty pages of notes, covered over thirteen hundred pages. In terms of cost, the research was also unprecedented—the equivalent of roughly three million current dollars. In the midst of the Depression, Myrdal was paid an annual salary that was the equivalent of roughly $200,000 in current dollars.[2] Large sums were also paid out to collaborators who were commissioned to conduct independent studies and to write memoranda that provided much of the raw material that Myrdal, together with Richard Sterner and Arnold Rose, wove into *An American Dilemma*. Published under the imprimatur of the prestigious Carnegie Corporation, the book was widely reviewed in the popular press and was an instant success.[3]

On the other hand, success does not a monument make. What explains the book's extraordinary appeal and its enduring reputation?[4] How is it that this study, in the words of Myrdal's biographer, "established a liberal orthodoxy on black-white relations and remained the most important study of the race issue until the middle of the 1960s"?[5] Clearly, *An American Dilemma* was the right book at the right time. To say this, however, begs the issue unless we specify exactly what it was about the book and the times that made them "right" for each other.

One clue may be found in the factors that prompted the august Carnegie Corporation—the creation of one of the progenitors of American capitalism—to undertake a major study of race in America. According to John Stanfield, author of *Philanthropy and Jim Crow in American Social Science*, the Carnegie Corporation previously was "the most racially exclusive of the major foundations and was very supportive of white supremacy in apartheid societies."[6] It had paid little attention to race, with the exception of small grants to black colleges in the South and to the National Urban League.[7] What explains its newfound interest in race?

An American Dilemma was the brainchild of Newton D. Baker, a trustee of the Carnegie Corporation board who proposed a study on the Negro in America at a meeting of the board in October 1935. Baker, the son of a Confederate soldier, was an erstwhile mayor of Cleveland who served as Secretary of War during the First World War and subsequently became active in civic affairs in Cleveland and Washington. His reasons for proposing a study of the Negro in America can be surmised from private correspondence unearthed by historian Walter Jackson, author of *Gunnar Myrdal and America's Conscience*.[8] In a letter to the Carnegie Corporation in 1934 Baker spoke of the danger of racial conflict in public housing projects in Cleveland. As Jackson writes of Baker: ". . . he had learned about the desperate situation of blacks in northern cities, the inability of private charitable groups to cope with these problems, and *the danger of mounting racial tensions*."[9] This last phrase is worth underscoring because, as will be seen, throughout the twentieth century it was the danger of mounting racial tensions that served as the primary catalyst of both scholarship and political action with respect to "the Negro problem." Indeed, it was this danger that made "the Negro problem" a problem in the first place.

My point is that fear, not philanthropy, was the driving force behind the Carnegie Corporation's decision to underwrite a major study of race in America. Newton Baker was hardly motivated by an altruistic impulse to render assistance to downtrodden blacks. Consider the following paean to slavery by this son of a Confederate soldier, excerpted from a letter that Baker wrote in 1935 to Frederick Keppel, president of the Carnegie Corporation:

I think anybody who has read Anthony Adverse will share my feeling of unlimited amazement at the courage of the white people in this country who received the slaves from slave ships and undertook to make useful laborers of them. How many white civilizations could have dared to receive so many wild savages, who were practically uncaged animals, and spread them around over their farms in contact with their own families passes human comprehension. What has been done for the Negro in a

hundred years is an unparalleled achievement and nothing but a theoretical democratic impatience can make us critical of it, though, of course, much more remains
to be done. [10]

Of course, it would not be fair to use Baker's paternalism and un-
varnished racism to impugn the motives of the Carnegie trustees who
made the decision to underwrite Myrdal's study. This decision was
not made in a vacuum, however. Nor was it primarily motivated by
any sense of moral outrage over the wrongs visited upon blacks: their
abject poverty and the systematic violation of their civil rights had
never captured the attention of the trustees before. What was new was
that "the Negro problem" had migrated from South to North, where
the pressures emanating from the expanding urban ghettos were beginning to capture *national* attention. America's racial pariah was
about to be resurrected from what Orlando Patterson calls "a social
death" and to be thrust onto the stage of history.

The most important factor was the Depression—not because "depression" was new to blacks, but because it set into motion a series of
changes that would lead inexorably to the civil rights revolution two
decades later. The collapse of Southern agriculture, compounded by
New Deal policies that paid subsidies to landowners who took their
land out of production, uprooted hundreds of thousands of black
sharecroppers and tenant farmers, many of whom gravitated to black
communities in the North. Arriving at a time when even "Negro
jobs" were being taken over by whites, these newcomers were often
unable to find employment. In Harlem, for example, unemployment among blacks in 1932 ran between 40 and 50 percent, twice the
level of the city's white population. [11] Nationally, two million blacks,
half the urban black population, were on relief, though the benefits
were meager. With increasing pauperization came broken families,
crime, and the other "social ills" that Newton Baker fretted about in
his letter to the Carnegie Corporation.

Baker's apprehension about mounting racial tensions did not reflect any unusual prescience on his part. In March 1935—seven
months before Baker made his proposal before a meeting of the Carnegie board of trustees—a riot had erupted in Harlem. Unlike pre-

vious race riots where blacks were victims of white violence—"po-groms" would be a more apt term—the Harlem Riot was essentially a venting of black resentment, aimed at property rather than people. The precipitating factor was the arrest of a teenager accused of pilfer-ing a penknife at Kress's Department Store on 125th Street. A crowd assembled and a rumor spread that the boy had been beaten to death by the police. In the mayhem that ensued, Kress's was ran-sacked and looted, and as the mob traveled down 125th Street, stores were trashed, looted, and set ablaze. By the time order was restored the next morning, the casualty list included 100 persons stabbed, beaten, or shot, 250 shop windows smashed, 125 men arrested, and 3 dead—killed by police bullets.

Thus, even from the Carnegie Corporation's gilded offices on Fifth Avenue, it was becoming clear that a sea change in race relations was in the making. More was involved than the social disorder emanating from Northern ghettos. Concentrated as they were in industrial states rich in electoral votes, blacks were emerging as a major factor in na-tional politics. The Depression severed black loyalty to the party of Lincoln, and in the 1934 Congressional elections Democrats openly bid for black votes for the first time, touting the benefits that had ac-crued to blacks under New Deal programs. "In no national election since 1860," according to *Time* magazine, "have politicians been so Negro-minded as in 1936."[12] Other signs of racial transformation abounded: Eleanor Roosevelt's personal crusade against discrimina-tion, disfranchisement, and lynching helped to strip racism of moral legitimation; the legacy of the Harlem Renaissance, snuffed out by the Depression, manifested itself in stubborn racial pride and politi-cal militancy; the development of a liberal social science challenged scientific racism and rejected notions of innate black inferiority; the emergence of Nazism cast America's racist practices in bold relief, and, as Harvard Sitkoff writes, "gave black and white authors an audience receptive to narratives of racial subjugation."[13] These factors combined to give issues of race and racism a new salience and urgency. As early as 1930, the *New York Times* announced it would henceforth spell "negro" with a capital "N" as "a tribute to millions who have risen from a low estate into 'the brotherhood of the races.'"[14] Indeed, the Negro was on the rise, as was awareness and concern with "the Negro problem." Other foundations—especially the Rosenfeld Fund—were funding research projects on race. Within this context, Frederick Keppel, president of the Carnegie Corporation, resolved that it was time "to do more for the Negro."[15]

The next question is why the Corporation decided to recruit a foreigner to direct the study, one who had done no previous research on race and had never even traveled south of the Mason-Dixon line. The official explanation is provided by Frederick Keppel, who writes in his foreword to *An American Dilemma* that the whole question was "so charged with emotion that it appeared wise to seek as the head of the undertaking someone who could approach his task with a fresh mind, uninfluenced by traditional attitudes or by earlier conclusions."[16] But what does it mean to have "a fresh mind" with respect to racial oppression? What were the "traditional attitudes" and "earlier conclusions" that the sponsors wished to avoid? Although the selection of someone far removed from America's racial conflict created an aura of objectivity, it was far from politically innocent. Its real significance becomes clear against the background of another study of race that was launched in 1935. Let us return to the so-called Harlem Riot.

The day after the riot was brought under control, Mayor La Guardia, whom the *Amsterdam News* once referred to as "one of the most fearless friends the Negro has ever had in or out of Congress," appointed a biracial commission composed of religious and civic leaders.[17] The Commission had an unmistakably liberal cast. It included Oswald Garrison Villard, the white publisher of *The Nation*, and A. Philip Randolph, president of the Sleeping Car Porters Union and the most militant black leader of the period. The Commission employed thirty researchers from the Home Relief Bureau, and recruited E. Franklin Frazier as its research director. Frazier was the nation's preeminent black sociologist and head of the Sociology Department at Howard University, where he was dubbed "Forceful Frazier" for his resolute personal style.[18] Frazier was chiefly responsible for the Commission's investigation and ultimate report. As Randolph later recalled, "Frazier was the brains of the group and everybody else, including me, was window dressing."[19]

Eight months later the Commission issued its report under the title *The Negro in Harlem: A Report on Social and Economic Conditions Responsible for the Outbreak of March 19, 1935.* As the title suggests, the Commission construed its mandate broadly. "This relatively unimportant case of juvenile pilfering," the report began, was only "the spark that set aflame the smoldering resentments of the people of Harlem against racial discrimination and poverty in the midst of plenty."[20] Much of the report dwelled on the inadequacies of the relief system, the schools, the health care system, and the police in meeting the needs of Harlem's population. However, the main focus was on the economic factor, which the Commission insisted was the root of the problem. It based this conclusion on a detailed examination of patterns of discrimination in industries and unions that either excluded blacks altogether or relegated them to the worst jobs. Among the facts uncovered by the Commission:

- In a work force of 10,000 the Consolidated Gas Company had only 213 Negroes, employed either as hallmen or porters. New York Edison also had a work force of 10,000 and employed only 65 Negroes in menial positions.

- Negroes accounted for 580 of the 10,000 employees of the Interborough Rapid Transit Company, but they were employed only as messengers, porters, and cleaners.

- The Commission's survey of 238 hotels showed that 60 percent had no Negro employees.

- The Metropolitan Life Insurance Company employed no Negro agents despite the fact that there were thousands of policy holders in Harlem.

- The local chapter of the International Brotherhood of Teamsters and Chauffeurs did not have a single Negro among its 2,000 members. The same was true of the Newspaper Printing Pressmen Union.

- The various locals representing building trades had fewer than 1,000 Negroes in a membership of 40,000.
- In the clothing and textiles unions, which had a membership of over 150,000, there were 6,704 Negroes, mostly in the International Ladies' Garment Workers' Union. Most other unions, including those in the public sector, excluded Negroes altogether.

The Commission concluded that "the first and most fundamental problem of the Negro citizens of Harlem is the economic problem."[21]

Nor did the Commission place the blame on the Depression since, as it observed, "the great mass of the workers in the community live even during normal times close to the subsistence level." Why then were blacks reduced to a state of "perpetual dependency"? Again, the Commission was forthright: "The main social factor which is responsible for this condition is racial discrimination in employment. It is this factor more than any other factor that arouses so much resentment in the Negro worker."[22]

The Commission's report ended with a long list of proposed reforms, but consistent with its view that employment discrimination was central to the other problems that beset the Harlem community, its first recommendation was "that the city enact an ordinance to the effect that no contracts may be given to any firm or labor union that discriminates against Negro workers."[23] This is a stunning proposal. It came ten years before Randolph's March on Washington forced President Roosevelt to issue an executive order imposing a non-discrimination policy on defense contractors, thirty years before the 1964 Civil Rights Act formally proscribed employment discrimination, and forty years before President Johnson issued his executive order mandating all federal contractors to practice non-discrimination, which was key in the development of affirmative-action policy. To say that Frazier and his Commission were ahead of the times is to misplace the emphasis. It would be more accurate to say that white society, including the academic establishment and the liberal foundations, were not ready to contemplate, much less embrace, the simple truths enunciated in Frazier's report.

Thus, when the Carnegie Corporation scoured the Western world for someone to head its study of race, it is clear that it had no interest in "Forceful Frazier" from Howard University, whose exposé of institutionalized racism in New York was combined with a searing analysis of the role that economic institutions played in the maintenance of blacks in a state of "perpetual dependency." Indeed, the report of his Commission was too controversial even for Fiorello La Guardia, who refused to release the report to the public. However, in July 1936, the *Amsterdam News* gleefully announced that it had obtained a copy of the report, which it printed in its entirety. If Frazier's report was suppressed, if its contents were too "controversial," then it behooves us to ask: What was it about *An American Dilemma* that made it politically acceptable?

Scientific Racism: A Paradigm in Crisis

"The last two or three decades," Myrdal wrote in *An American Dilemma*, "have seen a veritable revolution in scientific thought on the racial characteristics of the Negro."[24] Myrdal was alluding to the impact of the nascent social sciences in repudiating the cardinal principle of scientific racism: biological determinism. The idea that blacks were inferior beings—that they were a separate and permanently inferior species—was at least as old as slavery. In the mid-nineteenth century, however, this idea received scientific legitimacy from the biological sciences. The new science of phrenology held that brain size and other aspects of brain morphology were related to mental faculties and personality traits. Its leading practitioner, Dr. Samuel George Morton, author of *Crania Americana*, collected eight hundred skulls from around the world, and came to the conclusion that cranium size was correlated with intelligence.[25] Morton was a New England Quaker, apparently free of racial animus, but his book was seized upon by Southerners who saw it as providing scientific validation for slavery. When he died in 1851, the South's leading medical journal had this eulogy: "We of the South should consider him as our benefactor, for aiding most materially in giving to the negro his true position as an inferior race."[26]

Over the next half century craniometry emerged as an established science, practiced in leading institutions of higher learning. On the premise that mental capacity was located in the head, scientists labored for decades to identify the organic basis of intelligence. Every conceivable aspect of the skull was subjected to meticulous measurement: the size of the brain pan and the brain itself, the convolutions of the brain, the sutures between the skull and bones, the protrusion of the jaw, and the cranial index that distinguished between long and short skulls and was assumed to be related to intelligence. In *The Mismeasure of Man*, Stephen Jay Gould assures us that "the leaders of craniometry were not conscious political ideologues. They regarded themselves as servants of their numbers, apostles of objectivity." But, as Gould also points out, "they confirmed all the common prejudices of comfortable white males—that blacks, women, and poor people occupy their subordinate roles by the harsh dictates of nature."[27]

The idea that black subordination was related to the configuration of the negro skull held sway well into the twentieth century. Consider, for example, the following passage from the 1910 *Encyclopaedia Britannica*:

Mentally the negro is inferior to the white. The remark of F. Manetta, made after a long study of the negro in America, may be taken as generally true of the whole race: "the negro children were sharp, intelligent and full of vivacity, but on approaching the adult period a gradual change set in. The intellect seemed to become clouded, animation giving place to a sort of lethargy, briskness yielding to indolence. We must necessarily suppose that the development of the negro and white proceeds on different lines. While with the latter the volume of the brain grows with the expansion of the brainpan, in the former the growth of the brain is on the contrary arrested by the premature closing of the cranial sutures and lateral pressure on the frontal bone.[28]

Thus did this renowned compendium of knowledge ratify a stock tenet of phrenology which held that the mental capacities of blacks and whites were similar in childhood, but that the shape of the skull constricted the growth of intelligence in blacks. With an air of scientific probity, the *Encyclopaedia* conceded that the evidence was inconclusive, and it went on to speculate that another factor might be at work: "the arrest or even deterioration in mental development is no doubt very largely due to the fact that after puberty sexual matters take the first place in the negro's life and thoughts."[29]

How is it that the scientific establishment not only produced such a bogus theory but clung to it for so long even in the absence of corroborating evidence? There is a sobering lesson here. In *The Structure of Scientific Revolutions* Thomas Kuhn suggests that the acceptance or rejection of a paradigm does not necessarily follow the dictates of evidence because scientists rationalize away any empirical anomalies or counterinstances. As Kuhn writes: "They will devise numerous articulations and ad hoc modifications of their theory in order to eliminate any apparent conflict."[30] The research in craniometry was replete with such anomalies and counterinstances. As early as 1838 an anatomist at the University of Heidelberg compared the brains of fifty whites and blacks and found no appreciable difference.[31] His findings, however, were dismissed by Josiah C. Nott, America's leading exponent of phrenology, on the grounds that the investigator had included Egyptian and Hindu skulls in the white sample.[32] Other studies at the turn of the century found that African blacks and Australian aborigines had dolichocephalic (long and narrow) skulls that were supposedly related to intelligence. The crowning irony (the pun is intended) was when fossil Cro-Magnon skulls turned out to be larger than those of modern Frenchmen.[33] Despite such inconvenient findings, faith in the cephalic index persisted well into the twentieth century.

If the underlying appeal of craniometry was that it imparted racial hierarchy with scientific legitimacy, then part of the reason for its decline was that a new and more convincing methodology had become available: the intelligence test. "What craniometry was for the nineteenth century," Stephen Jay Gould writes, "intelligence testing has become for the twentieth."[34] Here was a *direct* measure of intelligence that obviated the vexing methodological and epistemological questions involved in cranial measurement. As Thomas Gossett observed in his history of racism, "Now it scarcely mattered how the races differed physically; the point was that a method had been devised which seemed to prove that all the nonwhite races are intellectually inferior."[35] Soon after the Stanford-Binet scales of intelligence were perfected in 1916, they were administered to no fewer than 1,700,000 men in the armed forces. Some of the findings were inconsistent with the claim that the tests measured native intelligence; for example, like other recent immigrants, Jews scored low on the tests. As with the cephalic index, such anomalies did not dislodge the investigators from their bedrock assumptions. The psychologist who headed the research team concluded that the tests "brought into clear relief . . . the intellectual inferiority of the negro. Quite apart from educational status, which is utterly unsatisfactory, the negro soldier is of relatively low grade intelligence."[36]

By the late 1930s, when Myrdal launched his research project, scientific racism—as it would eventually be called—had been effectively stripped of any claim to scientific validity, at least in the eyes of most of the nation's leading scholars and intellectuals. For several decades researchers had been whittling away at the core of the racist edifice. Chief among them was Franz Boas, a Jewish expatriate from Germany, whose studies of Eskimos and Indians in the Northwest led him to emphasize the infinite diversity of human cultures, and the preeminent role of environment in the genesis of culture. When the first *Encyclopaedia of the Social Sciences* was published in 1930, it was Boas who wrote the entry on "race." His renunciation of craniology could not have been more explicit:

The size of the brain depends not upon the number of nerve cells and fibers and their connections, but to a much greater extent upon tissue which has nothing to do with nerve activity. . . . There are relations between the form of the skull and the configuration of the brain, but the observation of artificially deformed heads suggests that there is no functional relation.[37]

Boas was equally critical of theories linking race with intelligence:

. . . Brigham found that among groups of Europeans who had immigrated at various times and had been subjected to intelligence tests those who had stayed longest in the

United States gave the best results. While originally he ascribed this to the immigration of more poorly equipped stock in later years, subsequently he withdrew this conclusion. It seems more plausible that the improvement is due to gradual assimilation to American speech and customs. Klineberg found this to be the case among Negroes migrating from rural districts to cities. The evidence in regard to mental differences between races has been assembled by Garth, who reaches the conclusion that no essential differences have been proved.[38]

In short, biological determinism had been relegated to the trashbin of history. As Harvey Sitkoff writes about the late 1930s:

A new consensus had emerged: that there are no inborn or innate racial differences in aptitude but only differences caused by educational, cultural, economic, and other environmental determinants. When the twenty-two thousand members of the American Psychological Association were called upon [in 1939] to affirm the validity of that view, only three publicly dissented.[39]

The triumph of liberal social science over scientific racism signified a major paradigm shift. As Kuhn reminds us, however, it would be simplistic to think that this change reflected an inherent tendency within science to rectify its own mistakes, or even the impact of new ideas emanating from the new social sciences. The genesis of these new theories, and their acceptance within the scientific fraternity, reflect the larger constellation of historical and ideological factors alluded to earlier that transformed both the reality and the image of "the Negro." This was the historical and social context in which science lost faith in its paradigmatic assumptions, and after long denial, saw through its own shibboleths.

Gunnar Myrdal: Walking the Fine Line

Thus, by the 1930s not only was the old racial order crumbling, but the pseudoscientific theories invented to legitimize this order had been jettisoned, at least within the community of scholars. At this historical moment the Carnegie corporation resolved to underwrite "a comprehensive study of the Negro in America."

After a lengthy search, Keppel wrote to Myrdal in April 1937, inviting him to serve as director. In explaining the decision to "import" a director, Keppel acknowledged that many devoted scholars of both races were working to improve the Negro condition, "but, as far as I know, there is not one of them whose thinking is not influenced by emotional factors of one type or another, and many are also under the influence of earlier environmental conditions, family or community traditions of the abolition movement on the one hand or of the old regime of the South on the other."[40] With this elliptical language, Keppel was defining the ideological agenda for the Carnegie study. It would break with "the old regime of the South," including the discredited theories that had been used to prop up that regime. But it would also eschew the "traditions of the abolition movement," presumably an allusion to the ideological fervor and political activism associated with the crusade against slavery.

In a lengthy letter two months later, in which he outlined his expectations for the study, Myrdal struck a similar ideological chord:

> During my stay in the States in 1929–30 I found myself having a purely questioning attitude to the Negro problem. My general attitude to race problems . . . is that I am on the one hand inclined to keep very critical against the popular insistence on great biological difference in intellectual and moral qualities between races but on the other hand not apt *a priori* to postulate perfect parity.[41]

This seems an astounding admission from the illustrious author of *An American Dilemma*. It is reminiscent of abolitionists a century earlier who repudiated slavery but stopped far short of proposing full equality between the races. Perhaps too much importance should not be attached to a single, unguarded comment in private correspondence, one that perhaps was pitched to his benefactors at the Carnegie Corporation. Yet such an unguarded comment can also expose the value premises that an investigator brings to his study. As Alvin Gouldner has suggested, "Like it or not, and know it or not, sociologists will organize their researches in terms of their prior assumptions; the character of sociology will depend upon them and will change when they change."[42] Similarly, in his book *What Is History?* Edward Carr enjoins the reader to "study the historian before you begin to study the facts."[43]

Indeed, this is precisely what the trustees at the Carnegie Commission did in their selection of the person in whose hands they would place the delicate and potentially explosive facts of race in

America.[44] Of paramount concern, as Stanfield comments, was that the person they selected be someone "who was devoted to the interests of foundations and who would not raise embarrassing issues."[45] There was good reason to place their faith in Gunnar Myrdal, who was already ensconced in the influential world of government, foundations, universities, and corporations. He first came to the United States in 1929 on a Rockefeller Foundation fellowship. Together with his wife, Alva, he traveled around the country, meeting with prominent scholars in leading universities.[46] During this visit Myrdal met Beardsley Ruml, a psychologist and erstwhile dean of social science at the University of Chicago. Ruml had once served as an officer at the Carnegie Corporation and then as director of the Laura Spelman Rockefeller Memorial, before entering the world of business as treasurer of Macy's department store. In addition, he was an influential political insider in the Roosevelt administration, and, like Myrdal, a champion of social planning. It was Ruml who first told Keppel about Myrdal, and when Myrdal vacillated about undertaking the Carnegie project, it was Ruml who prevailed upon him to accept the offer.[47] Given Myrdal's elite credentials and patronage, the trustees could rest assured that the person they had recruited and were paying so handsomely would cause them no embarrassment.

It might still seem strange that the conservative Carnegie Corporation would select a man who helped to lay the foundation for the Swedish welfare state. Myrdal was a committed social democrat, but he was still politically safe. Judged by his early writings, he was a neoclassical economist who believed in the unfettered operation of the free market. The Depression, with a soaring rate of unemployment and the concomitant danger of political instability—reinforced by the specter of fascism and communism—convinced Myrdal of the necessity of what he called "prophylactic social welfare policy."[48] As his biographer notes:

Hoping to shape a consensus in support of the party's policies, Myrdal asserted that the Depression required a dramatic new departure in Swedish politics. His approach represented a radicalism from the top down, however, and a prescription for granting extensive power to experts to act in the public interest.[49]

Myrdal was par excellence a social reformer. Not only was he a staunch anti-Communist, but he was also hostile even to expressions of intellectual Marxism. Even so, a few years earlier he might well have been regarded as too liberal by the Carnegie trustees, but in the context of the Depression his political colors blended in with the regnant politics in the Roosevelt Administration. For all intents and purposes, Myrdal was a New Dealer.

The Carnegie trustees also had reason to believe that Myrdal's social activism would be restrained when it came to the Negro problem. In the same letter in which Myrdal commented that he did not necessarily postulate "perfect parity" between the races, he indicated that the study should not emphasize practical solutions to the Negro problem, but should be a comprehensive analysis of "the facts" that would benefit policymakers.[50] As will be seen, Myrdal remained true to his word, and *An American Dilemma* advances few ideas insofar as social policy is concerned. Myrdal, the champion of "social engineering," ends up strangely reticent when it came to proposing solutions to "the Negro problem."

Thus, from the point of view of the Carnegie Corporation, Myrdal was the ideal person to head a study of the Negro in America. His liberal credentials would lend credibility to the study at a time of liberal ascendancy in American politics and increased militancy from within the black community. Besides, "fresh ideas" *were* needed to make sense of the breakdown of the old racial order, and to provide an intellectual foundation for the reconstituted racial order that was emerging. Yet it was clear that Myrdal would remain within safe political bounds, and would not roil the political waters as Frazier had done in his report on the Harlem Riot.

Thus, in terms of personal biography, intellect, and ideology, Myrdal represented the future, not the past, of race relations in America. Not a utopian future, but a proximate future. Not a future that would resolve the American dilemma, but a future in which blacks would make incremental progress but remain second-class citizens in all respects. Myrdal's ideological mission, one might say, was to provide an intellectual rationalization for the *future* status quo—precisely the one that emerged in the decade following the publication of his monumental study.

An American Dilemma: Rationalizing the *Future* Status Quo

A comprehensive study of the Negro in America could hardly be achieved by a single person, especially a foreigner who had never studied race before. The irony of the matter, as Stanfield points out, is that Myrdal's "great ignorance about American racial issues made him chronically dependent upon native researchers and consultants who ended up, in effect, writing his book for him."[51] This last barb perhaps goes too far. Myrdal seems to have been firmly in charge of the planning and direction of the research project. Not only did he assume major responsibility for the final draft of the book, but he also left his own indelible imprint on it. It is true, however, that Myrdal had an extraordinary amount of help. Scores of "experts" were consulted at various stages of the project and are acknowledged in Myrdal's preface.[52] Myrdal also commissioned dozens of studies on a plethora of subjects, and the list of collaborators reads like a Who's Who in American Social Science. Among the white scholars were Melville Herskovitz, Otto Klineberg, Ashley Montagu, Edward Shils, Samuel Stouffer, and Louis Wirth, not to mention Richard Sterner and Arnold Rose, who played major roles in writing the final volume and are listed as "assistants" on the book's jacket. Most of the leading black social scientists were also included among the collaborators: Sterling Brown, Ralph Bunche, Allison Davis, J. G. St. Clair Drake, E. Franklin Frazier, Charles Johnson, and Doxey Wilkerson. These scholars were commissioned to prepare "research memoranda" that served as the raw material which Myrdal synthesized and wove together in the process of writing *An American Dilemma*.

Thanks in no small part to the efforts of these scholars, the forty-five chapters and ten appendixes of *An American Dilemma* do provide a "comprehensive" account of the Negro in American society. Early chapters provide a detailed account of racist ideology and the caste system. No fewer than eleven chapters are subsumed under "economics," and explore the economic status of blacks in various sectors of the economy, in both the North and the South. Another four chapters deal with "politics"; another four with "justice." Ten chapters deal with social institutions within the black community: leadership, protest organizations, the church, schools, the press. Clearly, *An American Dilemma* is the product of a prodigious research effort, one that provides an invaluable historical record of the condition of blacks in America at a critical moment when the nation was on the cusp of a profound racial transformation.

Precisely because the book covers so much intellectual ground, I will not attempt to summarize its contents. Rather my purpose is to highlight the central ideas in the work, and above all to grasp how and why the book succeeded in establishing a new liberal orthodoxy on race in America.

In the first place, the master concepts in *An American Dilemma* were hardly "new." The idea that racism constituted a troubling contradiction between American ideals and practices was very much a part of the nation's self-serving way of acknowledging its shortcomings. This construction had also been part of the discourse on race over many decades. Consider, for example, the following passage from a book by John Daniels that dealt with blacks in Boston in colonial times. Entitled *In Freedom's Birthplace*, it was published in 1914:

Thus there arose, simultaneously with the Negro's advent, a contradiction between the abstract profession of the white citizens of Boston and their concrete treatment of this race. The Puritans had founded the town in devotion to the cause of spiritual freedom. Yet they did not refrain, within a few years, from placing Negroes in a state of bondage. . . . This contradiction was speedily to give trouble to the Puritan conscience, and was to have momentous consequences, in bringing that conscience to bear as a level to change the Negro's lot. It was a contradiction, moreover, which in modified degree and form has survived to the present, and which still troubles the Boston community.[53]

In another passage, Daniels enunciates yet another of Myrdal's master concepts, the vicious circle:

. . . the two vital factors here involved are, first, the past and present inferiority of the Negro himself; and, second, the resulting prejudice against him. These two factors, moreover, constantly react upon each other. The Negro's inferiority tends, on the one hand, to perpetuate the prejudice to which he is thereby subject. This very prejudice, on the other hand, possessing a semi-independent entity and influence on its own account, has the effect of perpetuating not only the prevailing assumption of the Negro's inferiority, but also the fact itself, by grievously handicapping this race in its efforts to obtain a fair fighting chance. *Such is the vicious circle which lies at the heart of the Negro problem.* [54]

Myrdal's iteration of this idea is as follows:

Throughout this inquiry, we shall assume a general interdependence between all the factors in the Negro problem. White prejudice and discrimination keep the Negro low in standards of living, health, education, manners and morals. This, in its turn, gives support to white prejudice. White prejudice and Negro standards thus mutually "cause" each other. [55]

Such were the "fresh ideas" that the Carnegie Corporation had imported from Sweden!

What *was* new in the Carnegie study, and of immense and enduring value, were the detailed empirical studies conducted by the numerous collaborators that Myrdal resourcefully incorporated into his book. A prime example is the chapter "Violence and Intimidation." Myrdal minces no words in describing how violence was routine and systematic in Southern life, and rested on the complicity of the state itself. Below are several key excerpts:

It is the custom in the South to permit whites to resort to violence and threats of violence against the life, personal security, property and freedom of movement of Negroes. There is a wide variety of behavior, ranging from a mild admonition to murder, which the white man may exercise to control Negroes. While the practice has its origin in the slavery tradition, it continues to flourish because of the laxity and inequity of the administration of law and justice.

But quite apart from laws, and even against the law, there exists a pattern of violence against Negroes in the South upheld by the relative absence of fear of legal reprisal. Any white man can strike or beat a Negro, steal or destroy his property, cheat him in a transaction and even take his life, without much fear of legal reprisal. . . . Negroes, of course, try to avoid situations in which such violence is likely to occur, and if Negroes do incur the displeasure of a white man, a mere command or threat is usually enough to control them without the use of actual violence. The Negro's economic dependence upon whites makes these verbal controls especially potent. But accidental insult, and sometimes nothing at all except the general insecurity or sadism of certain whites, can serve as occasion for violence.

There is little that Negroes can do to protect themselves, even where they are a majority of the population. They cannot easily secure the protection of police or court against white men. They cannot secure the protection of white employers against white men, unless the latter are poor or have had a bad reputation. They can, of course, strike back but they know that means a more violent retaliation, often in an organized form and with danger to other Negroes. In an important sense, lynching and the wholesale destruction of Negro property are often merely the extreme forms of organized white retaliation against Negroes who have struck back when they were struck or cheated first by whites. This retaliation more frequently takes a less violent form: the legal system may be called on to imprison the Negro for "attacking a white man"; white men may pretend that they are going to lynch the Negro but end up by only beating him or using the "tar and feather" technique; or the Negro may be "run out of town" and warned not to return.[56]

As is readily apparent from these excerpts, Myrdal did not equivocate in the least when it came to exposing the raw facts concerning racial violence and other heinous aspects of the caste system. Indeed, this is the most noteworthy achievement of *An American Dilemma*: it provides an extensive documentary record that, on its face, constitutes a powerful indictment of the entire system of racial oppression. Considering the time of the book's publication—1944—this was a monumental achievement indeed.

The problem with *An American Dilemma* lies not in a failure to adequately expose the raw facts of American racism, but rather with the conceptual framework in which it placed these facts. Like a pair of eyeglasses, a conceptual framework determines which facts come into focus and which become blurred or imperceptible. What I am suggesting here is that Myrdal's conceptual framework placed a gloss over the raw facts, and in doing so obscured them from full view and blunted their impact. He took facts that were potentially explosive, and he defused them by cramming them into insulated conceptual boxes. To see how Myrdal achieved this rhetorical feat, let us examine the key elements of his conceptual framework.

THE TITLE

A title trumpets a book's main point or theme. It also serves as its most salient point of reference. What are we to think of a book—heralded as a classic—whose title reduces racial oppression to a "dilemma"? At the very least, such terminology places an exculpatory gloss over racial oppression, much as terms like "the Jewish question" and "the final solution" masked the reality and horror of genocide. "Dilemma," furthermore, contradicts the book's own contents, which depict the systematic, willful, and ruthless subjugation of an entire people. Why, then, subsume this narrative under such a benign title? The decision to do so was certainly not politically innocent. Yet few of Myrdal's contemporaneous reviewers commented on this anomaly, with the notable exception of Herbert Aptheker, the acerbic Communist intellectual, who leveled the following attack on Myrdal:

It is perhaps understandable how an adviser to and an official of the government of Sweden, which treated the late war against fascism as a dilemma and preferred neutrality (especially a neutrality made lucrative by "necessary" trading with Nazi Germany) might decide to christen the fact of the exploitation and oppression of the American Negro people a dilemma—"a situation involving choice . . . between equally unsatisfactory alternatives."[57]

Aside from soft-pedaling racial oppression, Myrdal's title subtly shifts emphasis away from the victims of oppression whose freedoms are stomped upon, onto the oppressor who is depicted as conscience-stricken, torn between two poles of a dilemma, and in need of moral redress. Pity the oppressor!

RACISM AS A MORAL PROBLEM

Despite the many chapters that probe the political and economic dimensions of racism—which essentially treat racism as a problem of political economy—Myrdal's conceptualization of racism, developed on the very first page of his Introduction, is that racism is a *moral* issue. In grandiloquent language, italicized for emphasis, Myrdal writes:

The American Negro problem is a problem in the heart of the American. It is there that the interracial tension has its focus. It is there that the decisive struggle goes on. This is the central viewpoint of this treatise. Though our study includes economic, social, and political race relations, at bottom our problem is the moral dilemma of the American—the conflict between his moral valuations on various levels of consciousness and generality.[58]

Here, at the outset of his book, Myrdal informs his readers that all of
the myriad details concerning economic, social, and political race
relations are secondary to something else: a putative moral dilemma
whereby whites are split between their democratic and enlightened
ideals, and the racial practices so embedded in American history and
culture. Again, the emphasis is subtly shifted from the sordid realities
of racial oppression to a moral conflict that supposedly afflicts the
oppressor. Instead of the wrongs visited on blacks, racism is cast as a
problem whereby a nation wrestles with its own contradictions. Pity
the nation!

THE AMERICAN CREED

The selection of Myrdal to head the Carnegie study was predicated on
the notion that, as an outsider, he was free of bias. Ironically, Myrdal
rejected the idea that scientific inquiry could ever be free of bias, and
he aggressively exposed the hidden biases of laissez-faire economists
and others with whom he disagreed. However, he remained oblivious
to his own biases, one of which was a reverence for American democracy, heightened by the advent of fascism in Germany and the
tribulations of the Second World War.

At the center of Myrdal's conceptual framework was "the American Creed of liberty, equality, justice, and fair opportunity for everybody."[59] Myrdal had no illusions that this political nirvana existed in
American society. Indeed, his whole point was that American racist
practices were fundamentally at odds with the dictates of the American creed. However, he argued that all Americans internalized the
moral imperatives inherent in the American creed, that they experienced the dissonance between American ideals and racist practices
on a deeply personal level, and that this creed constituted the philosophical bedrock of American society and the basis for rectifying the
flagrant violations of its moral dictates.

Placing the American creed at the center of a study of American
racism has a paradoxical rhetorical effect: America's greatest crime is
seen in the penumbra of America's highest ideals. True, the founding
fathers erred in permitting the slave trade. True, the highest courts

had legitimated racial segregation within the framework of the Constitution. True, the caste system was a flagrant violation of democratic norms. Despite all this, Myrdal insisted, there is a transcendental commitment to the moral imperatives embodied in the American creed. This is rather like telling a mass murderer that he is, at bottom, a good person who has merely succumbed to the darker side of an otherwise healthy personality. If this statement seems far-fetched, consider Myrdal's panegyric to the Southern bigot:

. . . even a poor and uneducated white person in some isolated and backward rural region in the Deep South, *who is violently prejudiced against the Negro and intent upon depriving him of civic rights and human independence*, has also a whole compartment in his valuation sphere housing the entire American Creed of liberty, equality, justice, and fair opportunity for everybody. He is actually also a good Christian and honestly devoted to the ideals of human brotherhood and the Golden Rule.[60]

The emphasis placed on the American creed led one astute reviewer to ask whether Myrdal "has not flattered us so hugely with his American creed theory, as somewhat to obscure the true nature of the problem."[61] The wisdom of this comment becomes clear when one examines Myrdal's praxis. Instead of directly combatting racism and making restitution for past wrongs, Myrdal relies on a gradual strengthening of the American creed. As he wrote in his concluding chapter: "What America is constantly reaching for is democracy at home and abroad. The main trend in its history is the gradual realization of the American Creed."[62]

THE FOCUS ON RACIAL BELIEFS

Nowhere is the discrepancy between Myrdal's empirical analysis and his overarching conceptual framework more evident and more troublesome than in his treatment of racism. On the one hand, whole chapters deal with the complex ways in which racism was embedded in major political and economic institutions. Myrdal, to repeat, did not shirk the facts. The disfranchisement of blacks, the existence of patently racist laws, the exclusion of blacks from juries, the implication of police in racial violence, the restriction of blacks to the most exploitative and least desirable jobs, the segregation of schools and public accommodations, and the indignities of the caste system—these and other aspects of racial subordination received ample treatment in *An American Dilemma*. On the other hand, Myrdal took all of these elements of institutionalized racism and encapsulated them within a facile conceptual framework—one that reduced racism to the level of *beliefs* that whites held about blacks.

For Myrdal, this "racial dogma" undergirds the entire system of racial oppression. He acknowledges that particular beliefs originated as a rationalization for slavery and racial hierarchy, and that they are "opportunistic" in that they serve the interests of the white majority. Nevertheless, he treats racial dogma as a vestigial residue of pre-rational, pre-democratic, and pre-scientific modes of thought. The remedy, therefore, is to disabuse people of these retrograde beliefs, by substituting other "rectifying beliefs" in their place. Myrdal, furthermore, is optimistic about the prospects for the elimination of racial dogma. First, he presupposes that *"people want to be rational, to be honest and well-informed,"* and therefore would choose truth over error.[63] Second, he believes that, thanks to advances in science and in social science, "the popular race dogma is being victoriously pursued into every corner and effectively exposed as fallacious or at least unsubstantiated."[64]

Myrdal's most formidable critic, Oliver Cox, scoffed at the idea that racial beliefs were of more than epiphenomenal import. "If beliefs, per se, could subjugate a people," Cox wrote with searing irony, "the beliefs which Negroes hold about whites should be as effective as those which whites hold against Negroes."[65] For Cox, racial beliefs are merely a surface manifestation of something else: a system of racial domination and exploitation. It follows, therefore, that unless this system of domination and exploitation were changed, then efforts to attack racial beliefs would be to no avail. "The reformer," Cox wrote, "seeks to eliminate only the racial aspects of the exploitative system; he compromises with the system which produces the racial antagonism."[66]

Cox was both black and an avowed Socialist, and if that were not

enough to assure his marginality, he was uncompromising in his criticism of mainstream social science. His prolific essays, including his
critique of Myrdal, received little notice within the academic fraternity. Reviewers of his masterpiece *Caste, Class, and Race*, published
in 1948, dismissed it as the work of a Marxist and therefore tendentious.[67] Of course, it was Cox's Marxist bent that led him to recognize
the pitfall of treating racism as disembodied culture, severed from the
political and economic institutions that engendered and sustained
"racial dogma."

Nevertheless, Cox conceded that "as a source of information and
brilliant interpretation of information on race relations in the United
States," *An American Dilemma* is "probably unsurpassed."[68] Yet he
was unsparing in his criticism of "the theoretical structure" of Myrdal's opus, especially its failure to locate the structural basis and material sources of prejudice. Thus his rebuke: "Myrdal does not bring
to light the social determinants of this well-known dilemma; he
merely recognizes it and rails against its existence."[69]

In this epigrammatic sentence, Cox has identified both the
strength and the fatal weakness of *An American Dilemma*. In the context of the period in which it was written, and against the background
of previous scholarship, the fact that Myrdal "recognized and railed
against" the contradictions between America's democratic ideals and
its racist practices undeniably represented significant, if not monumental, progress. Nor can it be denied that *An American Dilemma*
established an invaluable historical record of the condition of blacks
in America at this crucial juncture in the nation's history. Not only
are the raw facts of racial violence and the caste system documented
in detail, but they are published in a book bearing the imprimatur of
the Carnegie Corporation. In all these respects, it can be said that *An
American Dilemma* played a historically significant role in the de-
legitimization of racism, a necessary first step in the eventual disman-
tling of official segregation.

On the other hand, there is Myrdal's defective theoretical structure. Myrdal, one might say, took all the racial arsenic compiled in
the substantive chapters and wrapped it in a sugar coating to make it

palatable not only to his patrons at the Carnegie Corporation, but to the academic establishment and the mass public as well. Here, perhaps, is where Myrdal's consummate skill as a politician came into play: his book exalted American democracy even as it fleshed out the ignominious details concerning American apartheid. In Myrdal's hands, "America's greatest failure" becomes "America's incomparably great opportunity for the future"—all within a single sentence.[70] And while he rails at racism throughout the book, he offers no specific proposals for social policy, despite his assertion in the very last paragraph of his book that the reconstruction of society is "the supreme task of social science." In this respect Myrdal was no different from other liberals of the period, who, as Peter Kellogg found, had come to regard race as a serious problem, but "only declaimed that something ought to be done without making specific suggestions for reform."[71] Myrdal remained true to the commitment he made to Keppel in 1937 to provide policymakers with the facts, and to avoid advocacy of "practical solutions."

If anything, Myrdal's conceptualization of the problem implied a conservative agenda for social action. This was noted by one contemporaneous critic, Leo Crespi, in a review in *Public Opinion Quarterly* entitled "Is Gunnar Myrdal on the Right Track?" Crespi contended that Myrdal's stress upon morality puts the emphasis in the wrong place: "It suggests treating the individual to eliminate Negro prejudice—with the remedies of ethical exhortation—whereas society is more properly the patient, and the remedies are social and economic planning which will remove the gain from prejudice."[72] Ethical exhortation that did not challenge racist structures—this was medicine that even the South could swallow, and it should come as no surprise that the publication of *An American Dilemma* aroused few howls of protest from journalists and other commentators in the South.[73]

In short, Myrdal had written a book that was politically safe, precisely along the lines that Keppel had broadly hinted at in his original letter to Myrdal in 1937. It broke with the old regime of the South by placing a final nail in the coffin of biological determinism and it re-

pudiated racism at least in principle. On the other hand, it did not directly challenge major political and economic institutions, or advocate reforms that would prove "controversial." One can scour the
thirteen hundred pages of *An American Dilemma*, including the
concluding chapter entitled "America Again at the Crossroads," and
find no mention of the need for civil rights legislation to secure the
rights of citizenship for blacks.[74] No mention even of the need for
anti-lynching legislation that had failed to pass through Congress for
decades, and that Roosevelt had refused to support because he did not
want to jeopardize Southern support for the New Deal.[75] No mention
of *strategies* to attack the caste system and legal segregation. No mention from this renowned economist of how blacks might be integrated
into the economic mainstream. No mention from this architect of
Sweden's welfare state about how the state might *act* to redress the
wrongs so copiously documented in the forty-five chapters of his
book.

These silences provide a striking contrast to the assertive and uncompromising demands for racial justice that are found in another
volume, entitled *What the Negro Wants*, also published in 1944. The
idea for the book originated with W. T. Couch, who was director of
the University of North Carolina Press. On the premise that the
country "ought to know what the Negro wants," Couch commissioned Rayford W. Logan, a black historian at Howard University, to
select contributors to the volume, with the stipulation that "equal
representation in the book be given to left-wing, moderate, and right-
wing points of view." When the manuscript was submitted for publication, however, Couch declared that it was "not publishable." According to Logan, "What disturbed Mr. Couch more than anything
else, I believed then and now, was the virtual unanimity of the fourteen contributors in wanting equal rights for Negroes."[76] After much
wrangling, Couch agreed to publish the book provided that it contained an introduction by him—in which he repeatedly invokes *An
American Dilemma* and disassociates himself from the contents of
What the Negro Wants.

Indeed, with a single voice the fourteen contributors demanded equal rights. Logan entitled his own essay, "The Negro Wants First-Class Citizenship." Included in his list of "irreducible fundamentals of first-class citizenship" were equality of opportunity, equality of suffrage, and abolition of public segregation. Not content with enunciating a set of goals, Logan also endorsed the idea of "non-violent resistance" which had been used in some cities and "has achieved a limited success in breaking down public segregation."[77] A. Philip Randolph went even further in spelling out both "a program of liberation," and "techniques of action," building on his successful March on Washington Movement.[78] Langston Hughes prophesied that "the wheels of the Jim Crow car are about to come off and the walls are going to burst wide open."[79] No less than the "radicals," the three contributors who represented the "conservative" or "right-wing" viewpoint argued for full equality. Leslie Pinckney Hill, a prominent educator, wrote: "What does the American Negro want? Full citizen status in our American Democracy."[80] Mary McLeod Bethune, another educator, issued nine demands, including "the protection of his civil rights and an end to lynching," "the free ballot," "equal access to employment opportunities," "elimination of racial barriers in labor unions," and "extension of federal programs in public housing, health, social security and relief under federal control."[81] Frederick Patterson expressed the difference between "conservatives" and "radicals" when he wrote: "the more conservative element of Negroes differ from those who hold the most radical views in opposition to segregation only in terms of time and technique of its elimination."[82] This juxtaposition between the contents of *What the Negro Wants* and *An American Dilemma* points up Myrdal's most stunning failure: despite his apotheosis of American democracy and the American creed, and despite his repudiation of American racism and second-class citizenship, he was unwilling to commit himself to a program or policy that would secure the rights of citizenship for African Americans.

Of course, had Myrdal presented himself as an advocate for civil rights, he would have been denounced as a dangerous radical, and a foreign one at that, and his book would have suffered a fate similar to

Frazier's report on the 1935 Harlem Riot. Myrdal's genius was to dispense only as much medicine as the patient was willing to swallow, and his book was perfectly tailored to the political and racial climate of the post-war decade. This was a period when racism lost its legitimacy, and while the forces for racial change were gaining momentum, the time was not yet ripe for a head-on challenge to racist structures.

In the final analysis, the "success" of *An American Dilemma* was its uncanny historical timing. This was not accidental, however. *An American Dilemma* was the product of the very forces that were reconstituting race relations in the society at large, and it was carefully honed by its author to remain within safe political limits. At one and the same time, Myrdal's opus served as an epitaph to the old racial order and as an intellectual baptism for a new racial status quo—the one that evolved during the first post-war decade and that would persist until it came under challenge from a grassroots protest movement.

2

Paradigm Crisis
The Decline of Liberal Orthodoxy

> Why did social scientists—and sociologists in particular—not
> foresee the explosion of collective action of Negro Americans
> toward immediate full integration into American society?
>
> Everett Hughes, presidential address to the
> American Sociological Association, August 1963

One historian of science has likened a "paradigm change" to "picking up the other end of the stick."[1] The facts of racism exist as before, but they are handled differently, and are placed within a new system of relations and a different framework of analysis.

An American Dilemma marked one such paradigm change. The "facts" associated with racial hierarchy that previously had been construed as evidence of the innate inferiority of blacks were now cast in a different framework, one that saw racial hierarchy as an artifact of environmental factors rather than a natural outgrowth of genes. To repeat, Myrdal did not singlehandedly effect this paradigm change. Long before he arrived on American soil, scientific racism and social Darwinism were in retreat. However, as Kuhn points out, "the decision to reject one paradigm is always simultaneously the decision to accept another."[2] *An American Dilemma* provided a politically acceptable alternative, and the acclaim that was showered on the book signified the culmination of this paradigm change.

Of course, the two volumes that composed *An American Dilemma* abounded with facts that might have been handled differently, and brought to a different conclusion, as some of Myrdal's contemporaneous critics contended. However, like the critics of scientific racism

50

during its heyday, Myrdal's critics were generally ignored or spurned. Marxists, like Aptheker and Cox, were dismissed as ideologues and virtually banished from respectable academic discourse. Blacks of whatever political stripe, like the fourteen who contributed to Logan's collection on *What the Negro Wants* and demanded the abolition of second-class citizenship, were simply met with a deaf ear. The response of the white world to "what the Negro wants" was captured by Du Bois, who compared blacks to prisoners trapped in a dark cave desperately trying to get the attention of passersby:

One talks on evenly and logically in this way but notices that the passing throng does not even turn its head, or if it does, glances curiously and walks on. It gradually penetrates the minds of the prisoners that the people passing do not hear; that some thick sheet of invisible but horribly tangible plate glass is between them and the world.[3]

Indeed, the marginalization of black voices in academia was facilitated by an "invisible but horribly tangible" color line that relegated all but a few black scholars to teach in black colleges far removed from the academic mainstream.

If Myrdal often picked up the wrong end of the stick, at least in the view of his critics, then civil rights was a "stick" that he refused even to pick up. As we have seen, his study contained voluminous evidence of the many ways in which blacks were denied elementary civil rights. Systematic violence, political disfranchisement, restriction to "Negro jobs," Jim Crow laws mandating segregation in schools and public accommodations—these "facts" might easily have led Myrdal to ratify the goals of the NAACP, which ever since its founding in 1909 had crusaded against disfranchisement and Jim Crow laws. Myrdal had devoted an entire chapter to describing the activities of Negro protest organizations that were agitating for protection of their civil rights, whether this came through the courts, the legislatures, or, as in the case of Roosevelt's executive order desegregating wartime industries, through the exercise of presidential power. Myrdal's failure to speak out forcefully as an advocate for civil rights is clearly his most glaring failure.

Nor can this be explained merely by the constraints placed upon

the study by its sponsor. True, in his foreword to An American Dilemma Keppel asserted that the "proper function" for a foundation is
"to make the facts available and let them speak for themselves," and
not "to instruct the public as to what to do about them."[4] However, in
his neglect of civil rights Myrdal was reflecting a stream of liberal/left
thought that consciously downplayed civil rights approaches to "the
Negro problem." Indeed, Henry Steele Commager, the distinguished
historian from Columbia University, lauded Myrdal for not endorsing a civil rights strategy to the Negro problem. To quote Commager:

A solution to the Negro problem—the American problem—is implicit in Black Boy
as it is both implicit and explicit in Myrdal's monumental study. Clearly it is not by
taking refuge in Constitutional guarantees or in the courts or even in direct political
action. It is not the constitutional or political citadel that needs to be stormed. Nor is
it by propaganda, or by abstract appeals for justice—appeals the validity of which no
one denies.[5]

According to Commager, racism was but a surface manifestation of
deeper economic inequalities, and "discrimination and oppression
spring, it is clear, from ignorance and insecurity." To get to the root of
the problem, therefore, it was necessary to launch a concerted attack
"on ignorance and poverty and insecurity."[6]

The irony of proposing a remedy that would uplift the oppressor
rather than the oppressed did not escape Commager altogether. At
least he added the following caveat: "By abstract moral standards it is
perhaps less important that white men have jobs than that Negroes
have justice. But it seems clear that unless white men have jobs, Negroes will not have justice."[7] Thus, the black demand to vote and to
secure the other rights of citizenship would have to wait for a liberal
crusade against ignorance, poverty, and insecurity among whites.
Preposterous as this logic may seem in hindsight, it continues to pervade liberal discourse on race, as will presently be seen.

At least two factors were behind Commager's neglect of civil rights.
One stemmed from a Marxist tradition of subsuming "race" to
"class." In this model, social class factors are at the root of the entire
system of racial domination and exploitation, and racism is seen as a
mere epiphenomenon of underlying class factors. This theoretical

orientation, which was shared by many black Marxists as well—cluding Oliver Cox—led to a view that reforming the racial aspects of capitalism without overhauling the system itself was shortsighted and futile. There was a second, more pragmatic concern, however. Liberals of the period feared that taking up the cause of the Negro would antagonize powerful Southern Democrats whose support, always tenuous, had been indispensable in passing New Deal legislation, and would continue to be necessary to advance the liberal agenda. This was not the first time, nor would it be the last, that the Negro was sacrificed on the altar of an unholy alliance between Northern liberals and Dixiecrats.

Similar reasoning is also reflected in a review essay of *An American Dilemma* written by Frank Tannenbaum, a leading historian and author of one of the first histories of slavery.[8] Tannenbaum carried his analysis of the economic foundations of racism to the point of asserting that "there is no caste system really, and . . . there is no Negro problem as such."[9] On this premise he reached the remarkable conclusion—remember that Tannenbaum is writing in 1944—that "there is no solution to the Negro problem, because there is, as we said before, no problem with a big 'P.'"[10] Even if discrimination and racial prejudice were to disappear, he explained, "the problem would still remain substantially what it is."[11] Namely, an economic problem involving a backward regional economy wedded to a single crop whose price was declining. "The way out," Tannenbaum concluded, "is not to concentrate upon the issue in hand, but to concentrate upon something else, concentrate upon opening up avenues for the good life for all of the people in the South, both white and black, and in time—in the long time—fears will diminish, memories fade, new practices and new attitudes replace the old, and the Negro will cease to be a Negro and become a man—just another Southerner, just another American."[12] In *An American Dilemma* Myrdal had singled out Tannenbaum for criticism, accusing him and other liberals of "explaining the problem away," much as average Southerners did when they denied that there was "a Negro problem."[13] Indeed, one has to ask whether the liberal argument about "opening up avenues

for the good life for all of the people of the South" was more than a
pious evasion for dealing with "the issue at hand."

It is tempting to assign the liberal default on civil rights to racial in-
sensitivity. At least one writer has suggested that white liberals "often
seemed to find it easier to empathize with the white South despite its
racism than with the apparently more remote blacks whose life style,
they assumed, was further removed from their own."[14] However,
many leading black intellectuals of the period, including those far to
the left of Myrdal, scoffed at the civil rights approach pursued by the
NAACP as too moderate. Chief among them was Ralph Bunche,
chairman of political science at Howard University and, according to
Myrdal's biographer, the American scholar who was closest to Myrdal.[15] Bunche accompanied Myrdal on a long trip through the South
in 1939, sleeping in different hotels and meeting surreptitiously at
night. Bunche's skepticism about a civil rights strategy was reflected
in an article that he published in the *Journal of Negro Education* in
1935, entitled "A Critical Analysis of the Tactics and Programs of Minority Groups." Bunche wrote:

Perhaps the favorite method of struggle for rights employed by minority groups is the
political. Through the use of the ballot and the courts strenuous efforts are put forth to
gain social justice for the group. Extreme faith is placed in the ability of these instruments of democratic government to free the minority from social proscription and
civic inequality. The inherent fallacy of this belief rests in the failure to appreciate the
fact that the instruments of state are merely the reflections of the political and economic ideology of the dominant group, that the political arm of the state cannot be di-
vorced from the prevailing economic structure, whose servant it must inevitably be.[16]

Bunche concluded that "the only hope for the improvement in the
condition of the masses of any American minority group is the hope
that can be held out for the betterment of the masses of the dominant
group. Their basic interests are identical and so must be their programs and tactics."[17] Thus for Bunche, as for many white leftists, a
civil rights strategy was misguided and illusory. Political redemption
could come only through larger political transformations that eliminated the political and economic conditions that constituted the material basis of racial division.

However, there were others on the left—C. L. R. James is the most notable example—who criticized the tendency to subsume "race" to "class." They actively supported independent black protest, which they viewed not only as legitimate in itself but also consistent with the larger goals of socialism.[18] As is often pointed out, the Communist Party stood practically alone in championing the cause of "the Negro" in the 1930s and 1940s.[19] It did so, not so much out of compassion for blacks, but because its paradigm, so to speak, allowed it to handle the facts of racial subordination differently. For these Communists, racial subordination was not only emblematic of capitalist exploitation, but also consistent with the Leninist doctrine that wars of national liberation were legitimate and useful in advancing the cause of socialism. Of course, the ability to see racial subordination "within a new system of relations" also proved to be a great pitfall, evident in the disenchantment and sense of betrayal that blacks within the Party felt once they realized that the race issue was being used only to further its own political ends.[20]

In any event, the most important thing to be said about liberalism in the decade spanning the Second World War is that it had no program whatsoever for dealing with the plight of black America. This has been documented in a doctoral dissertation by Peter John Kellogg, involving a content analysis of two leading liberal journals, *The Nation* and the *New Republic*, between 1936 and 1952. Kellogg found that these journals paid little attention to issues of race, except for knee-jerk reactions to periodic atrocities or sensational events like the Scottsboro trial, in which nine black men were charged with the gang rape of two white women. On other occasions the journals reflected a Marxist proclivity to subsume race to class. Indeed, they went so far as to portray lynching during the Depression as having more to do with class than with race. According to Kellogg:

Lynching was most commonly described as an anti-labor technique, occasionally as further evidence of the protofascist characteristics of the South. For example, three artistic studies of lynching reviewed in the *New Republic* between 1936 and 1938 each made the victim a white man.[21]

Kellogg also found that these arch-liberal journals paid little attention to the March on Washington Movement, and ignored employment discrimination altogether. It was not until 1955, when protest erupted in Birmingham, that they began the first sustained examination of racial issues.[22] Even then, they treated the growing racial crisis as a troublesome diversion from other problems, and failed to develop a coherent strategy for racial reform. At the conclusion of his study, Kellogg raises the key issue: "If even liberals asked no more, what chance was there that politicians or anyone else in a position of influence in the society would attempt more?"[23]

Nor is the record of social science much better. In a trenchant critique of the social science literature on race—one of the few of its kind—Stanford Lyman shows how leading sociological theorists (from Robert Park through Gunnar Myrdal to Talcott Parsons) avoided the issue of civil rights. Instead, they advanced theoretical models that projected racial improvement as part of an evolutionary process of societal change. "Since the time for teleological redemption is ever long," Lyman adds, "blacks might consign their civic and egalitarian future to faith in the ultimate fulfillment of the inclusion cycle's promise."[24] Lyman ends with an indictment of the entire discipline: "Sociology . . . has been part of the problem and not part of the solution."[25]

To state the matter bluntly, had blacks waited for liberals for deliverance from the caste system, they would still be consigned to the back of the bus. Blacks have had to overcome not just the vicious opposition of their political enemies, but the well-intentioned counsel of "friends" who, whether inspired by utopian ideals or swayed by practical politics, actively discouraged the aggressive pursuit of civil rights.

This is aptly illustrated by the strange career of A. Philip Randolph. Like Ralph Bunche and other black intellectuals of the period, Randolph had been influenced by the Depression and the radical politics of the thirties. The "radicals" defined themselves in opposition to the "race men," epitomized by Booker T. Washington, who shied away from politics, opting instead to promote economic development within a segregated black community, or Marcus Garvey, who sought to escape from America's racial abyss by emigrating to Africa. The radicals, on the other hand, believed that the problems of the black masses emanated from the exploitation of labor by private capital, and, consistent with this belief, put their political faith in a new coalition based upon the solidarity of black and white labor.[26] Socialism, labor unionism, and interracial class solidarity was their credo.[27]

Randolph, of course, rose to national prominence as the leader of the Brothers of Sleeping Car Porters, the first all-black labor union. However, several factors eroded Randolph's faith in the radical credo. First of all, there was the deep-seated racism within the labor movement itself. Despite the success of the Brothers of Sleeping Car Porters, it was still a segregated union in a federation—the AFL—that was riddled with racism. Second, Randolph could not escape the fact that, as he said in a 1936 speech, "Black America is a victim of both class and race prejudice and oppression."[28] Segregation, disfranchisement, and peonage were problems that plagued black Americans alone, and "in the final analysis, the salvation of the Negro, like the workers, must come from within."[29] Third, Randolph came to realize that rank-and-file blacks responded to appeals of race, not of class, and that racial solidarity could be a boon to political action.[30] Randolph's genius was to forge a new ideological and political amalgam: he combined labor union tactics of political action with Garvey's racial chauvinism. Here was "a race man" of a different kind: one who would use racial solidarity not as a surrogate for political action, but as a rallying cry for a collective assault on racist structures.

So far had Randolph strayed from his original faith in "the unity of labor" that when he organized the March on Washington Movement in 1941, he endorsed a provision excluding whites. This aroused considerable opposition, from blacks as well as whites.[31] Roy Wilkins argued that it was contradictory to exclude whites from a movement whose purpose was to protest against racial segregation. Others attacked Randolph for "isolationism" and "reverse Jim Crow." Randolph, however, insisted that blacks had to take control of their own liberation movement:

Negroes are the only people who are the victims of Jim Crow, and it they who must take the initiative and assume the responsibility to abolish it. Jews must and do lead the fight against anti-Semitism, Catholics must lead the fight against anti-Catholicism, labor must battle against anti-labor laws and practices. [32]

Randolph also argued that only a black-led and black-financed organization would allow blacks to develop self-reliance, and "to break down the slave psychology and inferiority-complex in Negroes which comes and is nourished with Negroes relying on white people for direction and support." [33] At the same time, Randolph was not opposed to "collaboration" with whites and inter-racial organizations. Racial exclusivity was a means to combatting racism, never an end in itself.

It was Randolph who pioneered a "politics of confrontation" that ultimately provided both vision and praxis for the civil rights movement. As early as the 1940s—a time when racial oppression was at or near its zenith and blacks had little leverage even in the North for fighting back—Randolph made it clear that blacks would settle for nothing less than complete equality in all spheres of national life. He also spelled out a praxis that included direct political action, non-violence, and civil disobedience as tactics that would allow blacks to prevail against a more powerful opponent.

Vision and praxis were backed up with another indispensable quality—spine! Randolph rejected the accommodationist stance that pervaded black politics—the temptation to "settle" for what you could get in the name of "political reality." Had realpolitik governed Randolph's thinking, he never would have planned a March on Washington in the midst of a war. Would blacks not be accused of being unpatriotic? Would they not be playing into the hands of the Nazis? Was it worth risking the patronage of President Roosevelt who had in fact included blacks in his New Deal? Weren't blacks making major strides despite the color line in defense industries? Besides, what guarantee was there that Randolph could turn out anywhere near the

100,000 marchers that he claimed? No doubt Randolph was bombarded with these arguments and more. President Roosevelt enlisted Eleanor Roosevelt and Mayor La Guardia—the two preeminent liberals of the period—to convince Randolph to cancel the march. When that failed, he summoned Randolph to a personal meeting, committed himself to work for better treatment for blacks, and demanded that the march be cancelled.[34] Randolph still refused to back down until Roosevelt promised to issue an executive order proscribing discrimination in defense industries and establishing a Fair Employment Practices Committee to assure compliance. There was no exaggeration in Randolph's claim that this was "the most significant and meaningful United States declaration affecting Negroes since the Emancipation Proclamation."[35] It also proved that the federal government could be pressured into active intervention on behalf of blacks, a lesson that was not lost on the nascent civil rights movement.

Randolph's March on Washington Movement, which was organized in the wake of the cancelled march, ultimately foundered, partly because of its difficulty in raising the necessary funds without white support. Besides, the times were not yet ripe to mobilize the mass movement that Randolph envisioned. By the mid-fifties, however, the missing elements were present. Some two million blacks had moved North, partly as a result of the war and the lowering of racist barriers in Northern industries. Finally it was possible, as Piven and Cloward have suggested, "to construct the occupational and institutional foundation from which to mount resistance to white oppression."[36]

The Southern economy was also undergoing a fateful process of modernization. Aside from unprecedented growth of an urban economy, Southern agriculture was becoming less dependent on black labor because of the introduction of labor-saving technology. With the development of automatic cotton pickers in the 1950s, even the harvest became mechanized. In short, black labor was rapidly becoming obsolete. As Harold Baron has written:

While the civil-rights movement and the heroic efforts associated with it were necessary to break the official legality of segregation, it should be recognized that in a
sense this particular form of racism was already obsolete, as its base in an exploitative
system of production had drastically changed.[37]

Thus, the transformation of the Southern economy was the single
most important factor in explaining why the civil rights movement
occurred when it did and why it ultimately triumphed. Other factors
were also at work. The black vote in the North had become important
in national elections, and provided blacks with leverage within the
Democratic Party, leading to a split between Northern liberals and
Dixiecrats. The Supreme Court decision invalidating segregation
provided the movement with a legitimacy that it previously lacked. In
addition, it transformed the nature of the conflict from one having to
do with blacks and whites to a constitutional crisis that forced the federal government to act, however grudgingly, on behalf of blacks. Finally, in an era of Cold War politics, with the United States and the
Soviet Union competing for the allegiance of the Third World, the
South's racial practices had become a national embarrassment and an
impediment to the conduct of foreign policy. Like tarot cards, all of
the historical elements were in place, auguring a fateful change in the
South's system of state-sponsored racism.

Inevitable as change was, it would not have occurred without the
courageous and often heroic acts of individuals and groups who participated in the civil rights movement. If the history of race in America has left us with one unambiguous truth, it is that without black
protest there would have been no change in the prevailing racial order. Nor did this protest wait for liberal sanction. To be sure, liberals
played an indispensable role in the civil rights movement. They provided money, resources, political support, front-line activists, and, in
some instances, martyrs who gave not only their lives, but also a vital
legitimacy to the struggle. Nevertheless, liberals from President Ken-
nedy down through the ranks usually had to be goaded, cajoled, provoked, shocked, embarrassed, and dragooned by escalating conflict
into supporting the liberation movement. Indeed, an underlying
purpose of mass demonstrations and the choreographed confronta-

tions with the guardians of Southern racism was to engineer a crisis that would raise consciousness among whites and jolt them out of their apathy. It took great and unrelenting pressure to break through "the invisible but horribly tangible plate glass" that prevented whites from so much as taking notice of the agonizing cries emanating from the nation's racial prison.

The next passage in Du Bois's cave analogy is even more apropos to the events of the 1960s:

They get excited; they talk louder; they gesticulate. Some of the passing world stop in curiosity; these gesticulations seem so pointless; they laugh and pass on. They still either do not hear at all, or hear but dimly, and even what they hear, they do not understand. Then the people within may become hysterical. They may scream and hurl themselves against the barriers, hardly realizing in their bewilderment that they are screaming in a vacuum unheard and that their antics may actually seem funny to those outside looking in. They may even, here and there, break through in blood and disfigurement, and find themselves faced by a horrified, implacable, and quite overwhelming mob of people frightened for their own very existence.[38]

Indeed, as black anger and militancy reached feverish heights, white America responded with bewilderment and fear. It is clear, at least in retrospect, that this conflict and polarization provided the dynamic for change. Just as the movement transformed race relations, it altered established ways of *thinking* about race.

Paradigm Crisis: The Fall of Myrdal's Liberal Orthodoxy

"Scientific revolutions," Kuhn writes, "are inaugurated by a growing sense, again often restricted to a narrow subdivision of the scientific community, that an existing paradigm has ceased to function adequately in the exploration of an aspect of nature to which that paradigm itself had previously led the way."[39] This passage accurately describes what transpired in the field of race relations when, under the weight of the escalating racial crisis, social scientists lost faith in the prevailing paradigm and its adequacy for explaining racial trends.

The unmistakable sign of a paradigm crisis—the intellectual version of the smoking gun—was Everett Hughes's presidential address to the American Sociological Association in August 1963. Events had forced Hughes to confront a hard truth: that sociology had failed to anticipate, much less predict, the rise of black insurgency and the ensuing conflict that threw the entire society into crisis. Thus Hughes's vexing question: "Why did social scientists—and sociologists in particular—not foresee the explosion of collective action of Negro Americans toward immediate full integration into American society?"[40]

Although Hughes asked the right question, his answer was sadly deficient. All that he was willing to concede was that "our conception of social science is so empirical, so limited to little bundles of fact applied to little hypotheses, that we are incapable of entertaining a broad range of possibilities, of following out the madly unlikely combinations of social circumstances."[41] No doubt, narrow empiricism obscured "the big picture," but this so-called narrow empiricism is not altogether innocent of politics. Much as an optometrist fits a myopic patient with an appropriate lens, so do the methods adopted by social scientists influence whether proximate or more distant determinants come into focus. For a discipline that did not *want* to see the big picture, narrow empiricism provided an ingenious smoke screen.[42]

Hughes comes closer to the truth when he writes: "Why should we have thought, apart from the comfort of it, that the relations of the future could be predicated in terms of moderate trends, rather than by the model of the slow burn reaching the heat of massive explosion?"[43] Unfortunately, he poses this question rhetorically instead of probing into the *reasons* that sociologists took comfort in believing that change would proceed with moderation and without undue heat. Could this reflect the fact that all but a few professional sociologists were white and middle class in origin, and that *they* could afford to be patient? Was it not also the case that the prevailing models of "race relations" were wedded to the existing racial order, or a liberal variant of it? Since the sociological establishment rarely heard, much less heeded, the voices emanating from the bottom of black society, how *could* it have anticipated black insurgency?

In point of fact, there were people who were not averse to "the slow

burn reaching the heat of massive explosion," and who did predict
black insurgency. They were mavericks on the left, some with Communist leanings, who were dismissed as ideologues who did not
share a commitment to objective sociology. Again, the best example
is C. L. R. James, who wrote a piece in 1947 under the title "The
Revolutionary Answer to the Negro Problem in the U.S." James well
recognized "the revolutionary potential" that existed within black
America:

Let us not forget that in the Negro people, there sleep and are now awakening, pas-
sions of a violence exceeding, perhaps, as far as these things can be compared, anything among the tremendous forces that capitalism has created. Anyone who knows
them, who knows their history, is able to talk to them intimately, watches them at
their own theaters, watches them at their dances, watches them in their churches,
reads their press with a discerning eye, must recognize that although their social
force may not be able to compare with the social force of a corresponding number of
organized workers, the hatred of bourgeois society and the readiness to destroy it
when the opportunity should present itself, rests among them to a degree greater than
in any other section of the population in the United States."[44]

Far from failing to anticipate black insurgency, James and others on
the left erred in thinking that insurgency would occur much sooner
than it did.

Whatever the inadequacies in Hughes's analysis of why sociology
failed to predict the civil rights revolution, the fact of overriding importance was that he posited the question in the first place, and did so
in his capacity as president of the American Sociological Association.
Here was a rare admission of intellectual failure. The civil rights upheaval had jolted establishment sociology out of its inveterate complacency, and this was reflected in the mood of self-doubt and self-
criticism that pervaded Hughes's address. On the other hand, this
admitted failure of sociological imagination signaled a willingness to
examine old assumptions, to consider new ideas, and to heed those
radical and minority voices that had previously been excluded from
mainstream discourse. The forces were again in motion for a paradigm change.

Between 1961 and 1962 *Social Forces*, which exhibited more of a critical bent than the *American Sociological Review*, published three articles critical of *An American Dilemma*. The first, by Ernest Campbell, was entitled "Moral Discomfort and Racial Segregation—An Examination of the Myrdal Hypothesis." Campbell began by observing that Myrdal's assumption that whites suffer from moral conflict over racism had never been put to an empirical test. On the basis of questionnaires administered to nearly three hundred college students in a Southern college, Campbell found little evidence of racial guilt. To whatever extent students were committed to democratic norms, they had no trouble in rationalizing them away when it came to blacks. Campbell concluded that "Gunnar Myrdal performed a disservice to our understanding of segregated social systems by his drastic simplification of the normative dimensions of the issue."[45]

The same issue of *Social Forces* contained an article by Lewis Killian and Charles Grigg that put another of Myrdal's key concepts to an empirical test. Myrdal had postulated "a rank order of discrimination" that mirrored the degree of importance that whites and blacks give to various kinds of discrimination. Myrdal based his analysis entirely on personal impressions. On the basis of interviews conducted in Florida, Killian and Grigg found that whites showed more resistance to equal job opportunities than Myrdal had estimated. Blacks put job discrimination at the top of their list just as Myrdal had claimed, but they ranked political disfranchisement lower and segregation in public facilities higher than Myrdal assumed.[46]

Another article a year later also began on the premise that "Myrdal's thesis has become so well institutionalized among sociologists that its assumptions have never been systematically examined," and proceeded to take issue with Myrdal's conceptual framework, much as Cox had done twenty years earlier (and far more effectively).[47] Finally, in 1965 the *American Sociological Review* published an article by Frank Westie entitled "The American Dilemma: An Empirical Test." Like Campbell's earlier study, Westie found that bigots had little trouble reconciling their racism with the imperatives of the American creed.[48] Clearly, the aura surrounding Myrdal's "monumental study" was beginning to fade. Note, however, that these early attacks on Myrdal rested primarily on narrow empirical issues. Wounds were inflicted, but the paradigm as a whole stood intact.

The coup de grace, however, was administered in 1969 in a trenchant critique entitled "The Negro in America: Where Myrdal Went Wrong," written by historian Carl Degler. By 1969 the civil rights stage of the liberation struggle had already passed, and the battleground had shifted to cities in the North that were reeling from a series of riots. The historical moment was right for a total reassessment of Myrdal's liberal orthodoxy. It is noteworthy that this intellectual flogging took place in the public square, so to speak—the pages of the *New York Times Magazine*.[49]

Where had Myrdal gone wrong? Degler made a number of incisive points:

1. Myrdal had predicted increased militancy on the part of blacks after the Second World War, and he foresaw the possibility of race riots. However, he regarded the South as infinitely more racist than the North, and grossly underestimated the depth and virulence of Northern racism. Consequently, as Degler points out, "Myrdal's book missed entirely the great fact of the nineteen-sixties—namely, the outbreak of overt racial antagonism and violence in the cities of the North."[50]

2. Like most liberals, Myrdal believed that much of the dynamic for change would come from labor unions. This was wrong on two counts. First of all, Myrdal underestimated the depth and virulence of racism in the ranks of organized labor, and the extent to which unions would be a major impediment to racial progress. Second, he underestimated the extent to which the impetus for change would come from *within* the black community. To quote Degler:

Undoubtedly, the most striking error of omission in Myrdal's delineation of the course of race relations in the United States over the last quarter-century was his failure to recognize that the greatest peaceful pressure for change would come from Negroes in the South."[51]

Myrdal's error was that he accepted the "passivity" of the Southern Negro at face value. However, writers far to the left of Myrdal read this behavior differently, or one might say, picked up the other end of the stick. Consider, for example, Langston Hughes's 1949 poem "Warning":

> Negroes,
> Sweet and docile,
> Meek, humble, and kind:
> Beware the day
> They change their mind!
>
> Wind
> In the cotton fields,
> Gentle Breeze:
> Beware the hour
> It uproots trees![52]

3. Myrdal also underestimated the potential of the black church as an instrument for change. "In the South," Myrdal had written, "[the black church] has not taken a lead in attacking the caste system or even in bringing about minor reforms; in the North it has only occasionally been a strong force for social action."[53] Nor was it the case that the church changed in the years after Myrdal's book was written. In 1948 C. L. R. James singled out "the churches in particular" as a source of organized protest against racial oppression.[54]

4. According to Degler, "Myrdal's optimism . . . is the greatest weakness in his book."[55] This optimism was based, first of all, on a romantic view of human nature and of Americans in particular. Myrdal held that people, at bottom, want to be rational and just, and that Americans were conscience-stricken over their treatment of blacks. Second, Myrdal's philosophical idealism led him to treat racism as an "idea" that could be altered or exorcised through education. It followed that racism could be ameliorated by making people aware, with the help of social science, of their mistaken beliefs about blacks. By 1969 it was painfully evident that racism was too complex a problem to remedy through education alone.

5. Degler concluded that "if there is one thing that has been learned in the past quarter-century, it is that merely removing barriers to Negro opportunity is not enough if true equality of opportunity is the goal." Myrdal, according to Degler, failed to anticipate a next stage that would require compensatory programs:

His model of how change would take place did not envision the need for compensatory action. Yet it is evident from the last 25 years and from the experience of Brazil that compensatory measures are required if the black man is to overcome the burdens of slavery and discrimination. [56]

Nor can it be said that, writing in the 1940s, Myrdal could hardly have been expected to foresee the need for compensatory programs. When this issue eventually surfaced in the 1960s, Myrdal went on record as opposed to compensatory programs because, he argued, the effects of discrimination could only be diminished through race-neutral policies that would "lift *all* the poor people" out of poverty. [57]

Aside from the particulars of Degler's retrospective critique of *An American Dilemma*, its real significance was to render the harsh verdict of history: that, like most books, Myrdal's opus did not stand the test of time. This is not to deny its importance at the time it was written, or the role that it played in the evolving civil rights struggle. As noted earlier, *An American Dilemma* brought unprecedented national attention to the "Negro problem" and established an immensely valuable historical record of the condition of blacks in American society at this pivotal historical moment. It also helped to delegitimize racism, and provided political leaders, courts, journalists, and other opinion makers with an authoritative text with which to buttress their liberal edicts. However, by 1969 even liberals could not escape the conclusion that Myrdal's conceptual framework was of little use in explaining the racial crisis that engulfed the nation. The time had come to put Myrdal's "monumental study" on a back shelf. [58]

The demise of Myrdal's liberal orthodoxy, however, signaled the onset of yet another paradigm shift.

3

The 1960s and the Scholarship of Confrontation

> What we are discovering . . . is that the United States—
> all of it, North as well as South, West as well as East—
> is a racist society in a sense and to a degree that
> we have refused so far to admit, much less face.
>
> Charles E. Silberman, *Crisis in Black and White*, 1964

The process of racial change in the 1960s was exactly opposite to what Gunnar Myrdal would have predicted. Myrdal's concept of social engineering presupposed that change would occur through the rational application of principles of science and planning. Instead of this "top-down" approach, the impetus for change came from the "bottom up." It was a grassroots political movement, with its own organizational structure, that was the vehicle of racial change. Much the same thing happened in the realm of ideas. It was not a momentous intellectual breakthrough—a discovery, a brilliant treatise by some acolyte, an epiphany of some kind—that changed how scholars thought about race. Rather it was the pressure of ideas and events *outside* the academy that provided the catalyst for intellectual change.[1]

A paradigm shift produces something of a vacuum as the hoary old texts associated with a discredited paradigm are suddenly rendered insignificant. What, after all, was the fate of the vast body of scholarship in phrenology once *An American Dilemma* was accepted as a classic? To collect merciful dust on our bookshelves!

Of course, over time another canon of scholarship was developed, consistent with the axiomatic principles of Myrdal's liberal orthodoxy. As Thomas Pettigrew has pointed out, "the postwar years were characterized by psychological analysis of race relations with emphasis upon 'prejudice.'"[2] The cardinal assumption, rarely subjected to critical examination, was that the crux of "the Negro problem" had to do with prejudice. The prejudice directed against blacks was assumed to stem from the same factors as the prejudice against other groups that were "different"—namely, from ignorance and limited contact. It followed, therefore, that racism could be eliminated through a re-socialization of the bigot, either through education or through inter-cultural programs that fostered better "race relations." If this were done on a large enough scale—or so it was assumed—then America could achieve the promise of its creed. As the racial crisis deepened in the 1960s, this entire model was thrown into question.

By 1966 Pettigrew sounded the alarm of paradigm crisis: "I think one of the great fallacies we have had in the field of race relations for many, many decades has been to worry about attitudes rather than about conditions. It is a crude but, I think, generally correct statement to say that attitudes are more often a result than a cause of most of our race-relation situations."[3] As noted earlier, such confessions of intellectual failure were therapeutic in that they reflected an open-ness—even a hunger—for new voices and perspectives that might shed light on the forces that were tearing American society apart.

Scholars, however, are chronically slow to respond to social change, especially when it occurs suddenly. It is not just that, like Rodin's sculpture of "The Thinker," the scholar is transfixed, too absorbed in thought to respond to ephemeral events. Scholars by training are prohibited from spouting off until they have collected evidence to substantiate their claims. The obligatory collection of evidence requires time and money. For better or worse, it takes years before the academic wheel is sufficiently greased to turn out a significant body of scholarship, even on a major new development like the civil rights upheaval and, later, the outbreak of ghetto riots.

Perhaps for this reason, much of the early writing on the intensi-fying racial conflict came from the movement itself. A score of books were written by movement leaders and activists who suddenly found themselves with a white audience. Below is a chronological list of such books published between 1958 and 1978, mostly by leading publishing houses:

Martin Luther King, Jr., *Stride toward Freedom: The Montgomery Story* (Harper & Row, 1958).

Martin Luther King, Jr., *Why We Can't Wait* (Harper & Row, 1964).

Malcolm X, *The Autobiography of Malcolm X* (Grove Press, 1964).

Whitney M. Young, Jr., *To Be Equal* (McGraw-Hill, 1964).

James Farmer, *Freedom—When?* (Random House, 1965).

Eldridge Cleaver, *Soul on Ice* (McGraw-Hill, 1967).

Martin Luther King, Jr., *Where Do We Go from Here?* (Harper & Row, 1967).

Whitney M. Young, Jr., *Beyond Racism* (McGraw-Hill, 1969).

Bobby Seale, *Seize the Time: The Story of the Black Panther Party and Huey Newton* (Random House, 1970).

George Jackson, *Soledad Brother: The Prison Letters of George Jackson* (Coward-McGann, 1970).

Stokely Carmichael, *Stokely Speaks* (Random House, 1971).

Bayard Rustin, *Down the Line* (Quadrangle Books, 1971).

James Forman, *The Making of Black Revolutionaries* (Macmillan, 1972).

Huey P. Newton, *To Die for the People* (Random House, 1972).

Huey P. Newton, *Revolutionary Suicide* (Harcourt Brace Jovanovich, 1973).

Angela Davis, *Angela Davis—An Autobiography* (Random House, 1974).

H. Rap Brown, *Die Nigger Die!* (Dial Press, 1978).

It is noteworthy, of course, that the first "movement book" was Martin Luther King's inspiring account of his role in the Montgomery bus boycott and his ascent to national prominence. The genre got a big boost in 1964 with the publication of *The Autobiography of Malcolm X*, written with the assistance of Alex Haley. Originally Doubleday was slated to publish the book, but reneged out of fear of violence after the assassination of Malcolm X, much to the good fortune of Grove Press.[4] By 1966 it had already sold some 25,000 copies, and the paperback edition ultimately sold well over a million copies. The lesson was not lost on other publishing houses which eagerly signed on books by protest leaders. The paperback edition of King's *Where Do We Go From Here?*, issued by Beacon Press in 1968, sold over 24,000 copies in its first year. Eventually establishment publishers overcame their qualms about publishing books by young volatile authors, and books with titles like *Revolutionary Suicide* and *Die Nigger Die!* began to appear on the lists of leading houses.

By 1969 the *New York Times Book Review* declared that there was a "Black Revolution in Books."[5] The surging demand for books by and about blacks, augmented by rising college admissions among blacks, not only changed the practices of establishment publishers, but was also reflected in a doubling of commercial black publishing houses— from eighteen in 1960 to thirty-seven in 1974.[6] The boom was especially pronounced in fiction and autobiography.[7] Not only were these works self-consciously political, but in many instances—James Baldwin, Ralph Ellison, Richard Wright, Lorraine Hansberry, and Julius Lester come first to mind—black writers of fiction found themselves at the center of societal debates concerning race and politics. Race, for so long a taboo subject, was suddenly at the center of literary and political discourse, and the boundaries between art and politics were more blurred than at any time since the proletarian literature of the Depression.

Unlike academics, journalists do not hesitate to jump into the fray of newsbreaking events. Robert Conot wrote a riveting account of the 1965 Watts riot, entitled *Rivers of Blood, Years of Darkness*.[8] A similar book by John Hersey about the Detroit riot, *The Algiers Motel Incident*, became a best seller.[9] The journalist who had the greatest impact, however, was an editor at *Fortune* magazine, Charles Silberman, whose book *Crisis in Black and White* appeared on the *New York Times* Best Seller List for ten weeks in 1964.

Silberman began his book with Richard Wright's observation that

"American whites and blacks both possess deep-seated resistance against 'the Negro problem' being presented, even verbally, in all of its hideous fullness, in all of the totality of its meaning."[10] Now, nearly twenty years later, America had been forced to confront its racist legacy, and an editor from *Fortune* magazine was the unlikely purveyor of these belated truths to a nation jolted out of its apathy by years of racial strife. Gone, too, was the customary liberal gloss as Silberman declared that "what we are discovering, in short, is that the United States—all of it, North as well as South, West as well as East—is a racist society in a sense and to a degree that we have refused so far to admit, much less face."[11] In substance as well as tone, this was a far cry from Myrdal's characterization of racism as an unfortunate contradiction of the American creed. Silberman's repudiation of Myrdal was explicit:

> The tragedy of race relations in the United States is that there is no American dilemma. White Americans are not torn and tortured by the conflict between their devotion to the American creed and their actual behavior. They are upset by the current state of race relations, to be sure. But what troubles them is not that justice is being denied, but that their peace is being shattered and their business interrupted.[12]

Nor would moral suasion or melioristic reform suffice in redressing the evils of racism: "Nothing less than a radical reconstruction of American society is required if the Negro is to be able to take his rightful place in American life."[13] By the end of the book Silberman was invoking "the P-word"—preference—and quoted Whitney Young as follows:

> If those who make the decisions in this country are really sincere about closing the gaps, they must go further than fine impartiality. We must have, in fact, special consideration if we are to compensate for the scars left by 300 years of deprivation.[14]

If Myrdal gave the American people only as much medicine as they were willing to swallow, then by 1964 the patient had come to realize that the disease was life-threatening and required a more potent antidote. Silberman's book is remarkable for its forthright and uncompromising analysis of the extent to which American society was infected with racism.

As has been implied above, paradigms of racism involve not just theories that purport to explain racial subordination, but at least by implication, prescriptions for what should or should not be done to remedy the problem. Inasmuch as nineteenth-century Social Darwinists held that blacks were inherently inferior and destined by nature to occupy the lower rungs of society, it followed that any attempts to elevate blacks were misguided and futile. In Myrdal's paradigm, racial subordination was assumed to be rooted in a belief system that was pre-rational, pre-scientific, and pre-democratic. The "cure," therefore, was to marshal all the forces of reason and science to counter these retrograde beliefs, and to fortify democratic institutions. Silberman's position, clearly reflecting the assumptions of the protest movement, was that the society *as a whole* was racist. The logical extension of this premise was that its racist structures had to be overhauled. To the extent that racial subordination was the result of systemic racism, then extraordinary programs would be needed to compensate for past wrongs and to give blacks the job opportunities they had been so long denied.

In laying the blame for racial subordination on the doorstep of American society, Silberman spoke the simple truth that white America had so long feared, not because this truth was so painful to contemplate, but because it carried with it a moral and political obligation to revamp the entire racial order. Indeed, the anticipation of these changes is what explains the "deep-seated resistance against 'the Negro problem' being presented, even verbally, in all of its hideous fullness." The great lie of racism, from slavery down to the present, was that racial hierarchy was ordained by God or nature, or was rendered almost immutable by intractable social forces. Here was a radical new theory that shifted the blame onto American society and its major institutions, and that demanded an overhaul of the entire racial order. To repeat, Silberman was only expressing an idea at the heart of the protest movement. Still, the fact that it was embraced and given such lucid and resolute expression by a white editor of *Fortune*—in a book that received plaudits even from Malcolm X—indicates how profound an impact the message of the protest movement had had on white society.[15]

A steady flow of books throughout the 1960s confronted white society with its racism. Kenneth Clark's *Dark Ghetto,* published in 1965, began with a prologue entitled "The Cry of the Ghetto," consisting of poignant statements of Harlem residents, mostly youth. Although Clark dealt squarely with "the tangle of community and personal pathology," he did so within a larger context that fixed ultimate responsibility on white society. As he wrote: "Nothing short of a concerted and massive attack on the social, political, economic, and cultural roots of the pathology is required if anything more than daubing or displacement of the symptoms is to be achieved."[16] Clark also attacked the fashionable social deprivation theories as "merely substituting notions of environmental immutability and fatalism for earlier notions of biologically determined educational unmodifiability," thus absolving schools for their record of failure with respect to black children.[17] Finally, he ended with a trenchant attack on white liberals for acquiescing to the racial status quo, and for failing to combat racism even in spheres where liberals are powerful, such as labor unions, colleges, and politics.

The liberal faith in schools as a panacea for racial inequity also came under challenge by Jonathan Kozol's *Death at an Early Age,* which was a recipient of the National Book Award in 1967.[18] Kozol provided a grim picture of the experiences of black children in the Boston public schools. Like Clark, Kozol made it painfully evident that schools in the North, as well as the South, were riddled with racism. Far from being the solution, the schools were part of the problem.

In 1968 two black psychiatrists, William Grier and Price Cobbs, wrote *Black Rage.*[19] Published with a foreword by U.S. Senator Fred R. Harris, the book probed one of the most taboo topics in the field of race relations: what Franz Fanon called "the rage of the oppressed." At last, it would appear, white America was willing to confront the rage of its victims, as suggested by the fact that *Black Rage* was a Book-of-the-Month Club special alternate selection and a top seller in hard and soft covers. [20]

While social scientists were still puzzling about what was wrong with their models and designing research projects that would turn up the facts that had apparently eluded prior generations of scholars, another influential book was published, this time based on a collaboration between a political activist and an ivory-tower scholar. *Black Power* was written by Stokely Carmichael, the former chairman of SNCC who was catapulted into the national limelight in 1966 when he issued a call for "black power" at a political rally, and Charles Hamilton, a black professor of political science at Lincoln University in Pennsylvania. As a young activist, Hamilton had met Carmichael at SNCC workshops and retreats in the early sixties, and after "black power" emerged as an issue in 1966, they agreed to collaborate on a book. [21]

"What is racism?" So began *Black Power*, as the authors signaled their intention to challenge the cardinal element of racial discourse. Carmichael and Hamilton advanced a bold, new conception of racism, one that would have far-reaching implications for theory and politics alike. Their well-crafted formulation is worth quoting at length:

Racism is both overt and covert. It takes two, closely related forms: individual whites acting against individual blacks, and acts by the total white community against the black community. We call these individual racism and institutionalized racism. The first consists of overt acts by individuals, which cause death, injury or the violent destruction of property. This type can be recorded by television cameras; it can frequently be observed in the process of commission. The second type is less overt, far more subtle, less identifiable in terms of *specific* individuals committing the acts. But it is no less destructive of human life. The second type originates in the operation of established and respected forces in the society, and thus receives far less public condemnation than the first type. [22]

To this theoretical statement, Carmichael and Hamilton added a compelling illustration:

When white terrorists bomb a black church and kill five black children, that is an act of individual racism, widely deplored by most segments of the society. But when in that same city—Birmingham, Alabama—five hundred black babies die each year because of the lack of proper food, shelter and medical facilities, and thousands more are destroyed and maimed physically, emotionally and intellectually because of conditions of poverty and discrimination in the black community, that is a function of institutional racism. When a black family moves into a home in a white neighborhood and is stoned, burned or routed out, they are victims of an overt act of individual racism which many people will condemn—at least in words. But it is institutional racism that keeps black people locked in dilapidated slum tenements, subject to the daily prey of exploitative slumlords, merchants, loan sharks and discriminatory real estate agents. The society either pretends it does not know of this latter situation, or is in fact incapable of doing anything meaningful about it.[23]

Of course, the notion that racism was embedded in major institutions was not altogether new—it was central to the radical analysis of racism and received copious documentation in *An American Dilemma*. However, Carmichael and Hamilton highlighted the essential difference between intentional and unintentional racism, and encapsulated this important distinction in a succinct term that made its way into the discourse on race, both inside and outside the academy. "Institutionalized racism" did not deny the obvious—that a great many people harbor racist beliefs and stereotypes that form the basis for racist behavior. But it insisted that racism also includes practices that are not necessarily motivated by racial animus, but that nevertheless reinforce or perpetuate racial inequities.

The concept of institutionalized racism had powerful moral implications since it meant that liberal society could no longer purge itself of responsibility for racism solely by repudiating Southern-style racism. There were also the more subtle and insidious forms that racism assumed in the North, even in characteristically liberal institutions like the university, labor unions, and the Democratic Party. Without quite saying so, Carmichael and Hamilton were also raising the issue of collective guilt for racial oppression, which implicated whites generally—liberals included—for the wrongs visited upon blacks by a racist society. Malcolm X had come to a similar reckoning in his *Autobiography* when he wrote that "notwithstanding those few 'good' white people, it is the *collective* 150 million white people whom the *collective* 22 million black people have to deal with!"[24]

The concept of institutionalized racism had powerful political implications as well. It meant that laws securing the civil rights of blacks
and even laws specifically proscribing discrimination did not go far
enough. From the point of view of institutionalized racism, the *fact*
of black exclusion was prima facie evidence of racism. Whether exclusion was directly the result of willful acts of discrimination was, at
best, a secondary consideration. The conceptual groundwork was
being laid for a new policy initiative: one that would gauge the extent
of racism not by intent, but by results. Not until blacks were fully incorporated into all segments of American life, not until the statistical
disparities between whites and blacks in wealth, status, and power
were wiped out, not until impoverished racial ghettos were eliminated from the American landscape—only then could America erase
the stigma of being "a racist society."

The idea that racism could be an attribute of whole societies, and
not merely of discrete individuals, got another major boost in 1968
with the publication of the *Report of the National Advisory Commission on Civil Disorders,* better known as the Kerner Report. The
Commission was appointed by President Johnson to investigate the
causes of the riots that began in Newark and Detroit in the summer of
1967 and spread like wildfire to scores of cities across the nation. At
the time of its formation the Commission was severely criticized as
too "moderate."[25] Yet the report that it produced was a remarkably
radical document, in many ways comparable to Frazier's report on
the 1935 Harlem Riot that was suppressed by Mayor La Guardia.
Now, in the context of the 1960s, the Kerner Report was not only
published with fanfare, but was first on the *New York Times* paperback
best-seller list in 1968 and sold some two million copies.[26]

Unlike the McCone Commission that characterized the Watts riot
of 1965 as an "insensate rage of destruction," a "spasm," and a "form-
less, quite senseless, all but hopeless violent protest," the Kerner
Commission explicitly rejected the notion that the "disorders"
stemmed from mindless violence on the part of aberrant ghetto
youth.[27] Studies conducted by the Commission found that the typical
rioter was somewhat *better* educated than those who did not actively

participate in the riot, and that while most of the active participants were young males, they had the sympathy of a broad segment of the ghetto community. In effect, the Commission conceded that the riots constituted a form of protest. Even the looting and burning, according to the Commission, were usually directed "against symbols of white American society—authority and property—rather than against white persons."[28]

The keynote of the Kerner Report, however, was its declaration that "white racism is essentially responsible for the explosive mixture which has been accumulating in our cities since the end of World War II."[29] This was an astonishing and unprecedented declaration. At the time American society was reeling from a seemingly endless chain of riots, replete with daily television coverage of looting, burning, and sniping. Yet a "moderate" presidential commission was placing the ultimate blame on white racism. Furthermore, the Commission made it clear that the problem of racial segregation was far from solved by the passage of landmark civil rights legislation in 1964 and 1965. On the first page of its report, it issued its famous declaration that "our nation is moving toward two societies, one black, one white—separate and unequal."

The Kerner Report concluded with seventy-three pages of policy recommendations. Included were a plethora of reforms in the areas of education, housing, and welfare, but, as with Frazier's 1935 report on the Harlem Riot, the emphasis was on employment. In addition to opening up the existing job structures by strengthening enforcement of anti-discriminatory laws and extending affirmative action, the Commission proposed to create two million new jobs over three years, half of them in the public sector. That the Commission had no illusions that its proposals would be implemented is evident from the concluding paragraph of the report, which quotes Kenneth Clark's testimony before the Commission:

I read that report . . . of the 1919 riot in Chicago, and it is as if I were reading the report of the investigating committee on the Harlem riot of '35, the report of the investigating committee on the Harlem riot of '43, the report of the McCone Commission on the Watts riot.

I must again in candor say to you members of this Commission—it is a kind of Alice in Wonderland—with the same moving picture re-shown over and over again, the same analysis, the same recommendations, and the same inaction.

Clark's cynicism was borne out by events. The report never became the basis for legislative action or other public policy initiatives. [30] Small comfort could be taken from the fact that, unlike Frazier's report on the Harlem Riot, it was filed away after, rather than before, publication.

It is indicative of how far the political pendulum had swung that even the Kerner Report came under fire from the left. Robert Blauner wrote that "what makes the Kerner Report a less-than-radical document is its superficial treatment of racism and its reluctance to confront the colonized relation between black people and the larger society." [31] Andrew Kopkind also complained that "failure to analyze in any way the 'white racism' asserted by the commissioners in the Report's summary transformed that critical category into a cheap slogan." [32] Kopkind provided a detailed account of the schism that developed between "conservatives" and "radicals" on the Commission that, he claimed, led the majority to seek a safe middle ground. On the other hand, one of the embattled "radicals" on the Commission's staff, Gary Marx, called the report "the most significant and far-reaching statement of a programmatic nature ever made by a governmental unit on American race relations." [33]

Whatever its shortcomings, the Kerner Report represented a remarkable historical development. At a time when the peaceful tactics of the civil rights movement had given way to violent protest on the part of ghetto youth, a presidential commission had placed the ultimate blame for racial conflict on the doorstep of white America. The problem with the Kerner Report is not that it did not go far enough, but that its far-reaching policy recommendations were never acted upon. Nevertheless, the report did have an enduring impact on the nation's racial consciousness. Never before, except perhaps during the brief reign of the Radical Republicans after the Civil War, had the nation gone so far toward accepting collective responsibility for the terrible repercussions of "white racism."

Social Science and the Scholarship of Confrontation

The outpouring of books on race and racial conflict during the 1960s initially reflected the contributions of political activists, journalists, and, increasingly, black intellectuals and literary figures. Slowly a new canon began to emerge in the social sciences as well. The earliest works came from an older generation of stalwarts who had been active in the black liberation struggle even before it coalesced into a "movement." History had caught up with them, as it were, and they not only were strategically located to interpret the unanticipated course of events, but also enjoyed an unaccustomed respectability.[34]

In time a younger generation of scholars, many of whom were personally involved in the movements of the sixties, reached intellectual maturity.[35] Reflecting their immersion in Marxist theory, the Young Turks christened themselves students of "political economy." Their books and articles had titles that loudly trumpeted the new political gestalt:

Raymond Franklin, "The Political Economy of Black Power," *Social Problems* 16 (Winter 1967).

John C. Leggett, *Class, Race and Labor: Working Class Consciousness in Detroit* (Oxford, 1968).

Robert Allen, *Black Awakening in Capitalist America* (Doubleday, 1969).

James Boggs, *Racism and the Class Struggle* (Monthly Review Press, 1970).

William Tabb, *The Political Economy of the Black Ghetto* (Norton, 1971).

Michael Reich, "The Economics of Racism," *Upstart* 5, no. 1 (1971).

Harold Baron, "Black Labor: Historical Notes in the Political Economy of Racism," *Radical America* 5 (1971).

Raymond Franklin and Solomon Resnik, *The Political Economy of Racism* (Holt, Rinehart & Winston, 1973).

Martin Oppenheimer, "The Sub-Proletariat: Dark Skins and Dirty Work," *The Insurgent Sociologist* 4 (1974).

Each new turn in the course of the civil rights movement, each new bout of racial conflict, produced a spate of scholarly books and articles. The resurgence of black nationalism and the Black Muslims produced several fine studies.[36] The acrimonious debate that followed the publication of Daniel Patrick Moynihan's 1965 report on *The Negro Family* stimulated an enormous body of research and writing on the black family.[37] The emergence of the "black power movement" produced another slew of scholarly books and articles.[38] The outbreak of ghetto "riots"—"revolts" was the politically correct term—engendered a large body of research, much of it subsidized by governmental agencies and commissions.[39] The same was true of the never-ending conflict over school desegregation.[40]

Prior to the civil rights movement, historiography had produced few major studies of the black experience in America. In his 1935 study *Black Reconstruction*, W. E. B. Du Bois had good reason to denounce historiography on race as sheer propaganda that sought only to cover up the nation's ignominious past.[41] Indeed, it was not until 1959, with the publication of Stanley Elkins's *Slavery: A Problem in American Institutional and Intellectual Life*, that white historians began to take the question of slavery seriously.[42] By the late 1960s there was a veritable explosion in historical studies of the African-American experience. In 1969 Winthrop Jordan's study, *White Over Black: American Attitudes Toward the Negro, 1550–1812*, received the Bancroft Prize in history.[43] Over the next eight years, seven additional books dealing with the African-American experience received this prestigious award.[44] As historian Nathan Huggins wrote in 1990, "it was as if historians were bringing to life a people who had been both socially and historically dead."[45]

The new historiography, furthermore, was infused with the critical spirit of the 1960s. As Eric Foner has commented: "Reconstruction revisionism bore the mark of the modern civil rights movement. In the 1960s the revisionist wave broke over the field, destroying, in rapid succession, every assumption of the traditional viewpoint."[46] Icons fell like bowling pins, as an exciting new canon emerged that accorded blacks their proper place in American history.

Much the same can be said about each of the social science disci-
plines. In *Black Reconstruction*, Du Bois had written that "in propaganda against the Negro since emancipation in this land, we face one
of the most stupendous efforts the world ever saw to discredit human
beings, an effort involving universities, history, science, social life
and religion."[47] Now, in the aftermath of the civil rights revolution,
each of these fields began to produce a revisionist scholarship that
purged itself of its racist underpinnings, and confronted racism "in all
its hideous fullness."

Despite the burgeoning canon of scholarly books and articles that
reflected a new sensibility and perspective on issues of race and racism, no single study had the scope or achieved the stature of *An
American Dilemma*. Perhaps what was missing was a huge subsidy
from a foundation to underwrite another comprehensive study of
race in America. To be sure, the foundations responded to the racial
crisis by pouring money into research on race, but this research was
typically disguised as "poverty research," and the subsidies certainly
did not go to the Young Turks who would have been disqualified by
either their leftist politics or their unabashed identification with the
black protest movement.

Nor was it possible any longer to import a foreigner, on the pretext
that this would impart "value neutrality" to the study. In the ideolog-
ically polarized sixties, there was no neutral ground. As Irving Howe
wrote in *Dissent* in the summer of 1963: "The cant of 'moderation' is
at an end. It was always a lie, a supreme hypocrisy. It was the foul eva-
siveness by which our society made verbal concessions to its guilt
while doing nothing to help those whom it kept down."[48] In his repro-
bation of "moderation," Howe was reflecting the impact that the politics of confrontation had on white liberals—in forcing them to confront their own contradictions and to take sides. Who could claim
neutrality to the bloody battle waged on the streets of Selma when
civil rights marchers refused to back down from a phalanx of
mounted troopers recklessly swinging their truncheons? Could one
pretend to see "both sides" of the issue being battled out on the floor
of the 1964 Democratic Convention, when the Mississippi Freedom

Democratic Party refused to compromise on its right to replace the segregationists who had trampled over Democratic Party rules? With American cities under siege from angry youth, was even a pretense of dispassionate inquiry possible? By the 1960s there were no Swedes who could be summoned to rescue America from its own folly.

If there is a single work that meets Kuhn's criterion of "an exemplar study"—one that is representative of a paradigm—it is Robert Blauner's *Racial Oppression in America*. Published in 1972, the book brought together a number of Blauner's provocative essays on issues of race and politics. Obviously, *Racial Oppression in America* does not approach the size or scope of Myrdal's opus. Nor did Blauner enjoy the acclaim that was showered on Myrdal. By his own account, his book "was well received by minority scholars and by students but not by mainstream sociologists, especially by my own colleagues, whose dismissal of its merit resulted in my being turned down twice for a full professor promotion."[49] Of course, the fact that Blauner's work was spurned by mainstream sociologists is entirely consistent with the claim that he offered an alternative paradigm. As Kuhn writes, when new paradigms are proposed, "rather than a single group conversion, what occurs is an increasing shift in the distribution of professional allegiances."[50] At least among a segment of scholars of race, *Racial Oppression in America* was embraced as a pioneering work that had the rudiments of an alternative paradigm.[51]

Blauner makes no secret of his disenchantment with establishment sociology. In the preface to *Racial Oppression in America*, he writes: "My own developing framework probably owes more to the social movements of the oppressed than to standard sociology. . . . Besides the writers and scholars whose work I cite within, the most important influence has been the students with whom I have tested and exchanged ideas on race relations and American society."[52] A few pages later, he adds: "Virtually all of the new insights about racism and the experience of the oppressed have been provided by writers whose lives and minds were uncluttered by sociological theory."[53]

Actually, Blauner's political odyssey began well before he wrote *Racial Oppression in America*. In a recent autobiographical essay, he describes his youthful immersion in radical politics, which included a stint in the Communist Party. By the mid-fifties, however, he wanted "to settle down, to be respectable," and embarked on an academic career that led to a position in Berkeley's prestigious Department of Sociology, where he taught a course on social movements and began research on the sociology of death. A year later, however, the monastic ambience of the Berkeley campus was shattered by the Free Speech Movement. The civil rights movement was also reaching an explosive climax, and the fledgling professor resolved that "it was the problems of the living and not of the dead or dying that needed attention."[54]

Blauner pinpoints "the radicalization of my thinking" to the Watts "riot" in August 1965. In July he had drafted a paper on blacks in which "I used an ethnic group model in which 'the Negro' was the problem, not American society." Barely five months later he wrote "Whitewash Over Watts," a trenchant critique of the McCone Commission's report on the Watts "riot." In his capacity as a professor of sociology at Berkeley, Blauner had been recruited to serve as a consultant to the Commission. His suggestion to do a field study of how the residents of Watts felt about the "riot" was initially accepted, but then quashed because, according to Blauner, it threatened the Commission's law-and-order orientation. The McCone Commission's report gave Blauner another jolt. As he describes it:

The commission's report, when it appeared, was even worse than I had feared. The hypocrisy of its carefully modulated concern angered me. My first experience with official power must have chipped away the faith that I still had that established institutions might respond creatively to the racial crisis.[55]

Blauner's political awakening (or re-awakening, to be precise) eventually resulted in *Racial Oppression in America*.

Clearly, Blauner was a consummate "sixties radical." Not surprisingly, his book is emblematic of the insurgent thinking on race. In the opening sentence of *Racial Oppression in America*, Blauner writes that "the present crisis in American life has led to the questioning of long-accepted frameworks."[56] He follows with what might best be described as a personal declaration of paradigm crisis:

As a sociologist who was attempting to analyze the big news of the 1960s, I found that general sociological theory, as well as the more specific "theories" in the race relations field, was pointing in the wrong direction. These theories not only failed to predict and illuminate new developments—the shift from civil rights to group power strategies, the outbreak of rebellions in the urban ghettos, the growth of militant nationalism and ethnic consciousness—in short, the deepening of racial awareness and conflict in America. The "theories" actually obscured the meaning of these issues, making them more difficult to comprehend. In 1965 I began searching for alternative ways of conceptualizing American racial realities. [57]

In developing his case for "an alternative framework," Blauner identifies four fallacies within traditional sociology:

1. "The view that racial and ethnic groups are neither central nor persistent elements of modern societies." [58]

According to Blauner, the thrust of social theory was to see racial and ethnic identities "as essentially parochial survivals from preindustrial societies and fundamentally opposed to the logic of modernity." [59] Thus, on the one hand, the prevailing sociological framework could not explain the stubborn persistence of racial divisions, except as vestigial elements of premodern belief systems that were presumed to be withering away. On the other hand, it did not allow for "the possibility that racial minorities might prefer to build their own cultures and community institutions rather than choose absorption into the mainstream." [60] Contrary to the optimistic scenario projected by liberal social science, the end of the civil rights stage of the protest movement was associated not with greater integration, but with greater polarization.

2. "The idea that race and racial oppression are not independent dynamic forces but are ultimately reducible to other causal determinants, usually economic or psychological." [61]

Here Blauner lashes out at those on both the right and the left who, for different reasons, underestimate the depth and pervasiveness of racial oppression. The right likes to pretend that racism is a thing of the past, and denies its present-day reality. The left, on the other hand, reduces race to class, thus denying its existence as an autonomous force to be reckoned with on its own terms. Thus the irony: al-

beit for different reasons, both the color-blind right and the color-
blind left oppose public policies targeted for blacks.

3. "The position that the most important aspects of racism are the
attitudes and prejudices of white Americans."[62]

It had been an article of faith for several decades that prejudice was
waning and blacks were making steady progress. Thus, as Blauner observes sardonically, "there were still sociologists celebrating the impressive decline in racial prejudice at the very moment that Watts
burst into flames."[63] The escalating racial conflict forced social scientists to acknowledge that there was more to racism than racial prejudice, thereby repudiating the psychological reductionism that had
pervaded the vast literature on "prejudice." A distinction had to be
drawn—to quote Blauner—"between racism as an objective phenomenon, located in the actual existence of domination and hierarchy, and racism's subjective concomitants of prejudice and other
motivations and feelings."[64]

4. "The so-called *immigrant analogy*, the assumption, critical in
contemporary thought, that there are no essential long-term differences—in relation to the larger society—between the *third world* or
racial minorities and the European ethnic groups."[65]

Sociologists thought they were being liberal when they held that
blacks were only white Americans in black skin. Their intention, of
course, was to reject the racist canards that equated difference with
inferiority. However, this conceptualization also tended to negate
what was culturally unique about African Americans. Similarly,
when liberal sociologists compared blacks to other immigrants, they
thought they were projecting a hopeful scenario that in time blacks
would follow in the footsteps of European immigrants on the road to
success. However, this conceptualization obscured the ways in which
the black experience was fundamentally different from the experience
of other ethnic groups. It also obscured the ways in which racist structures prevented blacks from following in the footsteps of immigrants,
and the need, therefore, to develop alternative paths of mobility.

Given these conceptual foundations, it is hardly surprising that sociology failed to anticipate the civil rights movement, much less the ensuing ghetto uprisings. Events had exposed the utter uselessness of the prevailing models within social science to shed light on the forces that were tearing American society apart.

Blauner thus set out to develop an alternative framework. This begins with the idea that blacks are not just another "minority." Unlike immigrants from Europe who came voluntarily in pursuit of a better life, Africans were abducted from their homelands and imported as a source of cheap labor in the South's evolving plantation system. From these different starting points, the histories of blacks and immigrants proceeded along two altogether different trajectories. In the half-century after the abolition of slavery, the North imported tens of millions of immigrants to provide labor for its burgeoning industries. Although exploited, these immigrants were at least strategically located near the center of an expanding industrial economy, and in time they or their children moved up the economic and social ladder. Blacks, on the other hand, were categorically excluded from employment in the entire manufacturing sector, and, as Blauner points out, were confined to "the most unskilled jobs, the least advanced sectors of the economy, and the most industrially backward region of the country."[66] This racial division of labor engendered and reinforced vastly different systems of prejudice and control. Immigrants *did* encounter prejudice and discrimination, and their social ascent was not easy, but their troubles paled in comparison to the all-encompassing system of domination and exploitation that was the lot of the average Negro.

These crucial differences between blacks and immigrants received scant attention within the prevailing models in the field of race relations. The very terms of discourse—"race relations," "minority," and "prejudice and discrimination"—were ahistorical abstractions that, if anything, obscured the unique aspects of racial oppression alluded to above. Whether by intent or not, liberal sociology had effectively whitewashed racial oppression! It had glossed over the atrocities of slavery and the caste system by obscuring the fact that the obstacles that blacks confronted differed in kind—not merely in degree—to those encountered by other ethnic groups. To break out of the linguistic straitjacket, new constructs would be needed.

Blauner adopted the language and the model of "colonialism" that had come to be accepted in "the movement."[67] Beginning in the early 1960s, black intellectuals and activists seized upon the unmistakable parallels between the struggle against racism in this country with the anticolonial revolts that were raging throughout the Third World.[68] There was this difference, however. In the case of classic colonialism, Europeans used their superior technology and power to conquer vast territories in Africa and Asia, subjugate their people, and plunder their resources. In the American instance, the process had been reversed, and Africans had been forcibly imported to American soil where they, in effect, constituted an *internal colony*. Not only was African labor ruthlessly exploited, but these Africans and their descendants were consigned to live essentially as a conquered people outside the normative order as it applied to whites.

Nor did the colonial analogy apply only to slavery. "Internal colonialism" also seemed to describe the contemporary Northern ghetto which, like European colonies, existed as a world apart, administered by politicians, police, social workers, educators, and others whose primary relationship to the community was one of social control. Property, businesses, and virtually anything of value were owned and controlled by outsiders. If ghettos constituted a kind of colony, then it followed that the so-called riots were actually a form of "revolt," analogous to uprisings in the Third World. Liberation meant more than securing civil rights. It also meant taking control of one's communities.

Here was a mind-boggling alternative to the race relations model that dominated sociological thinking on race for several decades. No longer were blacks "white Americans in black skin." No longer were they merely the objects of the prejudice and discrimination that all minorities encounter. No longer was the ghetto "a temporary waystation," like the neighborhoods once occupied by immigrants before they moved to the suburbs. The colonial model swept away all of these premises, and portrayed blacks as a minority of a different kind: a permanent minority, an oppressed people, a "colonized group."[69]

This conception called the entire liberal project into question. By refuting the immigrant analogy, it implied that the traditional remedies—the processes and mechanisms that had worked for immigrants—could not be counted on to deliver blacks from the social and economic margins. As Herbert Gans had concluded in his refutation of the immigrant analogy, which was incorporated into the Kerner Report, "new channels of escape" would have to be found.[70]

The colonial analogy also challenged another key liberal assumption—that economic mobility on the part of individual blacks would necessarily result in racial integration. No longer was it certain that blacks could be—or *wanted* to be—integrated into white communities. Would another model have to be found that would allow blacks to be, as Harold Cruse has suggested in the title of his last book, *Plural but Equal?*[71]

Nathan Glazer was among the first to take issue with the colonial model, particularly the claim that the immigrant model did not fit blacks. As he wrote in a 1971 essay:

If it is generally believed that there has been a radical break between white immigrant experience and black experience, people will be impelled to adopt new and unprecedented measures to achieve for blacks the measure of status that white immigrant groups reached without such measures. . . . On the other hand, if people believe there is a substantial degree of similarity between the experience of white ethnic groups and black experience, arguments for unique and extreme measures to end black deprivation will be undermined.[72]

Glazer's syntax is revealing. He seems to be saying that if one does not approve of the "unique and extreme measures to end black deprivation," then one should not "believe" the argument that immigrant and black experiences are fundamentally different. Because he does not like where it leads, in terms of social policy, Glazer rejects the entire internal colonialism model, insisting that the black and immigrant experiences are *not* fundamentally different. Let us closely examine Glazer's counterargument.

1. According to Glazer, all ethnic groups display a degree of self-segregation. At least the evidence is "inconclusive" whether segregation is "voluntary or forced, or, if forced, whether it is based on economic or discriminatory factors."[73] Here Glazer, with apparent innocence, strikes a refrain used by segregationists through the ages —that blacks like things the way they are! Or in Glazer's more rarefied terms: "there are the positive attractions of a community of people of common descent and culture, one that plays probably as strong a role among blacks as among white ethnic groups."[74] Never mind that no white ethnic groups, with the exception of the Mormons or the Amish, has ever displayed the degree of "concentration" characteristic of blacks. Never mind that blacks were denied the *choice* that white ethnics have had to live in ethnically homogeneous or ethnically mixed neighborhoods. Never mind that even middle-class blacks have generally been excluded from white communities. Never mind that Jews and other immigrants fled their cozy ethnic neighborhoods as quickly as they could, and generally moved to communities that were far more ethnically diverse. Glazer asks us to believe that the racial ghettos of America are not a product of institutionalized racism, but merely an expression of ethnic cohesion and voluntary self-segregation.

2. Contrary to his own position, Glazer concedes that "the ghettos of the 'older immigrants' (Irish and German) have indeed largely disappeared."[75] But, he argues, blacks arrived in northern cities only recently, long after the great waves of European immigration had subsided. Thus, not enough time has elapsed to allow the process of mobility and assimilation to play itself out. Implicit here is a great leap of faith, hardly validated by events over the past two decades, that racial segregation would gradually decline.[76]

3. Glazer parries Blauner's point that, unlike immigrants, blacks have never gained control over their own communities with the following casuistry. It depends, he asserts, *which* immigrants blacks are compared to. Some, like Irish, have made great strides in politics; others, like Jews, in business and the professions; others, like Japanese, in education. Still others, like Italians and Slavs, have reaped far less success. True, blacks lag behind even Italians and Slavs, but the differences are not so great as to support so radical a notion as "internal colonialism." Thus are racism and the terrible realities of American apartheid explained away![77]

Glazer acknowledges that immigrant groups had more political and economic control over their communities. But, he asserts, this is because they had economic enterprise that was lacking among blacks. Racism, he concedes, may have destroyed black business "in pre-immigrant America," but—beware of the debater's trick—this "cannot be an *exclusive* explanation," since Chinese and Japanese also met "vicious racism," and this did not prevent their entrepreneurial success.[78]

As for politics, Glazer insists that blacks have been no slower at acquiring political power than other immigrants, with the exception of the Irish. To the extent that blacks lack their fair share of political power, this is because rates of registration and voting are abnormally low. And while gerrymandering is a problem, it "was not invented to keep blacks underrepresented."[79] Again, the conclusion: blacks are not victims of some unusual system of oppression as suggested by the internal colonialism model.

Why then, in 1971, are blacks so mired in problems? Some of Glazer's answer has already been insinuated: blacks lack the political acumen of the Irish, the business enterprise of the Jews, and the ingenuity and perseverance of the Chinese and Japanese. Although Glazer tiptoes through his argument, no doubt fearful that he will be accused of resorting to ethnic and racial stereotypes, the gist of his argument is clear: much of the blame for economic stagnation among blacks has to do with blacks themselves, specifically with cultural deficiencies that prevent them from following in the footsteps of earlier waves of immigrants.

Glazer even takes issue with Gans's contention that, because of a secular decline in blue-collar jobs, blacks migrating to Northern cities encountered a far less favorable structure of opportunity than immigrants had in earlier decades. Unskilled jobs have declined, Glazer writes, but so have the number of people competing for these jobs:

"the fact that many jobs for the unskilled are not filled shows that there has not been a substantial decline in the ratio of jobs to applicants."[80] What accounts for the high levels of black unemployment? First, because of social programs, "fewer people are driven to unpleasant and low-paying jobs by the need to feed their families." And second, "Expectations have changed, and fewer blacks or whites today will accept a life at menial labor with no hope for advancement, as their fathers and older brothers did and as European immigrants did."[81]

All of Glazer's sophistry was driven by a single purpose: to refute the claim that the black experience has been fundamentally different from that of immigrants, assuming one begins the comparison at the point that blacks arrive in Northern cities. But this proviso asks us to disregard two centuries of slavery and another century of Jim Crow, and to pretend that history began in New York City in the 1950s when white liberals worked with black leaders to pass some ineffectual ordinances banning housing discrimination. In another leap of faith, Glazer asks us to construe today's urban ghetto as merely a temporary way station on the road to some suburban mecca. Only by constructing these preposterous premises, and ignoring massive evidence to the contrary, does Glazer reach his conclusion that "the gap between the experience of the worst off of the white ethnic groups and the blacks is *one of degree rather than kind*."[82]

Since Glazer has essentially defined internal colonialism out of existence, and redefined blacks to be latter-day immigrants, he is sanguine about the future: "It is possible to see the position of blacks in northern cities in ethnic terms, that is, to see them as the last of the major groups, badly off at present, but due to rise in time to larger shares of wealth and power and influence."[83] Thus has Glazer contrived a logic that obviates the need for "unique and extreme measures to end black deprivation."

I have devoted considerable space to Glazer's criticism of Blauner for two reasons. First, Glazer was one of the preeminent scholars of race and ethnicity during the years spanning the black protest movement, and as a frequent contributor to *Commentary* and other liberal journals, his influence reached far beyond the academy. Second, Glazer's rejoinder to Blauner serves as an apt example of how the old guard responded to the challenge to their cherished assumptions. One can marvel at the mental gymnastics that Glazer employed—his artful hairsplitting, his evasions, his circumlocutions, his waffling, and his devious manipulation of facts—in an effort to parry the compelling arguments advanced by Blauner and other exponents of the new paradigm, all the while pretending to be a "friend of the Negro." It was Glazer's self-imposed mission to pick up the other end of the stick, and even to bend it as necessary, in order to restore the sullied paradigm to its former luster.

Just as black insurgency produced a scholarship of confrontation, the ensuing white backlash eventually produced "a scholarship of backlash." Glazer deserves the dubious distinction of being on the vanguard of a liberal retreat from the positions that were advanced in the sixties and early seventies, but he was not alone. In an ironic reversal of the pattern observed for the scholarship of confrontation, the scholarship of backlash began with an older generation of scholars who, like Glazer, anteceded the "radical sixties" and bided their time until they could launch a counterattack and reclaim their earlier pre-eminence. Gradually, a younger generation of scholars joined the stream, including a new genre of "black conservatives," and the retreat—at first halting—broke into a full-scale rout. Emboldened by the praise and institutional rewards heaped upon them, these writers stepped up the effort to "get beyond civil rights" and to discredit the core tenets of the scholarship of confrontation. No longer would the focus of attention be on societal structures that engender and maintain glaring racial inequalities. Once again, the focus of blame for the tangle of problems that beset black America would be placed on blacks themselves.

II

THE SCHOLARSHIP
OF BACKLASH

4

Backlash Outside and Inside the University

There has never been a solid, unified and determined thrust to
make justice a reality for Afro-Americans. The step backward
has a new name today. It is called the "white backlash." But the
white backlash is nothing new. It is the surfacing of old
prejudices, hostilities and ambivalences that have always been
there. It was caused neither by the cry of Black Power nor by
the unfortunate recent wave of riots in our cities. The white
backlash of today is rooted in the same problem that has
characterized America ever since the black man landed in
chains on the shores of this nation. The white backlash is an
expression of the same vacillations, the same search for
rationalizations, the same lack of commitment that has
always characterized white America on the question of race.

Martin Luther King, Jr., *Where Do We Go from Here?*, 1967

Backlash" is defined by the *American Heritage Dictionary* as "a sudden or violent backward whipping motion; an antagonistic reaction to
some prior action construed as a threat, as in the context of social or
race relations." The first manifestation of a white backlash to the black
protest movement occurred in the 1964 election when George Wallace shocked the nation by winning 34 percent of the Democratic vote
in the Wisconsin primary. Wallace went on to garner 30 percent of the
Democratic vote in the Indiana primary, and 43 percent of the vote in
the Maryland primary, thanks largely to working-class ethnic voters.[1]
Insofar as Wallace's ascendancy preceded both the "Black Power"
movement and the outbreak of ghetto "riots," this substantiates Martin Luther King's claim, in the passage quoted above, that the white
backlash was not triggered by these events. Yet it can hardly be denied

that Wallace's triumph signified an ominous new turn in racial politics, one that might well be described as "a violent and sudden backward whipping motion." In this sense, "backlash" is an apt metaphor for the period beginning with the ascendancy of George Wallace in 1964 and culminating with the election of Richard Nixon in 1968.[2]

Nixon's election marked the beginning of a major realignment of the two major political parties. Except for the election of Eisenhower, a war hero, Democrats had won every national election since the Depression through an unholy alliance of Northern liberals and Southern conservatives. This coalition was predicated on the acquiescence of the Northern wing of the Democratic Party to the segregationist practices of its Dixiecrat partners. The civil rights movement gradually drove a deep wedge between them, which first erupted in the bitter credentials fight at the 1964 Democratic Convention over the Mississippi Freedom Democratic Party. The final stroke came with the 1965 Voting Rights Act. When Lyndon Johnson proposed this legislation, he well understood that this fragile coalition was imperiled, if not doomed. The worst fears of the party pragmatists were realized in the 1968 election when Hubert Humphrey lost virtually the entire South. George Wallace carried the Deep South states of Louisiana, Mississippi, Alabama, Georgia, and Arkansas. Nixon narrowly won in Florida, South Carolina, North Carolina, Virginia, and Tennessee. The next time the "Solid South" voted in unanimity, it was for Nixon in 1972.[3]

Nor was racial backlash restricted to the South. At the height of Wallace's popularity, 22 percent of white blue-collar workers in the North considered voting for him, though only 9 percent did so in the actual election. Still, Wallace's showing was proof of a serious erosion of the Democratic Party's traditional base of support among blue-collar workers. Three out of every ten whites who voted for Johnson in 1964 voted for Nixon or Wallace in 1968.[4] This was indeed an ominous development. It meant that white flight was not just something that happened when blacks moved into previously white neighborhoods. White flight was also occurring within the Democratic Party.

In the 1968 election reporters dubbed Nixon's overt appeal to the white backlash his "Southern strategy." Once elected, Nixon lost no time in turning the clock back on the civil rights revolution. He began to dismantle the programs and policies established under Johnson's War on Poverty. He tried, unsuccessfully, to substitute a weaker version of the Voting Rights Act when it expired in 1970. He fulminated against "forced integration," thereby undermining the movement toward school desegregation. He sought to shift responsibility for school desegregation to the federal judiciary, and then nominated two Southerners with pro-segregationist records to the Supreme Court. Through the Omnibus Crime Control and Safe Streets Act of 1968, huge revenues were delegated for riot control. Finally, the Justice Department colluded with the FBI in a covert war against the Black Panther Party. Meanwhile, black leaders and organizations were denied entree to the Nixon White House. To demonstrate their ire, members of the black caucus boycotted Nixon's State of the Union message in 1970.[5]

The entire thrust of the civil rights movement had been to break through the "invisible but horribly tangible plate glass" that spared white America from even hearing the cries that were emanating from black America. Nixon, in effect, restored and even reinforced that plate glass. This was presaged by his response to the publication of the Kerner Report in March 1968. Nixon criticized the blunt language of the report because, he said, it only served "to divide people." Shifting the focus of blame, he insisted that "until we have order, there can be no progress." And, mounting the pulpit, he added: "What we need is more talk about reconciliation, more about how we're going to work together, rather than the fact that we have this terrible division between us."[6] With these words, Nixon was urging white America to once again don its racial blinders, and to pretend that "terrible division" could somehow be ameliorated with "more talk about reconciliation." Here was the death knell to the spirit of confrontation that, for a time, had forced the nation to face up to its racial divisions and to initiate a process of racial reconstruction.

For a number of reasons the protest movement ebbed by the early 1970s. First of all, the civil rights movement had succeeded in achieving its legislative agenda, effectively bringing an end to "the civil rights era." Second, the two principal protest leaders—King and Malcolm X—had been assassinated, precipitating a "crisis in black leadership" that persists even today. Third, to whatever extent the Black Panther Party posed any threat to the racial status quo, it was effectively neutralized through police subversion and repression.[7] Finally, the protest movement simply ran out of steam. In the best of times, it is difficult to sustain political activism. The civil rights movement had drained the energy and resources of the black community for some fifteen years. Now, with the civil rights issues resolved, the movement confronted far more ambiguous and daunting obstacles to racial progress. Gradually idealism gave way to cynicism, resolve to resignation. Perhaps, as some have argued, the black middle class had been effectively coopted, and lost its appetite for protest. Far more convincing (to pick up the other end of this stick) is the argument that the political establishment had made the concessions that were necessary to restore order and to take the steam out of the protest movement. With the ebbing of protest the nation and its power elites lapsed into their traditional mode of dealing with racism: evasion and denial.

Nothing better illustrates this than Moynihan's memorandum, leaked to the press in February 1970, urging President Nixon to adopt a policy of "benign neglect." With characteristic hyperbole, Moynihan wrote: "The issue of race has been too much talked about . . . has been too much taken over by hysterics, paranoids, and boodlers on all sides. We may need a period in which Negro progress continues and racial rhetoric fades."[8] Behind Moynihan's vituperation was an animus that he harbored against the liberal left—those "hysterics, paranoids, and boodlers" who had heaped criticism and scorn on him after the publication of his "Report on the Negro Family."[9] Whatever his personal motivations, Moynihan's oxymoron (after two centuries of slavery and another century of Jim Crow, can neglect ever be benign?) seemed to capture the political spirit of the post–civil rights era.

Nixon milked the white backlash to maximum advantage, but he could not totally ignore the pressures still emanating from the black community. Memories of the "riots" following King's assassination were still fresh, and served as a vivid reminder that black America could not be pushed too far. The brazen activism of the Black Panthers and other militant groups also fueled apprehensions concerning the possibility of renewed riots. Furthermore, black protest organizations, including the Congressional black caucus and the growing cadre of black mayors in cities across the nation, kept up the pressure on the Administration. A stream of noisy demonstrations by local grassroots organizations also protested discrimination in the construction trades. Speaking to indignant civil rights workers in 1969, Attorney General Mitchell commented: "You will be better advised to watch what we do instead of what we say."[10]

Indeed, despite his overt appeal to the white backlash and the other retrograde policies alluded to above, Nixon simultaneously pursued policies that laid the foundation for affirmative action policy. This was done less as a matter of preconceived design than as a byproduct of a series of administrative decisions and compromises that, in their net effect, formed the basis for affirmative action as we know it.

In the first place, Nixon beefed up the Equal Employment Opportunity Commission. The agency grew from a staff of 359 and a budget of $13.2 million in 1968 to a staff of 1,640 and a budget of $29.5 million in 1972. The government's principal enforcement mechanism against discrimination is the contract compliance check, and Nixon's budget for fiscal year 1973 provided for a doubling of Office of Federal Contract Compliance (OFCC) checks from 22,500 in 1971 to 52,000 in 1973.[11]

Second, in 1973 the Nixon Administration concluded the landmark AT&T-EEO Consent Decree, in which the Bell System—then the nation's largest private employer—paid monetary damages to aggrieved classes and agreed to change its employment policies and meet employment targets for women and minorities. This case was a milestone in the federal government's enforcement of equal employment principles and in the evolution of affirmative action policy. As the authors of a study assessing the impact of the decree wrote: "The signing of the decree marked a new stage in EEO enforcement and induced the EEOC and other governmental agencies in the equal employment field not only to adopt a more aggressive attitude but also to seek punitive money damages as a regular course of action."[12]

Nixon's third and most important policy initiative was the Philadelphia Plan, which required all contractors working on large federally funded projects to adopt "numerical goals and timetables" to assure the desegregation of their work force. This policy was originally developed during the Johnson administration, but encountered adamant opposition from organized labor and contractors alike, and was rescinded shortly after Humphrey's defeat in November 1968. However, it was revived early in Nixon's first term by Secretary of Labor George Shultz. The plan was specifically aimed at the construction trades and craft unions where blacks barely had even token representation, and were systematically excluded from apprenticeship programs. Hugh Davis Graham, the author of the definitive study *The Civil Rights Era*, speculates that Nixon's motives were less than pure, and that Nixon and his strategists saw the Philadelphia Plan as an opportunity to drive a wedge into the coalition between blacks and Democratic trade unions.[13] However this may be, the Department of Justice under Attorney General John Mitchell successfully defended the plan in litigation before the federal courts. This ruling, according to Graham, "extended the Philadelphia Plan's scheme of numerical goals and timetables, proportionally based on minority population ratios, beyond construction to cover government contractors in all areas of service and supply throughout the country."[14] As Graham also observes, compared to school desegregation, Nixon did not have to fear a voter backlash, since the effects of the Philadelphia Plan were felt mainly by Democratic trade unions.[15] However, when it served his purposes, Nixon would characterize goals and timetables as "quotas" and openly appeal to the white backlash.[16]

Thus, the record of the Nixon Administration with respect to civil rights does not lend itself to a simple, categorical verdict. As Graham has noted:

. . . in the long view of continuity in civil rights policy, the real Richard Nixon was not only the demagogue of busing and the hypocrite of quotas during the warm months of 1972. He was also the expedient and successful defender of the Philadelphia Plan, the careful but quiet enforcer of school desegregation in the South, the architect of judicial empowerment for the EEOC. [17]

It is tempting to conclude that the Republican strategy was to use covert racist appeals to get elected. Once in office, however, politicians had to weigh the political gains accrued by catering to the white backlash against the potential political costs of exacerbating racial tensions, especially if tensions threatened to reach the boiling point.

The same contradiction between political rhetoric and official action marked the Reagan regime as well. In his book *Civil Rights Under Reagan*, Robert Detlefson—an unabashed opponent of affirmative action—puzzles about why Reagan was "unable to modify substantially or eliminate unpopular civil rights policies."[18] He found that the federal courts, and the Supreme Court in particular, blunted the efforts of Reagan's Justice Department to reverse policies with respect to affirmative action and busing. However, the actions of the courts also need to be seen within a larger political context. Despite popular opposition to "quotas and busing," these policies were still supported by what Detlefson contemptuously refers to as "the civil rights establishment," consisting of liberal politicians, journalists, some large corporations, and the array of civil rights organizations that stubbornly defended existing policies against the assaults of the Reagan administration and its front-man, Bradford Reynolds, who as Assistant Attorney General headed the Civil Rights Division in the Department of Justice. There is perhaps a political lesson in the fact that so much was achieved under Nixon and that these gains were successfully defended under Reagan: that less depends on which political party occupies the seat of power than on exerting sufficient pressure to force the hand of government.

Backlash and the University

There is, of course, great irony in the fact that the unsung heroes of affirmative action are George Shultz, John Mitchell, and Nixon himself.[19] The irony is compounded by the fact that liberals (or erstwhile liberals) have been in the forefront of the retreat from affirmative action. Once again, the names of Daniel Patrick Moynihan and Nathan Glazer turn up among the earliest critics of affirmative action. Both men had one foot in politics and the other in the academy—Moynihan as a scholar/politician, Glazer as a public intellectual who wrote frequently about politics and on occasion worked as a government official or consultant. [20] It is therefore not surprising that they were among the first to sound the alarm about the "dangerous" new turn in public policy that was quietly being engineered by politicians and bureaucrats within the Departments of Labor and Justice.

As early as 1964, in an article published in *Commentary* under the title "Negroes and Jews: The New Challenge to Pluralism," Glazer warned that blacks were now demanding not just equality of opportunity, but "equality of results or outcomes," which he construed as a mortal threat to pluralism in general and to Jewish interests in particular. [21] Moynihan—never given to Glazer's circumlocution—simply denounced the drift toward "quotas" as "a new racialism," adding that "if ethnic quotas are to be imposed on American universities and similarly quasipublic institutions, it is Jews who will be almost driven out." [22]

In 1975 Glazer devoted an entire book to an attack on affirmative action. [23] Mischievously entitling the book *Affirmative Discrimination*, Glazer insisted that, despite the fact that blacks had been oppressed for centuries on the basis of their group status, "rights attach to the individual, not the group." [24] On this premise Glazer accused the proponents of affirmative action of engaging in a racial classification reminiscent of the Nuremberg Laws. Note the theoretical sleight of hand as anti-racist policy is portrayed as the quintessence of racism itself. In opposing affirmative action, then, Glazer sanctimoniously projected himself as the champion of a color-blind society even as this so-called color blindness functioned as a spurious justification for maintaining the racial status quo.

Just as confrontation and crisis produced "a scholarship of confrontation," the political retrenchment over the past two decades has produced a corresponding "scholarship of backlash." As will be seen in the chapters that follow, this "new" canon is actually a throwback to positions held prior to the 1960s but eclipsed by the sheer force of the civil rights upheaval and the surge of radical politics and racial militancy within the academy. Like sailors on a stormy sea, the Old Guard hunkered down, waiting for the storm to pass. Once it was safe to do so, they reemerged and again raised their benighted sails.

For example, in the opening sentence of *The Limits of Social Policy*, published in 1988, Glazer tells the reader that toward the end of the 1960s "an insight came to me that was to dominate my response to social policy from that time onward."[25] What was Glazer's epiphany? That social policy has its "limits"—or, to put it in the vernacular, that government cannot solve all of our problems. Glazer then goes a step further to argue that, through its well-intentioned but misguided policies, government actually exacerbates the problems it is supposed to cure—for example, by undermining families and encouraging welfare dependency. On the basis of this revelation, Glazer renounces his erstwhile faith in liberal social policy, and takes refuge in the following bromide: "In our social policies we are trying to deal with the breakdown of traditional ways of handling distress. These traditional ways are located in the family primarily, but also in the ethnic group, the neighborhood, the church."[26] Was this a "new" insight, as Glazer would have us think, or was it merely a reiteration of an old position? In point of fact, the statement just quoted is indistinguishable from positions advanced in *Beyond the Melting Pot*, published twenty-five years earlier. Consider Glazer's analysis of why black children in New York City are not able to use schools as a vehicle of mobility:

There is little question where the major part of the answer must be found: in the home and family and community. . . . It is there that the heritage of two hundred years of slavery and a hundred years of discrimination is concentrated; and it is there that we find the serious obstacles to the ability to make use of a free educational system to advance into higher occupations and to eliminate the massive social problems that afflict colored Americans and the city.[27]

Here Glazer struck a chord that would resonate through mainstream sociology down to the present: that centuries of racism had ravaged "home, family, and community," and that this impaired culture was now the major obstacle to progress. Here was another theoretical sleight of hand that shifted the analytical focus from racism to culture, and shifted blame from societal institutions onto blacks themselves. The implication for policy was that progress hinged not on combatting racism (the civil rights revolution had substantially accomplished that!), but on repairing the defective institutions within the black community.[28]

Thus, Glazer's analysis of race and class had changed little between 1963 and 1988. What *did* change was the surrounding political culture. In the liberal 1960s, Glazer did not embrace, and perhaps did not even recognize, the conservative elements in his scholarship on race. By 1970 Glazer trumpeted his own swing to the right with an article in *Commentary* entitled "On Being Deradicalized."[29] Having publicly disavowed his liberal persona, he was now free to carry his analysis to its logical conclusion, thus bringing his politics into belated symmetry with his scholarship.

In his political odyssey from liberalism to neoconservatism, Glazer personified a liberal retreat from race that would be the hallmark of social science scholarship during the post–civil rights era.

5

The Liberal Retreat
from Race during the
Post–Civil Rights Era

> In all crises, at all times, white liberals have two basic aims,
> to prevent polarization and to prevent racial conflict.
>
> Lerone Bennett, "Tea and Sympathy:
> Liberals and Other White Hopes," 1964
>
> A moderate is a cat who will hang you from a low tree.
>
> Dick Gregory, circa 1964

Racial backlash was not an affliction only of the political right. As early as 1963, *The Atlantic Monthly* published an article entitled "The White Liberal's Retreat." Its author, Murray Friedman, observed that "the liberal white is increasingly uneasy about the nature and consequences of the Negro revolt."[1] According to Friedman, a number of factors contributed to the white liberal retreat. For one thing, after school desegregation came to Northern cities, white liberals realized that the Negro was not just an abstraction, and not just a Southern problem. Second, the rise of black nationalism exacerbated tensions with white liberals, especially when they were ejected from civil rights organizations. Third, escalating tensions and violence tested the limit of liberal support. As Friedman wrote: "In the final analysis, a liberal, white, middle-class society wants to have change, but without trouble."[2]

The liberal retreat also manifested itself in a rift between white intellectuals and blacks. As an example, Friedman cited Nathan Glazer's laudatory review of Nathaniel Weyl's *The Negro in American Civilization*. Weyl cited the results of IQ tests to argue that "a large part of the American Negro population is seriously deficient in mental ability," and warned against the dangers of "random race mixing without regard to learning ability."[3] According to Friedman, Glazer was critical of Weyl's biological determinism, particularly his reliance on African brain-size data, but nevertheless declared that Weyl "is clearly free of any prejudice and deserves credit for having raised for public discussion crucial aspects of the Negro question which receive little discussion in academic and liberal circles, and which are usually left in the hands of bigots and incompetents."[4] Then Glazer posed the rhetorical question that leaves the answer to the racialized imagination: "What are we to make of the high rates of [Negro] crime and delinquency, illegitimacy, family break-up and school dropout?"[5]

As Friedman observed, there was nothing new in the tendency for white liberals to withdraw support from the liberation movement—essentially the same thing had happened during Reconstruction. In both cases, liberals demonstrated a failure of nerve, and nudged blacks into curbing their demands. Friedman described the situation in 1963 in these epigrammatic terms: "to the Negro demand for 'now,' to which the Deep South has replied 'never,' many liberal whites are increasingly responding 'later.'"[6]

It did not take long for the intensifying backlash and the liberal retreat to manifest themselves politically. The critical turning point was 1965, the year the civil rights movement reached its triumphant finale. The 1964 Civil Rights Act—passed after a decade of black insurgency—ended segregation in public accommodations and, at least in theory, proscribed discrimination in employment. The last remaining piece of Civil Rights legislation—the 1965 Voting Rights Act—was wending its way through Congress and, in the wake of Johnson's landslide victory, was assured of eventual passage. In a joint session of Congress on voting rights in March 1965—the first such session on a domestic issue since 1946—President Johnson had electrified the nation by proclaiming, in his Southern drawl, "And we *shall* overcome." As a senator from Texas, Johnson had voted against anti-lynching legislation. Now, in the midst of a crisis engineered by a grassroots protest movement, Johnson embraced the battle cry of that movement as he proposed legislation that would eliminate the last and most important vestige of official segregation.

In retrospect, Johnson's speech represented not the triumph of the civil rights movement, but its last hurrah. Now that its major legislative objectives had been achieved, not only the future of the movement, but also the constancy of liberal support, were thrown into question. By 1965, leaders and commentators, both inside and outside the movement, were asking, "What's next?" However, this question had an ominous innuendo when it came from white liberals. In *Why We Can't Wait*, published in 1963, Martin Luther King provides this account of his appearance with Roy Wilkins on *Meet the Press*:

> There were the usual questions about how much more the Negro wants, but there seemed to be a new undercurrent of implications related to the sturdy new strength of our movement. Without the courtly complexities, we were, in effect, being asked if we could be trusted to hold back the surging tides of discontent so that those on the shore would not be made too uncomfortable by the buffeting and onrushing waves. Some of the questions implied that our leadership would be judged in accordance with our capacity to "keep the Negro from going too far." The quotes are mine, but I think the phrase mirrors the thinking of the panelists as well as of many other white Americans.[7]

By 1965—even before Watts exploded—there was a growing awareness among black leaders that political rights did not go far enough to compensate for past wrongs. Whitney Young epitomized this when he wrote that "there is little value in a Negro's obtaining the right to be admitted to hotels and restaurants if he has no cash in his pocket and no job."[8] As Rainwater and Yancey have suggested, "The year 1965 may be known in history as the time when the civil rights movement discovered, in the sense of becoming explicitly aware, that abolishing legal racism would not produce Negro equality."[9]

If laws alone would not produce equality, then the unavoidable conclusion was that some form of "special effort"—to use Whitney

Young's term—was necessary to compensate for the accumulated disadvantages of the past. By 1965 the words "compensation," "reparations," and "preference" had already crept into the political discourse, and white liberals were beginning to display their disquiet with this troublesome turn of events.[10] In *Why We Can't Wait* King observed: "Whenever this issue of compensatory or preferential treatment for the Negro is raised, some of our friends recoil in horror. The Negro should be granted equality, they agree; but he should ask nothing more."[11]

The demand for "something more" than legal equality precipitated a crisis among white liberals. This was already evident in 1964 when *Commentary* magazine sponsored a roundtable discussion on "Liberalism and the Negro."[12] The event took place at Town Hall in New York City before an invited audience, which included many of the leading liberal intellectuals of the period. Norman Podhoretz introduced the discussion:

I think it may be fair to say that American liberals are by now divided into two schools of thought on what is often called the Negro problem. . . . On the one side, we have those liberals whose ultimate perspective on race relations . . . envisages the gradual absorption of deserving Negroes one by one into white society. . . . Over the past two or three years, however, a new school of liberal (or perhaps it should be called radical) thought has been developing which is based on the premise . . . that "the rights and privileges of an individual rest upon the status attained by the group to which he belongs." From this premise certain points follow that are apparently proving repugnant to the traditional liberal mentality.[13]

Behind this elliptical language was the specter of "preference." Traditional liberalism, Podhoretz explained, sought to integrate "deserving Negroes one by one into white society." But a newer school of liberals had emerged that "maintains that the Negro community *as a whole* has been crippled by three hundred years of slavery and persecution and that the simple removal of legal and other barriers to the advancement of individual Negroes can therefore only result in what is derisively called 'tokenism.'" Finally, Podhoretz laid his cards on the table:

This school of thought insists that radical measures are now needed to overcome the Negro's inherited disabilities. Whitney Young of the National Urban League, for example, has recently spoken of a domestic Marshall Plan, a crash program which he says need last only ten years, in order to bring the Negro community to a point where it can *begin* to compete on equal terms with the white world. Other Negro leaders have similarly talked about 10 percent quotas in hiring, housing, and so on. Negroes, they say, ought to be represented in all areas of American life according to their proportion in the population, and where they are not so represented, one is entitled to draw an inference of discrimination. The slogan "preferential treatment for Negroes" is the most controversial one that has come up in this discussion.[14]

The other white participants in the roundtable—Nathan Glazer, Sidney Hook, and Gunnar Myrdal—all declared their blanket opposition to any system of racial preference. Glazer touted the success of New York's Fair Employment Practices Law, implying that racial justice could be achieved within the same liberal framework that worked for other groups. Hook argued that, by lowering standards for Negroes, preference was patronizing and, in effect, treated blacks as second-class citizens. Myrdal cautioned that preference amounted to tokenism and that what was needed was a program to lift *all* poor people out of poverty.

James Baldwin stood alone, parrying the arguments thrust at him with his usual eloquence and resolve. To the optimistic view that the nation was making progress ("not enough progress, to be sure, but progress nevertheless"), Baldwin had this to say:

I'm delighted to know there've been many fewer lynchings in the year 1963 than there were in the year 1933, but I also have to bear in mind—I have to bear it in mind because my life depends on it—that there are a great many ways to lynch a man. The impulse in American society, as far as I can tell from my experience in it, has essentially been to ignore me when it could, and then when it couldn't, to intimidate me; and when that failed, to make concessions.[15]

As the discussion labored on, it became increasingly obvious that a vast difference in world view separated Baldwin and the others. When Hook gloated over the expansion of ethical principles in American society, Baldwin retorted:

What strikes me here is that you are an American talking about American society, and I am an American talking about American society—both of us very concerned with it—and yet your version of American society is really very difficult for me to recognize. My experience in it has simply not been yours.[16]

Speaking from the audience, Kenneth Clark was even more blunt in declaring his disaffection with liberalism:

How do I—a Negro in America who throughout his undergraduate years and the early part of his professional life identified himself with liberalism—how do I now see American liberalism? I must confess bluntly that I now see white American liberalism primarily in terms of the adjective, "white."[17]

Indeed, the day's proceedings seemed only to corroborate Podhoretz's initial observation of "a widening split between the Negro movement and the white liberal community."

Here in the spring of 1964 was an early sign of the imminent breakup of the liberal coalition that had functioned as a bulwark of the civil rights movement. One faction would gravitate to the nascent neoconservative movement. Another faction would remain in the liberal camp, committed in principle to both liberal reform and racial justice. This, however, was to prove a difficult balancing act, especially when confronted with an intensifying racial backlash. Even in the best of times, racial issues tended to exacerbate divisions in the liberal coalition on which Democratic electoral victories depended. As the polity swung to the right, liberals in the Democratic Party came under mounting pressure to downplay or sidestep racial issues.[18]

Thus, the liberal retreat from race was rationalized in terms of realpolitik. The argument ran like this: America is too racist to support programs targeted specifically for blacks, especially if these involve any form of preference which is anathema to most whites. Highlighting racial issues, therefore, only serves to drive a wedge in the liberal coalition, driving whites from the Democratic Party, and is ultimately self-defeating. That this reasoning amounted to a capitulation to the white backlash did not faze the political "realists" since their motives were pure. Indeed, unlike the racial backlash on the right, the liberal backlash was *not* based on racial animus or retrograde politics. On the contrary, these dyed-in-the-wool liberals were convinced that the best or only way to help blacks was to help "everybody." Eliminate poverty, they said, and blacks, who count disproportionately among the poor, will be the winners. Achieve full employment, and black employment troubles will be resolved. The upshot, however, was that blacks were asked to subordinate their agenda to a larger movement for liberal reform. In practical terms, this meant forgoing the black protest movement and casting their lot with the Democratic Party.

Thus, after 1965 many white liberals who were erstwhile supporters of the civil rights movement placed a kiss of death on race-based politics and race-based public policy. They not only joined the general retreat from race in the society at large, but in fact cited the white backlash as reason for their own abandonment of race-based politics. In this sense, the liberal retreat from race can be said to represent the left wing of the backlash.

The Howard Address: A Case of "Semantic Infiltration"

The ideological cleavage that would split the liberal camp was foreshadowed in a commencement address that President Johnson delivered at Howard University on June 4, 1965. The speech, written by Richard Goodwin and Daniel Patrick Moynihan, was riddled with contradiction, and for this very reason epitomizes the political limbo that existed in 1965, as well as the emerging lines of ideological and political division within the liberal camp. [19]

The speech, aptly entitled "To Fulfill These Rights," began with the most radical vision on race that has ever been enunciated by a president of the United States. After reviewing the series of civil rights acts that secured full civil rights for African Americans, Johnson declared: "But freedom is not enough." He continued:

You do not take a person who, for years, has been hobbled by chains and liberate him, bring him up to the starting line of a race and then say, "you are free to compete with all the others," and still justly believe that you have been completely fair. Thus it is not enough just to open the gates of opportunity. All our citizens must have the ability to walk through those gates.

Johnson's oratory went a critical step further:

This is the next and more profound stage of the battle for civil rights. We seek not just freedom but opportunity—not just legal equity but human ability—*not just equality as a right and a theory but equality as a fact and as a result.*

With these last words, Johnson adopted the logic and the language of those arguing for compensatory programs that would redress past wrongs. Equality, not liberty, would be the defining principle of "the next and more profound stage" in the liberation struggle.[20]

So far so good. Johnson's speech then took an abrupt detour away from politics to sociology, reflecting the unmistakable imprint of Daniel Patrick Moynihan who only a month earlier had completed an internal report focusing on problems of the black family. Johnson said:

. . . equal opportunity is essential, but not enough. Men and women of all races are born with the same range of abilities. But ability is not just the product of birth. Ability is stretched or stunted by the family you live with, and the neighborhoods you live in, by the school you go to and the poverty or the richness of your surroundings. It is the product of a hundred unseen forces playing upon the infant, the child, and the man.

Compare the language and logic of this passage with the one that follows:

Overt job discrimination is only one of the important hurdles which must be overcome before color can disappear as a determining factor in the lives and fortunes of men. . . . The prevailing view among social scientists holds that there are no significant differences among groups as to the distribution of innate aptitudes or at most very slight differences. On the other hand, differences among individuals are very substantial. The extent to which an individual is able to develop his aptitudes will largely depend upon the circumstances present in the family within which he grows up and the opportunities which he encounters at school and in the larger community.

This latter passage comes from a 1956 book, *The Negro Potential*, by Eli Ginzberg, who was a leading liberal economist of that period.[21] My point is not that Johnson's speechwriters were guilty of plagiarism. Rather it is to take note of their Machiavellian genius. With a rhetorical sleight of hand, Goodwin and Moynihan shifted the discourse away from the radical vision of "equal results" that emanated from the black protest movement of the 1960s back to the standard liberal cant of the 1950s which held that the black child is stunted by "circumstances present in the family within which he grows up." The conceptual groundwork was being laid for a drastic policy reversal: the focus would no longer be on white racism, but rather on the deficiencies of blacks themselves.

Having thus planted the seeds of equivocation, the speech then shifted back to a fretful discussion of the "widening gulf" between poor blacks and the rest of the nation, including the black middle class. Johnson cited a litany of statistics on black employment and income. Logically, this might have led to a discussion of policies that would move the nation in the direction of "equal results" in employment and income. However, as Tom Wicker shrewdly observed in the *New York Times*, "Mr. Johnson did not mention such specific remedies as job quotas or preferential hiring, which some civil rights leaders have advocated."[22] Instead, the speech shifted to more generalities on "the special nature of Negro poverty" and "the breakdown of the Negro family structure." Centuries of oppression, Johnson asserted, had eroded the ability of men to function as providers for their family, and, as a result, fewer than half of Negro children currently live out their lives with both parents. Inasmuch as the family "is the cornerstone of our society," the collapse of the family has dire consequences for individuals and communities alike. "So," Johnson concluded, "unless we work to strengthen the family . . . all the rest: schools and playgrounds, public assistance and private concern, will never be enough to cut completely the circle of despair and deprivation."

This last comment probably passed over Johnson's audience at Howard as mere political oratory. Only in retrospect can we fully appreciate the dire political implications of suggesting that government programs were futile "unless we work to strengthen the family." With another rhetorical sleight of hand, Johnson (via Goodwin and Moynihan) shifted the focus from "equal results" to the black family which, it was said, was perpetuating "the circle of despair and deprivation." The speech conspicuously avoided any policy prescriptions, deferring these to a planned White House conference under the title "To Fulfill These Rights." However, the conceptual groundwork was being laid for policies that would change "them," not "us."

Thus, a presidential speech that began on a progressive note ended up in abysmal political regression. Was this self-contradiction merely the result of careless or muddled thought? Or did it reflect political calculation? There is reason to think that Johnson's advisors acted with deliberation and foresight. In a *New York Times* story on June 5, the day after the Howard speech, unnamed "White House sources" are quoted to the effect that the Howard address was the first major presidential civil rights speech conceived independently of the direct pressure of racial crisis. Reading between these lines, it would appear that Johnson's political strategists were seeking to wrest control over the troublesome direction that racial politics were headed. Indeed, the Howard speech is a prime example of what Moynihan calls "semantic infiltration."[23] This term refers to the appropriation of the language of one's political opponents for the purpose of blurring distinctions and molding it to one's own political position. In this instance Moynihan invoked the language of "equal results" only to redefine and redirect it in a politically safe direction. When semantic infiltration is done right, it elicits the approbation even of one's political opponents who, as in the case of the audience at Howard, may not fully realize that a rhetorical shill game has been played on them.[24]

Moynihan was already on record as opposing public policies targeted specifically for blacks. In a conference sponsored by *Daedalus* and the American Academy of Arts and Sciences only a month earlier, "preference" emerged as a key issue of debate. Below is an excerpt in which Moynihan presents his case against race-specific policies, insisting that they must be embedded in a race-neutral framework. The other speakers are Everett C. Hughes, the eminent sociologist from Brandeis, and Jay Saunders Redding, professor of English at the Hampton Institute in Virginia:

HUGHES: May I ask all these gentlemen a question? Are they or are they not saying that any reduction in the number and proportion of the very poor among the Negro will be accomplished not by addressing ourselves so much to the Negro but by addressing ourselves to the whole state of the economy in our society, to the nature of poverty in general?

MOYNIHAN: I will answer the question by saying that in order to do anything about Negro Americans on the scale that our data would indicate, we have to declare that we are doing it for *everybody*. I think, however, that the problem of the Negro American *is* now a special one, and is not just an intense case of the problem of all poor people.

REDDING: Why do we have to announce that we are doing this for everyone?

MOYNIHAN: Congressmen vote for everyone more readily than they vote for any one. Because the poverty program is a color-blind program, we can do what we could not have done otherwise. We could not have done it for West Virginia or for Harlem—either one of those opposite extremes—but we can do it in generalized terms—for people.

REDDING: Do you think, then, that the idea of compensatory or preferential treatment for the Negro specifically is a bad idea?

MOYNIHAN: I do not know about "good" or "bad." I would say that in terms of the working of the system we are trying to influence by our thinking here, it will be done for "everybody," whatever may be in the back of the minds of the people who do it. [25]

Here Moynihan speaks with the dispassionate voice of the political pragmatist, brushing aside questions of "good" or "bad," "right" or "wrong," and guided solely by realpolitik—one that accepts white racism as a given, or, at best, a political impediment to be circumvented. This leads him to a blanket rejection of policies targeted for blacks. Within this political framework, the politics of "equal results" has no place.

Aside from its intent, the significance of the Howard address was that it drew a line in the political sands marking how far the Johnson administration would go in supporting the escalating demands of the protest movement. In throwing his support behind the Voting Rights Act, Johnson had gone further than any of his predecessors in jeopardizing the Solid South. The rhetoric of "equal results" also threatened to antagonize blue-collar workers, Jews, and other elements of the Democratic coalition. The covert message in the Howard speech was that, as far as the Democratic Party was concerned, the impend-

ing Voting Rights Act marked the end of the Civil Rights Revolution
("the end of the beginning," Johnson said disingenuously, quoting
Churchill). If blacks were "to fulfill these rights," they would have to
get their own house in order. Literally!

Thus, behind the equivocal language in Johnson's address was a
key policy issue concerning the role of the state in the post–civil rights
era. Would future progress depend on an expansion of anti-racist policies—aimed not only at forms of intentional discrimination but also
at the insidious forces of institutionalized racism that have excluded
blacks categorically from whole job sectors and other opportunity
structures? Or would future progress depend on programs of social
uplift that contemplate "the gradual absorption of deserving Negroes
one by one into white society"?

These alternative policy options were predicated on vastly different
assumptions about the nature and sources of racism. The one located
the problem within "white" society and its major institutions, and
called for policies to rapidly integrate blacks into jobs, schools, and
other institutional sectors from which they had historically been excluded. The other assumed that racism was waning, but that blacks
generally lacked the requisite education and skills to avail themselves
of expanding opportunities. This latter school included both traditional liberals who supported government programs that "help blacks
to help themselves," and conservatives, including a new genre of
black conservatives, who adamantly opposed government intervention, insisting that blacks had to summon the personal and group resources to overcome disabilities of race and class.

Thus, what was most flagrantly Machiavellian about Johnson's
speech is that it camouflaged "self-help" behind a rhetorical facade of
"equal results." For the most part the liberal press responded with predictable gullibility. For example, the *New York Times* editorialized:
"President Johnson has addressed himself boldly to what is unques-
tionably the most basic and also the most complicated phase of the
civil rights struggle—the need for translating newly reinforced legal
rights into genuine equality."[26] On the other hand, based on un-

named White House aides, Mary McGory of the *Washington Star* gave the speech a very different spin: "President Johnson suggested that the time had come for them [Negroes] to come to grips with their own worst problem, 'the breakdown of Negro family life.' "[27]

From Infiltration to Subversion: The Moynihan Report

The polarity between anti-racism and social uplift became even more sharply defined by the controversy surrounding the publication of the Moynihan Report three months after Johnson's address at Howard University. Officially titled: "The Negro Family: The Case for National Action," the report presented a mound of statistics showing high rates of divorce, illegitimacy, and female-headed households. Although Moynihan paid lip service to the argument that unemployment and low wages contributed to family breakdown, he was practically obsessed with a single statistic showing that AFDC continued to increase between 1962 and 1964, despite the fact that unemployment was decreasing.[28] On this meager empirical basis, Moynihan concluded that poverty was "feeding upon itself," and that the "disintegration of the Negro family" had assumed a dynamic all its own, independent of joblessness and poverty. In yet another leap of faith, he asserted that family breakdown was the *source* of most of the problems that afflict black America. In Moynihan's own words: ". . . at the center of the tangle of pathology is the weakness of the family structure. Once or twice removed, it will be found to be the principal source of most of the aberrant, inadequate, or anti-social behavior that did not establish, but now serves to perpetuate the cycle of poverty and deprivation."[29]

Moynihan's critics accused him of inverting cause and effect, and, in doing so, shifting the focus of blame away from societal institutions onto blacks themselves. For example, Christopher Jencks wrote in 1965:

Moynihan's analysis is in the conservative tradition that guided the drafting of the poverty program (in whose formulation he participated during the winter of 1963–4). The guiding assumption is that social pathology is caused less by basic defects in the social system than by defects in particular individuals and groups which prevent their adjusting to the system. *The prescription is therefore to change the deviants, not the system.*[30]

The regressive implications of Moynihan's report for public policy were also noted by Herbert Gans:

The findings on family instability and illegitimacy can be used by right-wing and racist groups to support their claim that Negroes are inherently immoral and therefore unworthy of equality. Politicians responding to more respectable white backlash can argue that Negroes must improve themselves before they are entitled to further government aid. . . . . Worse still, the report could be used to justify a reduction of efforts in the elimination of racial discrimination and the War on Poverty.[31]

Thus, at this critical juncture in race history—when there was political momentum for change and when even the president of the United States gave at least verbal support for "a new phase" that would go beyond political rights to assuring equal results—Moynihan succeeded in deflecting policy debate to a useless dissection of the black family. With his considerable forensic skill as speechwriter for Johnson, Moynihan had brought the nation to the threshold of truth—racial equality as a moral and political imperative—and then, with rhetorical guile, deflected the focus onto the tribulations within black families. By the time that the promised White House conference "To Secure These Rights" actually took place, it degenerated into a debate over the Moynihan Report, which by then had become public. Whether by design or not, Moynihan had acted as a political decoy, drawing all the fire to himself while the issue of "equal results" receded into oblivion.[32]

Notwithstanding the efforts of a number of writers, including Moynihan himself, to portray the controversy over the Moynihan Report as fruitless and even counterproductive, it proved to be one of the most formative debates in modern social science. The debate crystallized issues, exposed the conservative assumptions and racial biases that lurked behind mainstream social science, and prompted critics of the report to formulate alternative positions that challenged the prevailing wisdom about race in America. The principal counter-position—encapsulated by William Ryan's ingenious term "blaming the victim"—blew the whistle on the tendency of social science to reduce social phenomena to an individual level of analysis, thereby shifting attention away from the structures of inequality and focusing on the behavioral responses of the individuals suffering the effects of these structures. The controversy also stimulated a large body of research—the most notable example is Herbert Gutman's now classic study of *The Black Family in Slavery and Freedom*.[33] This study demolished the myth that "slavery destroyed the black family"—a liberal myth that allowed social scientists and policymakers to blame "history" for the problems in the black family, thus deflecting attention away from the factors in the here and now that tear families apart.

Yet leading liberals today contend that Moynihan was the victim of unfair ideological attack. Moynihan set the tone for this construction of history in an article that he published in *Commentary* under the title: "The President and the Negro: The Moment Lost." Again, Moynihan begins on the threshold of truth: "For the second time in their history, the great task of liberation has been left only half-accomplished. It appears that the nation may be in the process of reproducing the tragic events of the Reconstruction: giving to Negroes the forms of legal equality, but withholding the economic and political resources which are the bases of social equality."[34] Moynihan goes on to argue, as I have here, that 1965 represented a moment of opportunity: "The moment came when, as it were, the nation had the resources, and the leadership, and the will to make a *total* as against a partial commitment to the cause of Negro equality. It did not do so."[35]

Why was the opportunity missed? According to Moynihan, the blame lies not with the forces of racism and reaction, and certainly not with himself, but with "the liberal Left" who opposed his initiative to address problems in the black family. Specifically, opposition emanated:

. . . from Negro leaders unable to comprehend their opportunity; from civil-rights militants, Negro and white, caught up in a frenzy of arrogance and nihil-

ism; and from white liberals unwilling to expend a jot of prestige to do a difficult but dangerous job that had to be done, and could have been done. But was
not.[36]

Thus, in Moynihan's recapitulation of events, it was his political enemies who, in "a frenzy of arrogance and nihilism," had aborted the
next stage in the Negro revolution that Moynihan had engineered as
an influential advisor to the President.

Moynihan's account is predicated on the assumption that "the
civil-rights movement had no program for going beyond the traditional and relatively easy issues of segregation and discrimination."[37]
But this is an inaccurate and patently self-serving construction of
events. The civil rights movement was evolving precisely such a program, and it involved a sure-fire method for achieving equal results:
instituting a system of preference that would rapidly integrate blacks
into job markets and other institutions from which they had been excluded historically. Moynihan, as we have seen, was adamantly opposed to such an approach, and he did what he could, as speechwriter
for Johnson's duplicitous Howard address and as author of the report
on the Negro family, to derail any movement in this direction. Yet he
portrays himself sanctimoniously as the innocent victim of "the liberal Left," and shifts the blame for "the moment lost" to his critics. He
seems to forget that these critics were only reacting to a political position that he had advanced—one that, despite Moynihan's many
disclaimers, did shift the focus of policy away from a concerted attack
on racist structures to an inconsequential preoccupation with the
black family.

In recent years there have been attempts to rehabilitate Moynihan,
and to portray him as the hapless victim of the ideological excesses of
the sixties. For example, in *The Undeserving Poor*—a book that traces
the poverty debates since the 1960s—Michael Katz asserts that "because most critics distorted the report, the debate generated more passion than insight." One result of the attack on Moynihan, he adds
mournfully, "was to accelerate the burial of the culture of poverty as
an acceptable concept in liberal reform."[38] William Julius Wilson
goes even further in suggesting that "the controversy surrounding the

Moynihan report had the effect of curtailing serious research on minority problems in the inner city for over a decade."[39] Yet thanks to Wilson and others, Moynihan's theoretical and political positions would be given new life in the 1980s.

The Intellectual Reincarnation of Daniel Patrick Moynihan

Joyce Ladner's 1973 declaration of "the death of white sociology" turns out to have been premature.[40] A remarkable thing happened: "white sociology" underwent a black reincarnation. Indeed, Moynihan would be able to gloat over the fact that Wilson and other black scholars had taken up the very positions for which he had been vilified years earlier. As he commented in his Godkin lectures at Harvard in 1984: "The family report had been viewed as mistaken; the benign neglect memorandum was depicted as out-and-out racist. By mid-decade, however, various black scholars were reaching similar conclusions, notably William Julius Wilson in his 1978 study, *The Declining Significance of Race.*"[41]

In point of fact, Wilson struck a number of themes that were at the heart of Moynihan's political analysis in 1965: that blacks had their political rights, thanks to landmark civil rights legislation; that there was "a widening gulf" between the black middle class, which was reaping the benefits of an improved climate of tolerance, and the black lower class, which was as destitute and isolated as ever; that blacks were arriving in the nation's cities at a time when employment opportunities, especially in the manufacturing sector, were declining; and that future progress would depend less on tearing down racist barriers than on raising the level of education and skills among poor blacks.[42] The underlying assumption in both cases was that the civil rights revolution was a watershed that more or less resolved the issue of "race," but that left unaddressed the vexing problems of "class." By "class," however, neither Moynihan or Wilson were advancing a radical theory that challenged structures of inequality, or that envisioned a restructuring of major political and economic institutions. All they meant was that lower-class blacks needed to acquire the education and skills that are a prerequisite for mobility and that explain the success of the black middle class.[43]

In *The Truly Disadvantaged*, published in 1987, Wilson spelled out the implications of his "declining significance" thesis for politics and public policy. Again, he arrived at a position that Moynihan had articulated in 1965: that there was no political constituency for policies targeted specifically for blacks, and therefore "we have to declare that we are doing it for *everybody*." In the very next sentence, Moynihan added an important caveat: "I think, however, that the problem of the Negro American *is* now a special one, and is not just an intense case of the problem of all poor people."[44] But, he insisted, blacks could be helped only through color-blind programs that defined poverty—not race—as the basis for social action. Here, alas, was the "hidden agenda" that Wilson proposed twenty-two years later.

Originally Wilson intended to use "The Hidden Agenda" as the title of *The Truly Disadvantaged*.[45] Instead he used this as the title for Chapter 7, in which he contended that, because there is no political constituency for policies targeted for blacks, it becomes necessary to "hide" such programs behind universal programs "to which the more advantaged groups of all races and class backgrounds can positively relate."[46] Ironically, Wilson's language reveals that he is a poor Social Democrat. It suggests that his first priority is to help the ghetto underclass, and that he opts for "universal programs" only out of political expediency.

The notion of a "hidden agenda" also contradicts Wilson's claim that racism is of "declining significance." Indeed, it is *because* of racism that Wilson feels compelled to "hide" his agenda in the first place. The underlying premise is that America is *so* racist—so utterly indifferent to the plight of black America, so implacably opposed to any indemnification for three centuries of racial oppression—that it becomes necessary to camouflage policies intended for blacks behind policies that offer benefits to the white majority.

At first blush it might appear odd to portray Wilson as a political clone of Moynihan. Wilson, after all, is an ivory-tower scholar and a political outsider who has described himself as a Social Democrat.

Moynihan gave up any pretense of political chastity to become a major player within the Democratic Party. On closer scrutiny, however, Wilson is far from a detached intellectual. In two national elections he has gone on record, via op-ed pieces in the *New York Times*, to advocate race-neutral politics in order to enhance Democratic electoral prospects.[47] And he has quietly served as President Clinton's exculpation for the administration's failure to develop policies to deal with the plight of the nation's ghettos. Whenever Clinton is confronted with this issue, his stock answer is to defend his do-nothing policy by invoking the name of "the famous African-American sociologist William Julius Wilson," explaining how profoundly influenced he was by his book *The Truly Disadvantaged*, and ending with glowing projections about how blacks stand to benefit from his economic policies.[48] It should come as no surprise that Wilson has been mentioned as a possible Cabinet appointee.[49]

Thus, whatever differences exist between Moynihan and Wilson, the factor of overriding importance is that both repudiated race-based politics and race-based public policy. Here we come to the delicate but unavoidable issue concerning the role that the race of a social theorist plays in determining what Alvin Gouldner refers to as "the *social career of a theory*."[50] Not only was Moynihan white, but he wrote at a time of heightened racial consciousness and mobilization, both inside and outside the university. As a white, he was susceptible to charges of racism and of resorting to stereotypes in his depiction of black families. Even the voluble Moynihan was reduced to silence when it came to parrying the charges leveled against him by black scholars and activists.

Wilson, too, has had his critics, but at least he has been immune to charges of "racism." Furthermore, Wilson appeared on the stage of history at a time when racial militancy was ebbing. The nation, including the academic establishment, had grown weary of racial conflict, and was eager, like the Democratic Party, to "get beyond race." Wilson, clearly, was the right person in the right place and the right time, and, as if this were not enough, his book *The Declining Significance of Race* had the right title—one that satisfied the nation's yearning to put race behind, to pretend that racism was no longer the problem it had been in times past.

To be sure, Wilson did not cause the retreat from race that has occurred over the past two decades. He did, however, confer on it an indispensable mark of legitimacy. This is the significance of Wilson's elevation to national prominence and even to celebrity status. It has meant that the retreat from race could no longer be equated with racism and reaction.[51]

Cornel West: The Left Wing of the Backlash

If books could be judged by their titles, one would think that a book entitled *Race Matters* would be the antithesis of a book entitled *The Declining Significance of Race*.[52] But then again, one must beware of semantic infiltration, and the possibility that titles are subversive of meaning.

Of course, the title has an intentional double meaning. The first—*race* matters—serves as a catchall for the disparate essays that West has compiled in this volume. The second meaning—race *matters*—is more substantive, but still leaves the reader to wallow in ambiguity. In what sense does race "matter" in the *Weltanschauung* of Cornel West? Is this an ironic comment on whites' obsessive preoccupation with the happenstance of skin color? Or does it allude to the fateful influence that race has on the lives of African Americans? Nor is the meaning of "race" clear. Is this an affirmation of race—that is, of black culture and identity? Or does "race" refer to "racism" and the extent that *it* "matters" in the lives of African Americans? Or is the ambiguity purposeful, to point up the paradoxical and sometimes contradictory nature of the phenomenon itself?

Suffice it to say that many or all of these elements appear in West's book: topics range from the crisis in black leadership, to black conservatism, to Black-Jewish relations, to black sexuality. These are all race matters, to be sure, but they are only marginally related to the question that preoccupies us here: the extent that race (read: racism) matters, and the consequences that ensue for politics and public policy. These issues are explored in two of West's essays that serve as the

basis of the following discussion: "Nihilism in Black America" and "Beyond Affirmative Action: Equality and Identity."[53]

The term "nihilism" invites semantic confusion. Invoked by a professor of philosophy, the term conjures up hoary philosophical debates concerning the nature of existence and the possibility of objective knowledge. But West surely is not claiming that the ghetto is an enactment of some dubious philosophical doctrine. Invoked by a political activist, "nihilism" calls up associations with Russian revolutionaries who believed that the old order must be utterly eradicated to make way for the new. Again, it is doubtful that West, the political activist, is imputing these motives to ghetto youth. Nor does his use of "nihilism" suggest the angst and denial of meaning that are often viewed as endemic to modernity. No doubt West could expound on all of these themes, but in describing the urban ghetto, he uses the word specifically to refer to destructive and self-destructive behavior that is unconstrained by legal or moral norms. But this meaning comes dangerously close to the prevailing view of ghetto youth as driven by aberrant and anti-social tendencies. Alas, does "nihilism" merely provide an intellectual gloss for ordinary assumptions and claims?

Any such doubts are seemingly dissipated by the book's opening sentence: "What happened in Los Angeles in April of 1992 was neither a race riot nor a class rebellion. Rather, this monumental upheaval was a multiracial, trans-class, and largely male display of justified social rage." With this manifesto, West establishes his credentials as a person on the left. By the end of the same paragraph, however, West says that "race was the visible catalyst, not the underlying cause."[54] Already the reader is left to wonder: Does race matter or doesn't it?

In the next paragraph West assumes the rhetorical stance that pervades his book: his is the voice of reason and moderation between liberals and conservatives, each of which is allegedly trapped in rigid orthodoxies that leave us "intellectually debilitated, morally disempowered, and personally depressed."[55] Liberals, West avers, are burdened with a simplistic faith in the ability of government to solve our racial problems. Conservatives, on the other hand, blame the problems on blacks and ignore "public responsibility for the immoral circumstances that haunt our fellow citizens." Both treat blacks as "a problem people." West thus presents himself as mediator between ideological extremes. He is a leftist who does not resort to a crude economic determinism that denies human freedom and that relieves the poor of moral responsibility for their actions. And he is a theologian who does not use morality to evade public responsibility for social wrongs.

Thus for West racism and poverty are only part of the problem. Of equal concern is the "pervasive spiritual impoverishment" that afflicts ghetto dwellers. With these false dichotomies, West has set the stage for a morality play involving a contest between material and spiritual forces and between Left and Right. Enter the protagonist: a Man of Vision who sees through the mystifications of both sides, a Great Conciliator who transcends political schism and will point the way to an Eden of racial harmony and social justice.

A captivating tale, to be sure. But the critical issue is this: where does West's otherwise laudatory attempt to bridge the ideological chasm lead him? According to West, "the liberal/conservative discussion conceals the most basic issue now facing black America." The reader waits with bated breath: what is this "most basic issue"? West has already conveyed his skepticism of the left's monistic emphasis on issues of racism and political economy. And he claims to reject the conservative emphasis on "behavioral impediments" with its bootstrap morale. The most basic issue now facing black America, according to Cornel West, is *"the nihilistic threat to its very existence."*[56] West continues:

This threat is not simply a matter of relative economic deprivation and political powerlessness—though economic well-being and political clout are requisites for meaningful black progress. It is primarily a question of speaking to the profound sense of psychological depression, personal worthlessness, and social despair so widespread in black America.[57]

Now, there can be no doubt that "psychological depression, personal worthlessness, and social despair" abound in ghettos across

America. So do "battered identities," "spiritual impoverishment," "social deracination," "cultural denudement," and a host of related afflictions that leave West groping for words to convey the gravity and horror of this situation. Certainly West should not be faulted for bringing such conditions to light. This point is worth underscoring because Wilson and others have claimed that discussion of ghetto "pathologies" has been taboo ever since Moynihan was clobbered, as they would have it, for reporting some unpleasant statistics on black families. This is a totally unfounded allegation. The only issue, both then and now, concerns the theoretical claims advanced concerning the *causes* of these well-known afflictions, together with the related issue of what is to be *done* about them. This was the basis of the attack on Moynihan, and it is on these same issues that West must be judged.

According to West, despite the tribulations going back to slavery, blacks have always been endowed with "cultural armor to beat back the demons of hopelessness, meaningless, lovelessness."[58] He points out that until the 1970s the rate of suicide was comparatively low among blacks, but today young blacks have one of the highest rates of suicide. Thus for West the question becomes: what has happened to "the cultural structures that once sustained black life in America" and "are no longer able to fend off the nihilistic threat?" His answer focuses on two factors:

1. *The saturation of market forces and market moralities in black life.* By this West means that blacks have succumbed to the materialism and hedonism that pervade American culture, and that "edge out nonmarket values—love, care, service to others—handed down by preceding generations." If blacks are more susceptible to these corrupting influences than others, it is because the poor have "a limited capacity to ward off self-contempt and self-hatred."[59]

2. *The crisis in black leadership.* Here West bemoans the failure of black leaders to carry on a tradition of leadership that was at once aggressive and inspirational. One reason for this failure is the corruption of the new middle class by their immersion into mass culture.

But another reason that "quality leadership is on the wane" has to do with "the gross deterioration of personal, familial, and communal relations among African-Americans."[60] With families in decline and communities in shambles, the basis for effective leadership is lost.

Thus, West harkens back to the halcyon days when there was "a vital community bound by its ethical ideals."[61] Unfortunately, oppression does not always produce such pleasing outcomes, and the victims of oppression are not always ennobled by their experience and an inspiration to the rest of us.

West's problem, to repeat, is not that he discusses crime, violence, drugs, and the other notorious ills of ghetto life. Rather the problem is that he presents social breakdown and cultural disintegration as a problem sui generis, with an existence and momentum independent of the forces that gave rise to it in the first place. Moynihan, too, had held that centuries of injustice had "brought about deep-seated structural distortions in the life of the Negro American." But he added a remarkable addendum: "At this point, the present pathology is capable of perpetuating itself without assistance from the white world."[62] Similarly, West traces nihilism to centuries of injustice, but goes on to claim that nihilism is so embedded in the life of the ghetto that it assumes a life all its own. At least this is what West implies when he writes that "culture is as much a structure as the economy or politics."[63] Indeed, the whole point of West's critique of "liberal structuralism" is that nihilism is not reducible to political economy. It is precisely because nihilism is so deeply embedded that this "cultural structure" must be addressed as a force in its own right.

It takes hairsplitting distinctions that do not bear close scrutiny to maintain that West's view of nihilism is different from the conservative view of ghetto culture as deeply pathological, and as the chief source of the problems that beset African Americans. Despite his frequent caveats, West has succeeded in shifting the focus of blame onto the black community. The affliction is *theirs*—something we shall call "nihilism."

It is also theirs to resolve. As with the Moynihan Report, the regressive implications of West's theory become clear when one examines his praxis. West asks: "What is to be done about this nihilistic threat?" But his answer is sadly deficient. He calls for "a politics of conversion"—a frail attempt to use radical vernacular as a cover for ideas that are anything but radical. "Like alcoholism and drug addiction," West explains, "nihilism is a disease of the soul."[64] How does one cure a disease of the soul? West's prescription (to paraphrase Jencks) is to change the nihilist, not the system. To quote West again:

> Nihilism is not overcome by arguments or analysis; it is tamed by love and care. Any disease of the soul must be conquered by a turning of one's soul. This turning is done through one's own affirmation of one's worth—an affirmation fueled by the concern of others. A love ethic must be at the center of a politics of conversion.[65]

Here, alas, is the reason for the acclaim that has been heaped on *Race Matters*. The cure for the nihilism that so frightens white America is not a resumption of the war on poverty. Nor is it a resumption of the movement against racism. West, of course, would endorse both, but he has also been explicit in saying that "liberal structuralism" is not equipped to deal with "the self-destructive and inhumane actions of black people."[66]

One can almost hear the national sigh of relief from those who feared that expensive new programs of social reconstruction and a renewed commitment to affirmative action might become necessary to control the disorder emanating from the ghettos of America. Instead we have an inexpensive palliative: a crusade against nihilism to be waged from within the black community. So much the better that this proposal is advanced not by another black conservative whose politics might be suspect, but by a self-proclaimed Socialist. Unfortunately, West, the philosopher and activist, adopts the idiom of the preacher who mounts the pulpit, pounds the lectern, and enjoins his flock to "have the audacity to take the nihilistic threat by the neck and turn back its deadly assaults."[67]

One cannot fault West for trying to bridge the chasm between religion and politics. However, he has not placed himself in the tradition of Martin Luther King, who invoked religious symbols and appealed to spiritual values in order to mobilize popular support behind a political movement. King did not believe that a love ethic could ever serve as an antidote to spiritual breakdown. The only remedy was a political transformation that eliminated the conditions that eat away at the human spirit. West, on the other hand, offers no political framework for his so-called politics of conversion. Indeed, he explicitly divorces nihilism from political economy, thus implying that moral redemption is to be achieved through some mysterious "turning of one's soul."[68]

West cannot escape the retrograde implications of his position with disclaimers that "unlike conservative behaviorists, the politics of conversion situates these actions within inhuman circumstances."[69] He ignores his own admonition that "to call on black people to be agents makes sense only if we also examine the dynamics of this victimization against which their agency will, in part, be exercised."[70] And while he is guided by "a vision of moral regeneration and political insurgency for the purpose of fundamental social change for all who suffer from socially induced misery,"[71] he fails to translate this prophetic ideal into a political praxis. The practical implication of West's position is to substitute a vapid and utterly inconsequential "politics of conversion" for a genuine political solution—one that would call upon the power and resources of the national government for what is at bottom a national problem and a national disgrace.

It should come as no surprise that the most prominent convert to West's politics of conversion is President Clinton. In a speech delivered to a Memphis church in 1993, Clinton practically echoed West in asserting that there is a crisis of the spirit. The ramifications for public policy should have been predictable: "Sometimes, there are no answers from the outside in. Sometimes, all of the answers have to come from the values and the stirrings and the voices that speak to us from within."[72] Thus are legitimate spiritual concerns used as a subterfuge for political and moral abdication. The irony is made still more bitter by the fact that Clinton gave his speech in the same Memphis church where Martin Luther King delivered his last sermon the night before his 1968 assassination.

Not only does West shift the focus of analysis and of blame away from the structures of racial oppression, but in his chapter entitled "Beyond Affirmative Action" he undercuts the single policy that has gone a decisive step beyond equal rights in the direction of equal results. West is *not* opposed to affirmative action, but he engages in a tortuous reasoning that subverts the whole logic behind it. Thus, he begins on the one hand by declaring that in principle he favors a class-based affirmative action (as does William Julius Wilson).[73] On the other hand, he knows that such a policy is politically unrealistic. He also knows that if affirmative action in its present form were abolished, then "racial and sexual discrimination would return with a vengeance."[74] Why, then, all this hairsplitting? Even if a class-based affirmative action could be enacted, few of the benefits would filter down to African Americans who are not only most in need, but also have unique claims for compensatory treatment. Nor would working-class whites who become lawyers and doctors on the basis of affirmative action provide the black community with the professional talent that it sorely needs.

In short, affirmative action is meant to counteract the evils of *caste*, not of class. It is predicated on a realization that blacks have been victims of a system of oppression that goes far beyond the disabilities associated with class disadvantage, and therefore warrants a special remedy. West's equivocation with respect to race-based affirmative action is the clearest indication of how little race matters in his theoretical framework and in his agenda for change.

Reminiscent of Moynihan and Wilson, West's approach for helping blacks is to help "everybody." Like them, he provides a respectable liberal cover for evading the issue of race, and still worse, backing off from race-targeted policies like affirmative action, all in the name of getting "beyond race." West prides himself on steering "a course between the Scylla of environmental determinism and the Charybdis of a blaming-the-victims perspective."[75] Unfortunately, he ends up in a political never-never land where, as Du Bois once said in his critique of historiography, "nobody seems to have done wrong and everybody was right."[76] And nothing changes.[77]

This nation's ruling elites need to be told that there is no exit from the current morass until they confront the legacy of slavery and resume the unfinished racial agenda. It is *their* nihilism that deserves our condemnation—the crime, the immorality, the self-destructive folly of tolerating racial ghettos and excluding yet another generation of black youth from the American Dream.

Conclusion

Martin Luther King's "Letter from a Birmingham Jail" has become a part of this nation's political folklore. However, its specific contents have been all but expunged from our collective memory. The letter was not a condemnation of racism. Nor was it, like his celebrated "I Have a Dream" oration—whose contents *are* remembered—an evocation of American ideals or a prophetic vision of better times ahead. King was responding to a letter signed by eight priests, rabbis, and ministers that appeared in the *Birmingham News* while he was imprisoned. The letter spoke sympathetically of "rights consistently denied," but criticized King's tactics as "unwise and untimely" and called for a "constructive and realistic approach," one that would substitute negotiation for confrontation. In his response King acknowledged their sincerity in seeking "a better path," but explained why confrontation and crisis were necessary in order to shake white society out of its apathy and intransigence. Mincing no words, King issued the following indictment of the so-called moderate:

I have almost reached the regrettable conclusion that the Negroes' great stumbling block in the stride toward freedom is not the White Citizens' "Counciler" or the Ku Klux Klanner, but the white moderate who is more devoted to "order" than to justice; who prefers a negative peace which is the absence of tension to a positive peace which is the presence of justice; who constantly says "I agree with you in the goal you seek, but I can't agree with your methods of direct action"; who lives by the myth of time and who constantly advises the Negro to wait until "a more convenient season."[78]

Was there hyperbole in King's assertion that the great stumbling block in the stride for freedom was not the Council or the Klan but those who seek a middle ground and would settle for a negative peace? Perhaps. As is often argued, liberals are not *the* enemy. However, the enemy depends on the so-called liberal to put a kinder and gentler face on racism; to subdue the rage of the oppressed; to raise false hopes that change is imminent; to modulate the demands for complete liberation; to divert protest; and to shift the onus of responsibility for America's greatest crime away from powerful institutions that *could* make a difference onto individuals who have been rendered powerless by these very institutions.

The liberal retreat from race during the post–civil rights era is full of political paradox. When forced to confront the issue, the liberal will argue that in a racist society, race-based politics are not viable precisely because blacks are an isolated and despised minority. As with much race-think, this is upside-down and inside-out. It is precisely because blacks were an isolated and despised minority that they were forced to seek redress outside of the framework of electoral politics. The civil rights movement was triumphant in part because it tapped the lode of revolutionary potential within the black community, and in part because it galvanized the support of political allies outside the black community, including white liberals. Furthermore, this movement not only achieved its immediate objectives, but also was the major catalyst for progressive change in the twentieth century. As Aldon Morris writes at the conclusion of *The Origins of the Civil Rights Movement*:

. . . the civil rights movement served as a training ground for many of the activists who later organized movements within their own communities. Indeed, the modern women's movement, student movement, farm workers' movement, and others of the period were triggered by the unprecedented scale of nontraditional politics in the civil rights movement.[79]

A common refrain from the right is that advocates of affirmative action are guilty of the very thing that they say they are against—namely, treating blacks as a separate class. Again, this reasoning is upside-down and inside-out. The truth is that it is the *refusal* to see race—the willful color blindness of the liberal camp—that acquiesces to the racial status quo, and does so by consigning blacks to a twilight zone where they are politically invisible. In this way elements of the left unwittingly join the right in evading any reckoning with America's greatest crime—slavery—and its legacy in the present.

6

The Underclass
A Case of Color Blindness,
Right and Left

> Until we summon up the courage to distinguish between the
> problems of poverty and the problems of race, we shall
> have to reckon with the consequences of our lack of candor.
>
> Otis Dudley Duncan, "Inheritance of
> Poverty or Inheritance of Race?" 1968

> The belief that class has now supplanted race in the life
> chances of American blacks remains a pitiful delusion.
> This is a dangerous delusion because it drains energy
> and diverts attention from the stark fact that racial
> injustices perpetrated against all blacks—middle-class
> and underclassed blacks—remain the unfinished
> business of American democracy. Confronting racism is
> difficult for whites and blacks. But as long as racism exists it
> cannot be avoided either by semantics or by delusions.
>
> Kenneth Clark, "Contemporary Sophisticated Racism" (1979)

In the 1980s poverty acquired a new "voguish stigma."[1] The term
"underclass" was added to the English language's expanding lexicon
of inequality. The term actually originated with Gunnar Myrdal,
who borrowed an old Swedish term for the lower class, *underklassen*.[2]
In *Challenge to Affluence*, written in 1962, Myrdal used the term to
refer to groups that did not share in the nation's affluence. They were
a "permanent underclass," which is to say that they languished in
poverty even during periods of economic growth and declining unemployment.[3] Ken Auletta rescued the term from academic obscu-

137

rity in 1982 with the publication of *The Underclass*.[4] Suddenly the underclass was a hot topic, the subject of articles in *U.S. News and World Report*, *The Atlantic*, *Fortune*, *Newsweek*, *Reader's Digest*, and *Time*.[5] By 1988 the term entered the political discourse of the presidential election, as candidates were queried about their policies for dealing with the underclass. Though camouflaged behind a smoke screen of innuendo and code words, the issue permeated the campaign as George Bush and Walter Mondale vied with each other to demonstrate their commitment to "values." The values cited concerned family, work, and education, precisely those values central to the American success myth and presumed to be lacking among the underclass.

Once again, social science lagged behind journalism. In due course, however, the academic wheel was lubricated with foundation grants to measure the size, location, racial makeup, and other germane characteristics of the underclass. Dozens of studies were conducted, and, according to a summary report issued by the Social Science Research Council in 1988, estimates of the size of the underclass ranged from 2 to 8 million people.[6] One widely cited study by Ricketts and Sawhill defined an "underclass area" as a census tract with a high proportion of high school dropouts; young males outside the labor force; welfare recipients; and female-headed households. On the basis of these criteria, Ricketts and Sawhill estimated that 2.5 million people live in these underclass areas, most of which are in cities. Fifty-nine percent of their residents are black and 10 percent are Hispanic.[7]

As social researchers scurried about measuring the underclass, the term underwent a conceptual transformation. Myrdal had used "underclass" to define an objective condition—one that was rooted in the class system and labor market processes, and that manifested itself in the existence of a group so removed from the regular economy that it was unaffected even by surges in the economy, defying the maxim that a rising tide lifts all boats. This idea had a crucially important implication for social policy: it suggested that macroeconomic policies to stimulate growth and jobs would *not* reach the underclass. In other words, special programs and policies targeted for this castaway population would be necessary.

Once again, however, methodological individualism played havoc with the sociological imagination, reducing a concept that pertained to social structure down to the level of individual behavior. Thus, in the hands of the empiricists the underclass was redefined to refer, not to objective conditions of chronic poverty and joblessness, but to the socially dysfunctional behavior of the poor themselves. In summing up the prevailing view, Ricketts and Sawhill write: "most observers agree that the underclass is characterized by *behaviors which are at variance with those of mainstream America* (such as joblessness, welfare dependency, unwed parenting, criminal or uncivil behavior, and dropping out of high school)."[8]

Although these empirical studies have all the trappings of objective social science, they are riddled with unexamined value assumptions. The class system itself is accepted as a given—an empirical if not normative fact of life. Thus, attention is shifted away from the structures of inequality that produce an underclass, to the attributes of the individuals who inhabit this lowly stratum. Hence, the individual becomes the focal point of change as well. The presumption is that we can eliminate the underclass by rehabilitating its victims.[9]

A still more serious flaw in the concept of the underclass is the conflation of race, class, and culture. The result is a conceptual muddle that obscures the distinctive roles of race, class, and culture in producing the underclass, the explanatory weight that is to be assigned to each, and the dynamic relationships that exist among them. There *are* people, not all of them minorities, who may be said to live "outside the class system" and to engage in "behaviors at variance with those of mainstream society." We do not need sociology to tell us that, and when sociology engages in this rhetoric, it only gives scientific sanction to ordinary perceptions and prejudices regarding race and class.[10] Where sociology *can* be useful is in shedding light on the social production of this underclass. To do so, we need to disentangle race, class, and culture, instead of blurring these crucial analytical distinctions and focusing only on surface manifestations.

The conflation of race, class, and culture has left the theoretical door open for different theorists to single out whichever factor serves their ideological position. For "the color-blind right," *culture* is the key factor in explaining the underclass. For the "color-blind left," it is *class*—which is to say, the economic factors that keep people trapped in poverty. What these positions have in common is a neglect of *race*—that is, the specifically racist structures that keep racial minorities trapped in poverty.

Like "underclass," the term "race" lumps together groups that are disparate from one another, not only in terms of their historical origins but even in terms of the extent to which they encounter racist barriers to mobility. This sloppy conceptualization has led to specious comparisons between various "racial" minorities. For example, following Nathan Glazer's lead, Thomas Sowell has used the success of Asians and West Indians to argue that "race" is not an insurmountable obstacle and cannot explain why so many African Americans are mired in poverty.[11] As I have argued elsewhere, the much touted "success" of Asians and West Indians is largely an artifact of selective migration—that is, the influx of large numbers of professionals and other educated and skilled workers.[12] Nor can it be assumed that Asians and West Indians encounter the same "racist" barriers as do African Americans. The reification of "race" has not only blurred these crucial distinctions, but has also had an adverse impact on social policy. Because eligibility for affirmative action generally has been defined in terms of "historical disadvantage," rather than in terms of specific injustices visited upon specific minorities, groups with very different historical and moral claims have crowded under the meager umbrella of affirmative action.

In point of fact, there are different underclasses—different in their origins, their social constitution, their circumstances, and their implications for the society at large. To lump these disparate groups together on the basis of common demographic traits is to obscure the historically specific factors that produced these various underclasses, and in particular, the role that racism has played in the production and reproduction of the *black* underclass.

The Underclass as Culture

As indicated earlier, most studies of the underclass assume aberrant culture and anti-social behavior in the very definition of the underclass, thus obscuring cause and effect. The issue here is not whether there is an underclass, or whether its members engage in "socially dysfunctional behavior." Rather, the issue is whether their behavior *explains why* they are in the underclass, or, conversely, whether these individuals first find themselves in the underclass (typically as a matter of birth) and only then develop "socially dysfunctional behavior." Also at issue is whether this behavior, while clearly dysfunctional for the society at large, is nonetheless functional for the actors themselves, given their restricted life chances. As Douglas Glasgow wrote in his book *The Black Underclass*:

Behaviors of young inner-city Blacks . . . are consciously propagated via special socialization rituals that help the young Blacks prepare for inequality at an early age. With maturity, these models of behavior are employed to neutralize the personally destructive effects of institutionalized racism. Thus, they form the basis of a "survival culture" that is significantly different from the so-called culture of poverty. Notwithstanding its reactive origin, survival culture is not a passive adaptation to encapsulation but a very active—at times devious, innovative, and extremely resistive—response to rejection and destruction. It is useful and necessary to young Blacks in their present situation. [13]

In contrast to Glasgow's careful delineation of the existential sources and functions of cultural patterns associated with the underclass, note how cause and effect are obscured in the following passage from a 1987 article by Myron Magnet in *Fortune* magazine:

They are poor; but numbering around five million, they are a relatively small minority of the 33 million Americans with incomes below the official poverty line. Disproportionately black and Hispanic, they are still a minority within these minorities. What primarily defines them is not so much their poverty or race as their behavior—their chronic lawlessness, drug use, out-of-wedlock births, nonwork, welfare dependency, and school failure. *"Underclass" describes a state of mind and a way of life. It is at least as much cultural as an economic condition.* [14]

In this treatment of the underclass as "a state of mind and a way of life," we have a clear retrogression to the culture-of-poverty school

of the 1960s, which was itself a retrogression to the cultural deprivation school of the 1950s. The common element is a presumption that
the culture of the poor is different from that of middle-class society,
and that it is this aberrant culture that keeps the poor trapped in poverty. Critics over several decades have advanced powerful counter-
arguments, but it seems that no sooner is the head of this theoretical
dragon severed than it regenerates another. Part of the reason for its
regenerative powers is that the cultural thesis has superficial validity
and squares with everyday observation, not to speak of the findings of
a plethora of demographic and ethnographic studies. Why social scientists think they have *discovered* something when they find that an
indigent and marginalized population lives according to "different
rules" from the middle classes is itself perplexing. The descriptive
reality is there to be observed and measured. The critical question, as
Elliot Liebow showed in *Tally's Corner*, is not whether these cultural
patterns exist, but whether they constitute an independent cultural
tradition with "a life of their own," or whether they merely represent
the cultural byproducts of extreme poverty and marginality, pro-
tracted across generations.[15]

It is all too easy to isolate the aberrant and antisocial behavior of the
underclass, to rail against it, and to propose programs to redeem these
deficient individuals. The problem, though, is that it is myopic and
futile to attempt cultural change without attacking the constellation
of social and structural conditions in which this culture is anchored.
So long as social scientists persist in treating the behavior of the underclass as though it is self-generated and self-explaining, and focusing on agency without regard to structure, we will end up with superficial truths, facile value judgments, and ineffectual policy.

The Class Interpretation of the Underclass

If some observers of the underclass give theoretical primacy to culture, others give theoretical primacy to class. Ever since the publication of *The Declining Significance of Race* in 1978, William Julius
Wilson has been in the forefront of those who see the underclass as a
by-product of economic dislocations that have transformed the urban

economy, wiping out millions of jobs in the industrial sector.[16] These dislocations, which are themselves the product of larger transformations in the global economy, have had an especially severe effect on blacks since they are concentrated in cities and job sectors most impacted by deindustrialization. According to Wilson, blacks migrating to Northern cities not only encountered a shrinking industrial sector, but they lacked the education and skills to compete for jobs in the expanding service sector. For Wilson, this explains why conditions have deteriorated for the black lower classes during the post–civil rights era, a period of relative tolerance that has witnessed the rise of a large and prosperous black middle class.

Furthermore, Wilson sees this endemic unemployment and underemployment as the root cause of the "tangle of pathologies" associated with the underclass. Wilson's agenda for change is consistent with his analysis. Because the causes are not race-specific—that is, based on patterns of deliberate racial exclusion—neither can the remedy be race-specific. Thus, in *The Truly Disadvantaged* Wilson proposes "a universal program of reform" that would attack unemployment and underemployment.[17] Essentially, Wilson's agenda involves a renewal and expansion of the forgotten War on Poverty. Thus, Wilson calls for a macroeconomic policy to promote growth and generate jobs, and improved welfare and social services, including job training, for those who need it.[18]

Over against the culture-of-poverty theorists, Wilson is mindful of the link between culture and social structure. He traces underclass culture primarily to the job crisis that afflicts ghetto workers, particularly males, destroying the basis for stable families and engendering various coping strategies that affront middle-class society. In terms of the discipline, Wilson's emphasis on economic structures and labor markets has enlarged the scope of analysis well beyond the antiquated race relations model, which presupposed that racial inequality was primarily a function of race prejudice. Wilson seems to be saying that even if Myrdal had his way, and all whites were exorcised of their racist beliefs, the underclass would still be as badly off as it is today.

There can be no doubt that deindustrialization has exacerbated the job crisis for working-class blacks. In the case of New York City, for example, the manufacturing sector was cut in half between 1955 and 1975, involving the loss of some 500,000 jobs.[19] As recently as 1990, New York City lost 34,000 jobs over the summer, including 5,200 jobs in manufacturing, 5,600 jobs in construction, and 6,500 jobs in retailing.[20] If these jobs could be magically restored, many blacks would surely benefit.

Nevertheless, there is reason to think that Wilson places far too much explanatory weight on deindustrialization as the reason for the job crisis that afflicts black America. As Norman Fainstein has argued in a paper on "The Underclass/Mismatch Hypothesis as an Explanation for Black Economic Deprivation," blacks were never heavily represented in the industrial sector in the first place. Fainstein's data indicate a pattern of "employment ghettoization" involving the exclusion of blacks from whole job sectors—not only those that require the education and skills that Wilson assumes to be lacking among young blacks, but also service-sector jobs that require minimal education and skills. Fainstein concluded that "the economic situation of blacks is rooted more in the character of the employment opportunities in growing industries than in the disappearance of 'entry-level' jobs in declining industries."[21]

Taking a cue from Fainstein's study, let us look more closely at the evidence for Wilson's thesis that deindustrialization is the major factor in explaining the growth of the underclass. To begin with, Wilson offers no direct evidence of the numbers of blacks affected by plant shutdowns and layoffs. Nor does he present data on the job experiences and qualifications of unemployed blacks to substantiate his claim that these workers lack the education and skills for jobs in the expanding service sector. Nor does he examine the racial attitudes and hiring practices of employers. Rather, his conclusions are based entirely on a macroscopic analysis of economic and occupational trends in cities of high black concentration. Here he relies heavily on John Kasarda's studies showing a shift from manufacturing to service industries, together with a corresponding increase in the number of

jobs requiring education beyond high school.[22] On the assumption
that blacks have low levels of education and skill, Wilson reasons that
this restructuring of the urban economy has been especially devastating for blacks. Quoting Kasarda, he concludes that there is "a serious
mismatch between the current educational distribution of minority
residents in large northern cities and the changing educational requirements of their rapidly transforming industries."[23]

Thus, the entire thrust of Wilson's analysis is to interpret the growing black underclass as the hapless victims of color-blind economic
forces. What role, if any, does racism play? Wilson grants that *past*
racism has left lower-class blacks vulnerable to the economic dislocations of a postindustrial economy, but, consistent with his thesis in
The Declining Significance of Race, he does not see contemporaneous racism as a major factor in its own right.[24] Again, he presents no
direct evidence to show that blacks do not encounter racism in job
markets. Rather, he *infers* this on the basis of an improved climate of
tolerance generally, together with the unprecedented success of the
black middle class.

Given the meager empirical foundation on which Wilson's conclusions are based, it is astonishing how widely they have been embraced by social scientists who usually insist upon higher standards
of empirical proof. Not only are his major propositions unsubstantiated, but they rest on assumptions that are implausible if not patently false. Specifically:

1. Wilson assumes that if not for the collapse of the manufacturing
sector, blacks would have found their way into these jobs. But there is
nothing in history to support this assumption since, as we have seen,
the entire thrust of Northern racism has been to exclude blacks from
blue-collar jobs in core industries. Even if three million manufacturing jobs had not disappeared, what basis is there for assuming that
they would have gone to blacks, rather than to working-class whites
or, as in the past, to new immigrants who have been pouring into the
nation's cities despite the collapse of the manufacturing sector? The
lesson of history is that blacks have gained access to manufacturing

only as a last resort—when all other sources of labor had dried up. Now we are asked to believe that blacks would have finally gotten their turn, except that the jobs themselves have disappeared.

2. Wilson assumes that an expansive economy will translate into jobs and opportunities for "the truly disadvantaged." Yet his faith in macroeconomic policy has not been sustained by subsequent events. As was noted in a recent story in the *New York Times*, "even during the robust economic recovery of the late 1980s when the white unemployment rate was—as it is now—under 5 percent, black unemployment never dipped below 10 percent, and sometimes topped 12 percent."[25] The same conclusion was reached in a recent survey of poverty research:

> The severity of poverty is greater today than at any point since the late 1950s. Most of the increased severity occurred between 1977 and 1982, a period of high inflation and two recessions, when the poor got poorer. *More surprising is that the long economic recovery of the 1980s did not reduce the severity of poverty.*[26]

Of course, this outcome is "surprising" only if one accepts the assumption that "a rising tide raises all boats." In point of fact, these economic trends lend credence to Myrdal's concept of the underclass as unaffected by increased prosperity and declining unemployment.

Yet Wilson has not wavered in his faith in universal as opposed to race-specific public policy. At a 1993 symposium at the University of Michigan, he reported the results of recent research in ghetto neighborhoods where the majority of adults are unemployed or have dropped out of the labor force, construing this as evidence of a "new urban poverty." Citing the "resistance to targeted programs for the truly disadvantaged," he called for policies that "address concerns beyond those that focus on . . . inner-city ghettos."[27] Roger Wilkins promptly responded that "the new American poverty has to be viewed as part of the old American racism," insisting that "if we don't face the fact that we have done unique and severe damage to poor blacks, then we will construct broad-based social policy programs where the money will roll away from the poor as it always does. When we had model cities programs for the poor we ended up building golf courses and parks in suburbs. That is the way it works when money is not targeted."[28]

Essentially the same conclusion was reached by Gary Orfield and Carole Ashkinaze in a case study of Atlanta, which underwent a decade of spectacular economic growth beginning in the mid-seventies. The city, furthermore, was a model of "black empowerment": it was run by two nationally prominent black mayors and had a legion of black professionals and businessmen with political clout. "If economic expansion and a tight labor market could create equal opportunity without targeted government action," the authors reason, "it should have happened in the Atlanta area."[29] They found, however, that many workers were drawn in from the outside, and inner-city blacks were generally denied access to jobs generated by economic development, much of which occurred in outlying suburban areas. The lesson of Atlanta, according to the authors, is that "because of the consequences of racial segregation, unequal opportunity and discrimination, the nonracial solution of tight labor markets is not likely to work as expected."[30]

3. Wilson assumes that affirmative action has primarily helped the black middle class. As he writes: "Programs of preferential treatment applied merely according to racial or ethnic group membership tend to benefit the relatively advantaged segments of the designated groups. The truly deprived members may not be helped by such programs."[31] Wilson has been widely cited by white liberals to legitimate their own retreat from affirmative action even though he provides no direct evidence to substantiate his claim that affirmative action has primarily been of benefit to the black middle class. Presumably Wilson has in mind affirmative action programs in higher education and the professions that obviously do not reach blacks who are "truly deprived." However, as William Taylor has written in the *Yale Law Journal*: "The focus of much of the effort has been not just on white collar jobs, but also on law enforcement, construction work, and craft and production jobs in large companies—all areas in which the extension of new opportunities has provided upward mobility for less advantaged minority workers."[32] For these workers, a pink slip is all there is between being "relatively advantaged" and being "truly deprived." Furthermore, given Wilson's emphasis on how deindustrialization has destroyed employment opportunity for lower-class blacks, it is incomprehensible that he should renounce the very policy that has resulted in the first significant racial integration of major blue-collar industries, despite an overall contraction in the size of their work force.

4. Wilson assumes that the principal reason blacks have not been absorbed into the expanding service industries is that they lack the requisite education and skills. As he writes:

> Basic structural changes in our modern industrial economy have compounded the problems of poor blacks because education and training have become more important for entry into the more desirable and higher-paying jobs and because increased reliance on labor-saving devices has contributed to a surplus of untrained black workers.[33]

Here Wilson falls into the familiar trap of assuming that the postindustrial economy is based primarily on an educated and skilled work force. While this holds true for some jobs in a few fast-growing areas of technology, most jobs in the service sector are notable for *not* requiring much education and skills. According to a recent study by the Bureau of Labor Statistics, the following ten occupations account for the largest percentage of projected job growth between 1990 and 2005: retail salespersons, registered nurses, cashiers, office clerks, truck drivers, general managers, janitors and cleaners, nursing aides, food counter workers, and waiters and waitresses.[34] Only two of these—registered nurses and general managers—require a college degree. Other studies show that blacks with a high school degree have a far higher rate of unemployment than whites who have not graduated from high school.[35] Given these facts, it makes little sense to blame the scandalously high rate of black unemployment on deficiencies in education and skills.

In the tradition of the color-blind left, Wilson has advanced a class analysis that totally subsumes race to class. The chief problem with this approach is that it obscures the role that racism plays in the production and reproduction of the black underclass.

Racism and the Black Underclass

First and foremost, the very existence of a ghetto underclass is prima facie evidence of institutionalized racism. Ultimately, the ghetto underclass is the stepchild of slavery itself, linked to the present by patterns of racial segregation and inequality that are still found in all major institutions. The fact that less than half of black men of working age are part of the labor force reflects the cumulative effect of institutionalized racism, past and present. It is a measure of the extent to which current labor markets are perpetuating patterns of racial inequality. It also reflects the dismal failure of public policy to address the problem.

As Wilson reminds his critics, his point about "the declining significance of race" was never that blacks were approaching parity with whites. He recognized that the success of the black middle class was offset by a serious deterioration in the condition of the black underclass, thus resulting in a growing "bifurcation" between the haves and the have-nots within black America. But he construed the success of the black middle class as proof of an improved climate of tolerance and a more favorable opportunity structure for blacks. Therefore, according to Wilson's logic, "racism" cannot explain why the underclass has actually increased in size at a time when the black middle class is larger and more prosperous than ever.

But does this conclusion follow from the premises? After all, racism has never been indifferent to class distinctions, and it may well be the case that blacks who have acquired the "right" status characteristics are exempted from stereotypes and behavior that continue to be directed at less privileged blacks. There is nothing new in this phenomenon. Even in the worst days of Jim Crow, there were blacks who owned land, received favored treatment from whites, and were held forth as "success stories" to prove that lower-class blacks had only themselves to blame for their destitution. For example, in his history of Jim Crow in Mississippi, Neil McMillen writes:

Nearly every plantation county in Mississippi could claim at least one substantial black farmer who through a combination of ownership and rental cultivated several hundred and sometimes even a thousand or more acres, employed numerous share-croppers, and otherwise operated on a scale normally thought to be limited only to the more successful whites. These "Negro Success Stories," as they were called in the reports of the United States Department of Agriculture, were objects of pride and envy to both races. Officials in the regional offices of the USDA found in them evi-dence of "the steady progress of Negro farmers throughout the . . . deep South." They were proof, as their more sympathetic white neighbors believed, that the crop-lien system was the "poor man's opportunity," that only the black sharecroppers' prof-ligacy, their penchant for excursions, crap games, and whiskey, kept them down.[36]

The existence of this black elite did not signify that racism was abating (though illusions to this effect were common even among blacks). On the contrary, the black elite was itself a vital part of the system of oppression, serving as a buffer between the oppressor and the op-pressed, and fostering the illusion that blacks could surmount their difficulties if only they had the exemplary qualities of the black elite.

Nor would one conclude from the recent success of women in the professions that the legions of women who still work in sex-typed oc-cupations are not victims of institutionalized sexism, past and pres-ent. By the same token, the success of the black middle class does not mean that racist barriers are not as impenetrable as ever insofar as lower-class blacks are concerned.

The race/class issue, usually confined to academic journals, sur-faced several years ago in Yonkers, New York, where whites fiercely re-sisted court orders to construct low-cost housing that would introduce poor blacks into their middle-class neighborhoods. According to the *New York Times*, then-Governor Mario Cuomo commented that white opposition was based on class, not race, and that these same people would accept Lena Horne or Harry Belafonte as neighbors. Perhaps so. But the whole point of racism is that an African American should not have to attain the stature of Lena Horne or Harry Belafonte to have his or her rights of citizenship secure or to be accepted into "white" neighborhoods. Furthermore, to whatever extent white resistance is motivated by class, it still has the effect of perpetuating racial distinctions and racial inequalities. History will judge the United States by its treatment not of Lena Horne and Harry Belafonte, but of the anonymous masses who inhabit the nation's ghettos.

Like Governor Cuomo and the apologists for Southern racism, Wilson would have us believe that "if only" blacks had the requisite education and skills, they would encounter few obstacles on the road to success. But this view is predicated on a blanket denial of complex ways that racism prevents blacks from acquiring the requisite education and skills, as well as the persistence of old-fashioned racism that affects even blacks who *have* education and skills. Totally absent from Wilson's analysis of black unemployment is any consideration of racism in occupations and labor markets.

The fault does not lie with Wilson alone. Given the vast literature on racism, one might suppose that there are countless studies on employment discrimination. This is not the case. As the authors of a recent volume assessing the status of blacks in American society observed: "The extent of discrimination against blacks in the workplace has apparently not been extensively investigated by direct tests similar in design to the audits of residential housing markets."[37] Instead, the extent of discrimination is gauged by examining racial differences in employment rates or wages within given job sectors. Because discrimination is not measured directly, the methodological door is left open for some to claim that blacks are underrepresented, not because of discrimination, but because they lack the requisite "productive capacities." The counterclaim is that blacks have lower "payoffs" than whites even when they have the same productive characteristics. Ultimately, this issue can only be resolved with studies that measure employment discrimination directly.

One such study was sponsored by the Urban Institute in 1991. The authors conducted 476 "hiring audits" in Chicago and Washington, D.C. In a hiring audit, two testers, one black and one white, are carefully matched with respect to all attributes that could affect a hiring decision. The sample was drawn from help-wanted ads in major newspapers; only low-skilled, entry-level jobs requiring limited experience were selected. The basic finding was as follows:

> . . . young black jobseekers were unable to advance as far in the hiring process as their white counterparts 20 percent of the time; black testers advanced farther than their white counterparts 7 percent of the time. Blacks were denied a job that was offered to an equally qualified white 15 percent of the time; white testers were denied a job when their black counterparts received an offer in 5 percent of the audits. [38]

As the authors of the report acknowledge, these are conservative estimates, since employers who discriminate against blacks are not likely to advertise in newspapers. Instead, they rely on employment agencies or employee networks to insulate them from the hiring process. Furthermore, the auditors were all college students with "conventional appearance," defined as "average height, average weight, conventional dialect, and conventional dress and hair." But it is precisely the blacks who may not be "average" in height or weight, or who do not conform to "conventional" styles of speech and self-presentation, who are most apt to be victims of discrimination. Although its estimates of the frequency of employment discrimination are unrealistically low, the Urban Institute study provides incontrovertible evidence that old-fashioned racism is still commonplace.

Other direct evidence of employment discrimination comes from periodic revelations about the racist practices of employment agencies. In 1990, for example, two former employees of one of New York City's largest employment agencies divulged that discrimination was routinely practiced against black applicants, though concealed behind a number of code words. Clients who did not want to hire blacks would indicate their preference for applicants who were "All American." For its part the agency would signal that an applicant was black by reversing the initials of the placement counselor. [39]

Such revelations are shocking less because they uncover facts that were previously unknown than because they breach the conspiracy of silence that surrounds employment discrimination. Although there is little in public discourse to suggest that employment discrimination is rampant, a different picture emerges from surveys of employers and rank-and-file workers. In 1990 the *National Law Journal* asked a national sample of adults whether they believed that "employers practice some form of discrimination in their hiring and promotion practices regardless of their official policies." Half of whites (48 percent) and two-thirds of blacks (64 percent) said that all or most employers are discriminatory.[40]

The evidence of widespread employment discrimination against blacks is so overwhelming that even Wilson has recently shifted his position. At least this is what can be garnered from a feature story on Wilson by Gretchen Reynolds in *Chicago* magazine.[41] According to Reynolds, Wilson has recently "rediscovered racism." With grants lavished on him after the publication of two books that downplayed racism, Wilson and his students have undertaken a series of surveys and ethnographic studies of poor neighborhoods in Chicago. They also interrogated employers about hiring minorities. What they found is that employers do in fact make race central to their hiring decisions, and that, generally speaking, they are predisposed against hiring blacks.[42] Reynolds quotes Wilson as now admitting that "racism is far more important than I once believed."[43]

This would be a most welcome revision on the part of Wilson, who seems to have convinced the entire Western world (with the exception of the ghetto population whom he had not previously consulted) that racism was "of declining significance." However, Wilson adds an ominous caveat to his retraction: "But cultural factors also play a strong, very strong, role."[44] He explains:

When I say culture is important, I'm not talking about some kind of innate behavior. People are not inherently "lazy," or less able to keep a job, as many conservatives would have you believe. Yes, the culture that has developed in many inner-city neighborhoods makes it more difficult for residents there to get and keep jobs. But this culture is not innate. It is a response to bad times. It is not the cause of bad times. It also cannot be ignored. If we are to develop effective antipoverty programs, we must acknowledge the self-destructive behavior so evident in the poorest neighborhoods.

Alas, in another reversal of his earlier writing, Wilson seems to have rediscovered not racism but the culture of poverty. Like the culture of poverty theorists of yore, Wilson stipulates that this dysfunctional culture is not innate (even conservatives do not make this claim), but a response to the exigencies of poverty and unemployment. Indeed, Wilson seems to be echoing the view of the employers whom he interviewed, that it is not because of racism that black youth are not hired, but because of their poor work habits.[45]

According to Reynolds, "some conservatives are greeting this new Wilson with almost smug glee." Lawrence Mead, for example, is quoted as follows: "Bill and I used to profoundly disagree about whether economics or culture [was the fundamental cause of poverty]. But look at the results of his own study. Mexicans, with their work ethic, were less likely to remain in poverty. That's strong evidence. Let's face it. I won."[46] Wilson's apparent flip-flop is less surprising in light of the fact that he has consistently had a blind spot to racism. Now that he is confronted with incontrovertible evidence, dredged up by his own students, that employers in fact are averse to hiring blacks, he has accepted the employers' rationalizations at face value. Therefore, Wilson's "rediscovery" of racism does not lead him to reassess his erstwhile rejection of race-specific public policy and affirmative action in particular. Rather, according to Reynolds, Wilson's new agenda consists of car pools, job-referral services, and scattered-site housing, all designed to integrate blacks into hiring networks. Conspicuously absent from his agenda is any mention of vigorous enforcement of anti-discrimination statutes, much less affirmative action, as a lever for prying open doors that will otherwise be closed to black youth.

By focusing narrowly on the work habits and attitudes of unemployed ghetto youth, Wilson loses sight of the larger picture. Even if one grants his point that the employment prospects of blacks are diminished because of a lack of education and skills, even if one grants that these youth often lack the qualities that employers look for when they make hiring decisions, these "facts" must be placed in larger historical and social context. How else are we to explain the paucity of skills and other job prerequisites among yet another generation of ghetto youth? These personal deficits are not random or individual events, but are part of a larger pattern of institutionalized racism, reflected in the very existence of racial ghettos and maintained through the complicity of such institutions as the schools, the banks, the housing market, the job market, the welfare system, and the criminal justice system. It is thus a denial of both history and present-day social reality to lump these racial pariahs together with other marginal workers, and on this basis to seek "universal remedies." For the black underclass is not merely the accidental by-product of color-blind economic forces, but the end product of a system of occupational apartheid that continues down to the present.

In the final analysis, this is what is most disturbing about Wilson's thesis regarding "the declining significance of race" and his advocacy of universal, as opposed to race-specific, public policy: it absolves the nation of responsibility for coming to terms with its racist legacy, and takes race off the national agenda.[47]

The Politics of Memory

> That which we remember is, more often than not,
> that which we would like to have been; or that which we
> hope to be. Thus our memory and our identity are ever at
> odds; our history ever a tall tale told by inattentive idealists.
>
> Ralph Ellison, 1964

Victims have fallen from political grace. The 1990s marks a third decade of retrenchment since the political upheavals of the sixties, when "victims" rose up in angry confrontation, demanding restitution for wrongs visited upon them in the course of American history. This began with the civil rights movement, which in essence was an anti-slavery movement, in that it was waged by the descendants of slaves and assaulted the structure of oppression that had been erected in the aftermath of slavery and served as its functional surrogate. Emboldened by the gradual success of this movement, other groups awakened to their victimization, and, like African Americans, laid prideful claim to symbols that previously had been spurned as badges of shame. Thus was victimhood turned on its ugly head, as erstwhile victims—with some posturing and self-deception, to be sure—engaged in displays of chauvinism that not only affirmed new identities, but also made their oppressors doubt their vaunted superiority. It was only a matter of time before non-victims—the powerful and privileged majority—would reclaim lost status and restore victims to their socially assigned place.

This counterattack has occurred on many fronts, and recently has involved certain writers who have assailed the very idea of "victim-

156

hood." An early volley came from Joseph Epstein, whose article "The Joys of Victimhood" was published in the *New York Times Magazine* on July 2, 1989, two days before the nation celebrated its 212th anniversary of independence from colonial oppression. Epstein does not disguise his contempt for anyone who emulates Gandhi, "the great teacher of the art of victimhood, of setting one's victimization on full public display."[1] (Presumably this comment does not apply to the annual pageantry about how the American colonies were mercilessly abused under King George.) Epstein allows that the early civil rights movement was "immensely impressive" because "the movement's appeal was unmistakably not to the guilt but to the conscience of the nation."[2] Later, however, it degenerated into an orgy of guilt, as other groups—he specifically names sixties students, feminists, homosexuals, Vietnam veterans, the handicapped, and artists—followed "the black model" and indulged in public displays of self-pity and demanded restitution for past wrongs. Though Epstein mocks the putative "joys of victimhood," he can hardly conceal his own titillation at lampooning his political enemies, especially university teachers at prestigious colleges who teach "victimological studies." He ends his polemic with some tutelage of his own on how victims should comport themselves. Alluding to "the people I know who are seriously handicapped," Epstein writes:

As it happens, these people are all intensely political (they are liberals and conservatives), but the last thing I can imagine any of them doing is using his [sic] handicap for political advantage or for that matter in any public way either to define or advance himself. Because they neither act as nor think of themselves as victims, in the end they seem, far from victimized, immensely dignified and quietly heroic.[3]

Immensely dignified and quietly heroic! Not howling with pain and moral outrage. Not even sullen and despairing. Certainly not angry and confrontational. Epstein has cast the ideological mold for the perfect victim: dignified and quietly heroic, an inspiration even to the oppressor.

Such a victim spares the oppressor the thing that Epstein cannot abide: guilt. In his self-preoccupation, however, Epstein misses the point: what "the victim" wants from the oppressor is not guilt, but an honest reckoning with the past. Not guilt as such, but a sense of moral responsibility that will translate into political action to remedy past wrongs. As Martin Luther King wrote in 1964: "America must seek its own ways of atoning for the injustices she has inflicted upon her Negro citizens. I do not suggest atonement for atonement's sake or because there is a need for self-punishment. I suggest atonement as the moral and practical way to bring the Negro's standards up to a realistic level."[4] This is where morality spills over into politics, and conversely, this is where Epstein's hidden political agenda blunts his moral sensibilities.

"Do you know *why* the white man really hates you?," Malcolm X would coax his followers. "It's because every time he sees your face, he sees a mirror of his crime—and his guilty conscience can't bear to face it." Then he continued down the rhetorical path that drives Epstein to apoplexy: "Every white man in America, when he looks into a black man's eyes, should fall to his knees and say 'I'm sorry, I'm sorry—my kind has committed history's greatest crime against your kind; will you give me the chance to atone?' But do you brothers and sisters expect any white man to do that? No, you *know* better!"[5]

For Malcolm X, the appeal of the Muslims was that it shifted blame from himself to the external enemy who, he came to realize, was responsible for his degradation. This was the historical and moral truth that made sense of his life and that purged him of self-hatred. Thus, his moral redemption occurred the moment he donned the mantle of "victim." Yet contrary to what Epstein alleges, the victim status is not a sanction for self-pity and passivity. For Malcolm X and countless others, it was a mandate to act, to take control of one's destiny, and above all, to confront precisely the enemies whom others now feel secure consigning to history.

Indeed, the preoccupation with the past that marked the civil rights movement was never escapist, but on the contrary served to legitimize a protest movement that demanded concessions from the white power structure. It is precisely because victimhood leads to political action that Epstein wants to do away with it, to reduce it to a self-fulfilling state of mind. Thus, he ends his piece with this homily: "the most efficient way to become truly a victim is to think and act like a victim." No victims, no guilt. No guilt, no obligation to redress wrongs.

In *An American Dilemma* Gunnar Myrdal contended that whites were conscience-stricken because their mistreatment of blacks contradicted cherished principles embodied in the American creed. It would probably be closer to the truth to say that it is not guilt, but desperation to *avoid* guilt, that is typical of the oppressor. George Orwell portrayed this brilliantly in a short story called "The Hanging." A Hindu man in colonial Burma is about to be hanged for unknown crimes. Like Epstein, his executioners hope that the condemned man will be "dignified and quietly heroic," but he is not so accommodating. As he stands on the gallows with the noose fixed, he cries out to his god with a rhythmical, repetitive chant that persists even after the hangman draws a bag over his head. His executioners want to end "that abominable noise." Yet they are not totally impervious to his humanity or, in the words of Orwell's narrator, "the unspeakable wrongness of cutting a life short when it is in full tide." Once their gruesome work is complete, their sense of relief verges on exhilaration, and they anesthetize themselves with whiskey and gallows humor.[6]

Indeed, all systems of oppression master the art of moral evasion, and develop a stockpile of antidotes to guilt. In the nineteenth century slavery was portrayed as a benevolent institution that rescued Africans from a life in the bush, and bestowed them with Christianity and civilization. Through an elaborate system of guises and distortions, whites convinced themselves that blacks were naturally cheerful and contented even as slaves, a view that was given validation by the nascent social sciences. Consider the following assertion by a Southern sociologist, published in the *American Journal of Sociology* in 1908:

The plain English of the situation was that the negro did not chafe or fret and harass himself to death, where the Indian would have done so, or massacred the white man as an alternative. In many respects the negro is a model prisoner—the best in this country. He accepts the situation, generally speaking; bears no malice; cherishes no ill will or resentment, and is cheerful under conditions to which the white man refuses to reconcile himself.[7]

Epstein wishes to resurrect the victim who does not chafe or fret and harass himself (or others) to death, who labors in quiet dignity to overcome adversity, without making moral or political claims on the rest of us.

Of course, Epstein is not alone in his scorn of "victims." He reflects a current nostalgia for times past when poverty was invisible, when blacks were quiescent, and when the homeless were warehoused in institutions, and not a menacing presence in our neighborhoods. America has grown weary of victims, and a number of writers, both white and black, have come out of the woodwork to proclaim an end to victimhood.

A recent example is Shelby Steele, a black professor of English at San Jose State University in California, whose polemic against affirmative action also appeared in the *New York Times Magazine* in 1990. At the center of Steele's rejection of affirmative action is his supposition that it "nurtures a victim-focused identity in blacks and sends us the message that there is more power in our past suffering than in our present achievements."[8] One is impelled to ask *whose* achievements he has in mind. Presumably his own, and others like him who have travelled far down the road to success. As for the 10.6 million blacks still living below the poverty line, not to speak of the additional millions on the economic margin, there is little to celebrate and the "enemies" associated with racial exclusion and class disadvantage are not faint memories, but an obtrusive force in their everyday lives.

Steele's most concerted attack on victimhood appeared not in the mainstream press, but in *Dissent*, a liberal/left journal of politics.[9] In "The Memory of Enemies," Steele's thesis is that blacks are saddled with memories of enemies who are no longer the formidable and baleful adversaries of times past, and that these memories prey detrimentally on black consciousness. In his own words:

I think one of the heaviest weights that oppression leaves on the shoulders of its former victims is simply the memory of itself. . . . What makes this a weight is that the rememberer will gird himself against a larger and more formidable enemy than the one he is actually encountering. . . . I believe that one of the greatest problems black Americans currently face—one of the greatest barriers to our development in society—is that our memory of oppression has such power, magnitude, depth, and nuance that it constantly drains our best resources into more defense than is strictly necessary.[10]

To claim their new selves, to take advantage of a society that has lowered racist barriers, blacks must shed the victim image and pursue expanding opportunity.

It is difficult to fathom what possessed the editors of *Dissent* to give their imprimatur to such a position. Even more perplexing is that the very same issue contained a piece by Alexander Stille, entitled "What the Holocaust Meant in the Thinking of Primo Levi and Jean Améry."[11] Could it be that *Dissent's* editors are willing to grant Jews a collective memory, with all that this implies in terms of a historical and political consciousness, that they would deny to blacks?

In any event, despite the assonance in their names, these writers present radically different views of the meaning of history for groups that have suffered extreme victimization. Ironically, one does not have to look further than the pages of *Dissent* to find, in Stille, an eloquent rebuttal of Steele.

Stille's essay was originally written as the foreword to a new edition of Jean Améry's *At the Mind's Limits*.[12] Améry was a survivor of Auschwitz, and Stille attempts to compare Améry's views of the Holocaust with those of Primo Levi. Unlike Steele, who is disdainful of those who look "backward rather than forward, outward rather than inward," both Améry and Levi devoted their lives to probing a past that was so irrevocably grafted on their consciousness as to vitiate simplistic dichotomies between "backward" and "forward," "outward" and "inward." Over against Steele's exhortation to shuck off memories of past enemies, ponder Améry's angry rejection of the idea of ever putting behind the past:

In two decades of contemplating what happened to me, I believe to have recognized that a forgiving and forgetting induced by social pressure is immoral. . . . What happened, happened. But *that* it happened cannot be so easily accepted. I rebel: against my past, against history, and against a present that places the incomprehensible in the cold storage of history and thus falsifies it in a revolting way.[13]

Indeed, the animating force behind the vast Holocaust literature is that remembering is a moral imperative, that it is the only way that we can honor the victims and exact a kind of retribution over history. To forget the victims, to allow the past to recede into oblivion, even in the truncated memories of later generations, is morally repugnant because it abets the obliteration of the obliterated. We become like the Germans who pleaded that they "did not know."

Nor do we "remember" for its own sake alone. As Stille writes of Améry: "Rather than trying to discard the memory of his pain, Améry held on to it and tried to use it as an internal compass in a morally distorted world."[14] In the preface to the reissue of his book in 1977, Améry looked back over the thirteen years since the original publication:

Sometimes it seems as though Hitler has gained a posthumous triumph. Invasions, aggressions, torture, destruction of man in his essence. A few indications will suffice: Czechoslovakia 1968, Chile, the forced evacuation of Phnom Penh, the psychiatric wards of the USSR, the murder squads in Brazil and Argentina, the self-unmasking of the Third World states that call themselves "socialist," Ethiopia, Uganda.[15]

Herein lies the moral imperative that emanates from the memory of enemies. As Isaac Deutscher wrote in *The Non-Jewish Jew*, the message to be drawn from the long history of Jewish suffering is "the message of universal human emancipation."[16]

In sad contrast, however, the only enemies that Steele recognizes are the Southern redneck, the lynch-mob, the hatemonger. In his myopia he does not see through the insidious new guises that racism has assumed, and that continue to deny genuine freedom to millions of blacks. And there is no hint that he finds in the tragic history of black suffering the message of universal human emancipation. Instead, he dismisses the memory of enemies as "a reenactment of past victimization that confirms our exaggerated sense of the enemy but also undermines our advancement."[17] And he takes special delight in deriding those who exhibit "a slave mentality," and who "see lizards and call them dragons." One wonders what he would tell Jean Améry or Primo Levi.

Yet no one, least of all Améry or Levi, would challenge Steele's observation that "these little battles with memory can also be deflating."[18] *Deflating!* Both men committed suicide. Who can say whether their obsessive preoccupation with the past sapped life of all meaning, or whether their mental torment prevented them from accepting Steele's nostrum to put the past behind? What is important is that they kept the eternal flame burning. In contrast to Steele's shallow sensibility, they engaged in a painful quest to find in their personal tragedy some higher philosophical or social truth, which they sought to share with those who would listen.

Are we then left with a choice between despair or banality? Is engagement of the grisly past necessarily debilitating? Can victims confront their rage without being consumed by it? These are questions that James Baldwin ponders at the end of his autobiographical essay, *Notes of a Native Son*:

It began to seem that one would have to hold in the mind forever two ideas which seemed to be in opposition. The first idea was acceptance, the acceptance, totally without rancor, of life as it is, and men as they are: in the light of this idea, it goes without saying that injustice is a commonplace. But this did not mean that one could be complacent, for the second idea was of equal power: that one must never, in one's own life, accept these injustices as commonplace but must fight them with all one's strength.[19]

Fighting injustice is what remembering is *about*. While Steele worries that a preoccupation with the past will hinder blacks from pursuing opportunity, subordinating the past to a mindless pursuit of private gain leads to another kind of paralysis—to complacency, moral lassitude, political inertia, and betrayal of those left behind.

When, then, can slavery be placed in "the cold storage of history"? Not until this nation rids itself of racial ghettos, and the terrible divisions of race and class that are so destructive of the human spirit, for blacks and whites alike. Even then, hopefully, we will continue to commemorate the triumph against the sinister forces of oppression, and keep alive the message of universal emancipation.

8

Affirmative Action and Liberal Capitulation

The liberal is an aesthete, much preoccupied with form and
means and techniques. He looks out on a raging battlefield and
sees error everywhere, and he thinks he can find the truth by
avoiding error. . . . By word and by deed, white liberals
insist that Negroes subordinate their claims to the emotions
of racists. In the liberal rhetoric, it is considered a provocative
act to irritate white racists. It never seems to occur to white
liberals that irritated or not they are still the same old racists.

Lerone Bennett, "Tea and Sympathy:
Liberals and Other White Hopes," 1964

The civil rights revolution was primarily a struggle for liberty, not
equality. That is to say, it sought to dismantle the system of official
segregation that had been erected in the aftermath of slavery, and to
secure full rights of citizenship for African Americans. The abiding
faith of the movement and its leaders was that once the walls of segregation came tumbling down, blacks would be free to assume their
rightful place in American society. No sooner were the historic civil
rights acts of 1964 and 1965 passed, however, than it became clear
that legislation alone would not address the deep-seated inequalities
that were the legacy of two centuries of slavery and another century of
Jim Crow. This fact was eloquently acknowledged by President Johnson in his 1965 commencement address at Howard University,
quoted earlier:

Freedom is not enough. You do not wipe away the scars of centuries by saying: Now
you are free to go where you want, do as you desire, choose the leaders you please.

You do not take a person who, for years, has been hobbled by chains and liberate him, bring him to the starting line of a race and then say, "you are free to compete with all the others," and still justly believe that you have been completely fair. . . . We seek not just freedom but opportunity, . . . not just equality as a right and a theory but equality as a fact and as a result.

. Affirmative action is the single policy of the post–civil rights era that sought equality, not just as a right and a theory, but as a fact and a result. However, affirmative action was never formulated as a coherent policy, but evolved through a series of presidential executive orders, administrative policies, and court decisions. Partly for this reason, the term itself is so fraught with ambiguity that it is not always clear what advocates and opponents are squabbling about.

To begin with, affirmative action must be distinguished from policies of non-discrimination. Although both seek racial justice in the workplace, policies of non-discrimination merely enjoin employers from practicing discrimination in the recruitment, hiring, and promotion of workers. It is essentially a passive injunction: *not* to discriminate. Affirmative action, on the other hand, commits employers to go a step beyond non-discrimination and to *actively* seek out protected groups in employment. In this form—essentially "outreach" programs reliant on the good-faith efforts of employers—affirmative action arouses little or no opposition.

Another version of affirmative action, however, goes a step beyond outreach and involves granting "preference" to minority applicants in order to guarantee the desired result. This is where controversy begins. For example, in his confirmation hearings to the Supreme Court, Clarence Thomas spoke passionately of his support for outreach programs to extend opportunity to women and minorities, but he was equally adamant in his opposition to affirmative action programs that involve preference. What Justice Thomas and most opponents of affirmative action forget is that good-faith efforts to increase minority representation were generally ineffective until they were backed up by specific "goals and timetables" that, in effect, gave preference to minority applicants who met basic qualifications but might not have been hired or promoted without affirmative action mandates.

A good example is the American Telephone and Telegraph Company, one of the nation's largest corporate employers and a major government contractor. In 1973—nine years after the passage of the 1964 Civil Rights Act—AT&T was an archetypal example of caste segregation in the workplace. The Bell System employed 351,000 persons in low-paying operator or clerical classifications, 95 percent of whom were women. Of 234,000 higher-paid craft workers, 95 percent were male and only 6 percent of these were black.[1] Virtually no women or blacks were in management positions, and even supervisory personnel in "female" departments were male. Although officials could point to "equal opportunity" policies that had increased black employment from 2.5 percent in 1960 to 7.9 percent in 1970, this mainly reflected the hiring of black women as operators to replace white women who were experiencing a high rate of turnover.[2] When AT&T filed a petition for a rate increase in long-distance telephone service in November 1970, the Federal Communications Commission, with President Nixon's backing, launched hearings into the company's employment practices. Eventually this action resulted in a landmark consent decree in which the Bell System agreed to change its employment policies and meet employment targets for women and minorities. According to a Wharton School study, the program got off to a poor start but by 1975, 97 percent of its short-term targets had been reached.[3] Furthermore, these gains occurred at a time when low-skilled jobs were being eliminated due to the impact of new technology.

As the AT&T case shows, affirmative action was never a desideratum pursued for its own sake, but rather a policy of last resort, invoked only after good-faith efforts to break down entrenched patterns of racial and gender segregation failed. Yet once it became established as policy, affirmative action had the potential to effect a major transformation in the American work force. Lyndon Johnson's 1965 executive order, as amended by Richard Nixon's 1974 executive order, applied to some 15,000 companies employing 23 million workers at

73,000 installations.[4] No other mechanism exists to influence employment practices and outcomes on such a large scale.

Contrary to the claims of its critics, furthermore, affirmative action has produced very significant results. Prior to the implementation of affirmative action mandates, blacks had only token representation in the nation's core industries. The "bourgeoisie" that Franklin Frazier lampooned in *Black Bourgeoisie* consisted of a small group of professionals and businessmen anchored in the ghetto economy. It was affirmative action that opened up access to mainstream occupational structures. Studies have found that companies subject to EEOC requirements have raised the level of black employment far more than companies not under EEOC scrutiny.[5] The occupational spheres where blacks have made the most progress—in government service, in major blue-collar occupations, in corporate management, and in the professions—are all areas where vigorous affirmative action programs have been in place over the past two decades.

Nor is it the case, as Wilson and others contend, that affirmative action has mainly helped the middle class. Although debates about affirmative action usually center on academia and the professions, affirmative action has in fact had a profound impact throughout the occupational world, including the blue-collar sector. It would be difficult to exaggerate the dramatic and historic impact of affirmative action in reconstituting the racial division of labor that has existed since slavery.[6]

Black employment gains have been especially pronounced in the public sector. Indeed, one study has found that the majority of employment gains for the black middle class during the 1960s occurred in the public sector.[7] During the 1970s blacks continued to increase their numbers in public employment at a rate that was double that of whites. As Andrew Hacker has shown, between 1970 and 1990 the number of black police officers rose from 24,000 to 64,000; blacks accounted for 41 percent of the new positions.[8] By 1982 1.6 million blacks—roughly a fourth of all black workers—were employed by government. Exactly how many of these government workers owe their jobs to affirmative action is impossible to say, but one thing is clear: without government, both as employer and as enforcer of affirmative-action mandates, we would not today be celebrating the achievements of the black middle class. Indeed, it is precisely because the stakes are so high that affirmative action is so fiercely contested.

In recent years there has been a rising chorus of criticism against affirmative action programs, and it does not come only from whites who feel that they are being asked to pay the price for crimes that they did not commit. A number of black writers have also spoken vehemently against affirmative action. One of the first was Thomas Sowell, who in 1976 wrote "A Black 'Conservative' Dissents." Sowell argued that affirmative action not only fails to achieve its stated objectives, but that it actually backfires, in that it undermines "the legitimacy of black achievements by making them look like gifts from the Government."[9]

This refrain has been echoed by other black writers, most recently by Shelby Steele. Like Sowell, Steele contends that preferential treatment arouses paroxysms of self-doubt among its recipients, and reinforces white belief in the inferiority of blacks, thus "stigmatizing the already stigmatized."[10] Both argue that the gap between black and white incomes has not narrowed despite years of affirmative action. Neither show how abolishing affirmative action would contribute to income parity!

With the 1991 publication of *Reflections of an Affirmative Action Baby*, yet another nail was driven into the coffin of affirmative action.[11] Its author, Stephen Carter, is a black law professor at Yale who once clerked for Justice Thurgood Marshall. Carter knows what is wrong with affirmative action because, as he reminds us at least five times, "So yes, I am an affirmative action baby." With this self-serving candor, he proceeds to recount all of the indignities that befall the beneficiaries of racial preference. According to Carter, affirmative action is patronizing and demeaning because it is predicated on the assumption that black people cannot compete on the same playing field as whites. Not only the recipients, but all blacks, are then tainted with the suspicion that they have not earned their success on the basis of merit alone. This is especially vexing to Stephen Carter, the son of a Cornell professor who scored 800 on his math achievement test, only to find himself sought after more for his race than for his personal abilities. He feels sorry for himself and others who are racked with doubt over whether they would have succeeded without preferential treatment.

Despite his disclaimer, Carter presumes to speak for other "victims" of affirmative action. No doubt he does, since the logic of affirmative action runs up against the values of individualism and merit that, notwithstanding their mythical dimensions, are deeply embedded in the American mind. Victims of racial oppression, however, have existential reason to be cynical about the prevailing ideology, and to develop their own perspective on affirmative action. Some of the beneficiaries may resent that they are *made* to feel demeaned by whites who have their own reasons for opposing affirmative action. Others may feel relieved that they have passed through doors that would otherwise be shut. Others may feel proud to be part of a new generation that can bring dignity to themselves and to the race. Still others may share Du Bois's vision that they are part of a talented tenth that will form a vanguard in the struggle against racism. Finally, others may not give a damn what whites think and find within themselves a sense of their personal worth and mission. This is not to deny that there are those, especially in the academic world where status insecurity is endemic, who share Carter's angst about affirmative action. If Carter's book were destined for the self-help sections of the nation's bookstores, it could perhaps be commended as a case study of the conflicting emotions of one "affirmative action baby." Unfortunately, Carter goes far beyond self-revelation to call into question the legitimacy and value of affirmative action itself.

Although Carter rails against affirmative action throughout his book, and lavishly quotes critics, like Clarence Thomas, who are uncompromising in their opposition, he takes a more equivocal position. He writes: "My own view is that, given training, given a chance, we as a people need fear no standards. This is why I want to return the special admission programs to their more innocent roots, as tools for providing that training and that chance for students who might not otherwise have it."[12] This is very ambiguous language, to say the least. Carter never spells out which "special admission programs" he would retain, or explains why these are any less demeaning than the ones he repudiates. He makes it clear that anything that smacks of racial "preferences" is anathema, but he does not tell us how we are to create "that chance for students who might not otherwise have it" *without* invoking some form of preference. Again, the problem for Carter's position is that the original affirmative action programs that he would return to were ineffectual until they were backed up with enforcement mechanisms. Not until goals and timetables were instituted under Lyndon Johnson's 1965 executive order, and compliance reviews were instituted under Richard Nixon's 1974 executive order, was there significant progress in increasing black representation.[13] Thus, there is nothing but self-delusion in Carter's statement that "Black professionals . . . should not do much worse without affirmative action than we are doing with it, and, thrown on our own resources and knowing that we have no choice but to meet the same tests as everybody else, we may do better."[14]

Indeed, this is what is most disturbing about *Reflections of an Affirmative Action Baby*: its author appears wholly ignorant of the history of affirmative action, of the wide range of programs subsumed under the rubric of "affirmative action," and of their achievements as a counterweight to institutionalized racism. Nowhere in his book does he so much as mention that affirmative action exists outside the professions. Instead, he accepts on faith Wilson's unsubstantiated claim that affirmative action has primarily helped the middle class. Nor does he attempt to wrestle with the thorny issue of "goals" as opposed to "quotas." Nor does Carter trouble himself with the political and constitutional aspects of affirmative action. No doubt he would respond that these concerns go beyond the scope of his personal narrative. How then are we to construe his polemic against affirmative action? That because it has been troublesome for *him*, affirmative action should be abolished? That because it arouses anxiety in some of its recipients, we should slam the affirmative action door shut on the next generation of aspiring youth? Contrary to what Carter wants to believe, this next generation will be irreparably harmed by the impending evisceration of affirmative action programs. This is not because blacks cannot compete with whites on a level playing field, but rather because, so long as institutionalized racism persists, the playing field can never be level.

Whatever animates Carter's writing, his book has only served to fuel the racial backlash. As Derrick Bell points out: "Today, as policy makers again seek to abandon civil rights enforcement, certain experts assert that the plight of blacks is the fault of blacks or of the social programs on which the poor rely. When such claims are expounded by blacks, they obtain a deceptive authenticity."[15] In this way black neoconservatives provide whites with the cover they need for their retreat from racial justice.

In recent years a number of leading liberals have thrown in the towel on affirmative action, not because they oppose it in principle, but because they decided that affirmative action is not politically viable. A notable example is Paul Starr, the founding editor of *The American Prospect*, who published an article in 1992 under the title: "Civic Reconstruction: What to Do Without Affirmative Action."[16] This article warrants close scrutiny, not because Starr has changed the course of history, but because his article epitomizes all that is wrong with the liberal case against affirmative action:

1. Starr treats affirmative action as a troublesome abstraction and his argument is predicated on false assumptions of what is actually at stake—that is, of what has been accomplished under affirmative action and why it is critically important in the struggle against racism.

2. While Starr pretends to be motivated by realpolitik, he is willing to relinquish a policy that is already in place for political goals that are unattainable.

3. While he purports to advance a universalistic politics that promises to liberate "everyone," in actual fact he is endorsing a political agenda that will deepen racial divisions and inequalities.

4. Finally, while Starr professes love for the Negro (so, remember, did Southern segregationists), he condones a policy that will visit

great harm on African Americans and set back the cause of racial justice. In the name of stemming the backlash, he is joining the backlash.

Like most critics of affirmative action, including Clarence Thomas
and Stephen Carter, Starr draws a distinction between the original
affirmative action programs that involved outreach for minority candidates and the later incarnations of affirmative action that give preference to minority candidates. Outreach, he concedes, does not raise
constitutional and political problems, but preference does, and because these problems have become "overwhelming," Starr would like
to dispense with preferential policies altogether. Like Thomas and
Carter, he believes that dispensing with affirmative action does not
imply "any diminished commitment to fight racial discrimination."[17]
What they forget is that the reason that policy evolved from outreach
to preference was that outreach was not working as long as it depended on good-faith efforts alone. Thus, there is no basis for Starr's
contention that "much of what is conventionally attributed to affirmative action will be sustained under antidiscrimination law."[18] On
the contrary, without "goals and timetables" and other such enforcement mechanisms, much of the progress made under affirmative
action will rapidly dissipate.

Starr claims that he would favor affirmative action "if, taking *all* its
effects into account, it were positively beneficial."[19] However, he relies on his own self-serving cost-benefit analysis, one that simultaneously underestimates the benefits of affirmative action and over-
estimates the costs. Thus, to convince himself and others that
affirmative action is not worth the political costs, Starr's first tack is to
depreciate the significance of affirmative action. As he writes: "The
direct effects of affirmative action on the structure of opportunity
have been modest, and its broader social and political ramifications at
best mixed."[20] He offers no evidence to support this proposition. He
merely cites William Julius Wilson's inaccurate claim, in the pre-
miere issue of *The American Prospect*, that affirmative action has primarily been of benefit to the black middle class, but has done little to
help the poor.[21]

Not content with arguing that affirmative action has been ineffec-

tive as anti-poverty policy, Starr goes on to argue that "affirmative action policies have helped to perpetuate racism."[22] Why? Because they
taint all blacks as lacking in qualifications, which arouses the ire of
whites and leaves blacks feeling "embattled, angry, and resentful."
"The whole atmosphere of race relations is poisoned,"[23] writes Starr,
in overtones reminiscent of Southern segregationists who used to argue that there would be harmony between the races if only the civil
rights activists would pack their bags and go home. For the sake of
good race relations, Starr is asking blacks to forgo opportunity, and to
withhold their demands for access to job sectors where they still confront pervasive racism. A comment by Frederick Douglass serves as
an apt riposte: "You sacrifice your friends to conciliate your enemies."

The real weight of Starr's argument, however, is not that affirmative action is bad for blacks—he knows better—but that the political
costs are too great. As he writes:

. . . affirmative action has taken a big political toll: deep and continuing antagonism
from whites, particularly in the working class, who believe their personal opportunities are being taken away from them by a coalition of minority groups and liberal
elites. The result has been more political support for the right, and less chance of en-
acting the kind of positive legislation that would especially benefit low- to middle-
income Americans of all races.[24]

Thus instead of repudiating racism among his working-class allies
within the Democratic Party, or disabusing them of their belief that
blacks are responsible for their shrinking opportunities, Starr finds it
easier or more expedient to ask blacks to give up affirmative action.
Since he knows that blacks are unlikely to sacrifice themselves in the
name of a unity that is predicated on racism, he seems to relish the
possibility that the Supreme Court will, once and for all, invalidate
racial preferences. This, he writes, could be "a blessing in disguise,"
because it will allow for "the formation of bi-racial political alliances
necessary to make progress against poverty."[25]

As recent headlines suggest, we may in fact be witnessing "the end
of affirmative action."[26] However, this is no blessing in disguise, but
an unmitigated disaster for African Americans and the cause of racial
justice. It signifies nothing less than an attempt to abort the Second

Reconstruction, and is reminiscent of the retrenchment at the end of the nineteenth century. America did not return to slavery, but it negated rights that were supposedly secured by the Thirteenth, Fourteenth, and Fifteenth Amendments to the Constitution. It is inconceivable today that there could be a return to official segregation. However, the nullification of affirmative action will reinforce patterns of occupational segregation and deepen the racial crisis.

Thus, the problem is stated falsely when it is suggested that we must choose between merit or preference, or between the rights of individuals or the rights of groups, or between a color-blind or a color-conscious society. Rather, the paramount choice is between racial progress or turning the clock back on the gains wrung from white society over the past three decades.

For liberals to yield this hard-won ground amounts to a spineless capitulation to racial backlash. Yet one of the ironies of the current national debate is that the corporate sector has not joined the backlash against affirmative action. At a time when liberal journals like *The New Republic* and *The American Prospect* are trouncing affirmative action policy, one finds far more favorable treatment on the pages of *Business Week*, *Personnel Journal*, and *Fortune*.[27] Corporations tout their success with affirmative action not only because they are proud of their record as corporate citizens, but also because they have come to appreciate the importance of expanding the pool of talent from which they can recruit personnel. Affirmative action has been under attack, not because it has failed as policy, but because it has been used by race-baiting politicians to deflect attention from other problems. It is unbecoming and hypocritical for liberals to succumb to this political scapegoating.

The liberal capitulation to racial backlash signifies more than a failure of nerve. It does incalculable damage to the black liberation struggle, not because liberals wield power, but because their capitulation serves as a signal to those who *do* wield power that they will encounter little opposition or political fallout from their attack on affirmative action. Like cascading political cards, the black conservative gives license to the white liberal who gives license to the white conservative—to withdraw support from affirmative action and to return to the status quo ante—to the situation around 1965 when the nation salved its conscience with laws on the books that did little or nothing to reverse centuries of occupational apartheid.

III

THE ENDURING LEGACY OF SLAVERY

9

Occupational Apartheid and the Myth of the Black Middle Class

> No greater wrong has been committed against the
> Negro than the denial to him of the right to work.
>
> A. Philip Randolph, "March on Washington Movement
> Presents Program for the Negro," 1944

> . . . the core of the civil rights problem is the matter of
> achieving equal opportunity for Negroes in the labor market.
> For it stands to reason that our other rights depend on that one
> for fulfillment. We cannot afford better education for our
> children, better housing, or medical care unless we have jobs.
>
> Whitney M. Young, Jr., *To Be Equal*, 1964

> If there is any one key to the systematic privilege that
> undergirds a racial capitalist society, it is the special
> advantage of the white population in the labor market.
>
> Robert Blauner, *Racial Oppression in America*, 1972

The essence of racial oppression is not the distorted and malicious stereotypes that whites have of blacks. These constitute the *culture* of oppression, not to be confused with the thing itself. Nor is the essence of racism epitomized by sitting in the back of a bus. In South Africa this was called "petty apartheid" as opposed to "grand apartheid," the latter referring to political disfranchisement and the banishment of millions of blacks to isolated and impoverished "homelands." In the United States the essence of racial oppression—*our* grand apartheid—is a racial division of labor, a system of occupational segrega-

179

tion that relegates most blacks to work in the least desirable job sectors or that excludes them from job markets altogether.[1]

The racial division of labor had its origins in slavery when some 650,000 Africans were imported to provide cheap labor for the South's evolving plantation economy. During the century after the abolition of slavery the nation had the perfect opportunity to integrate blacks into the North's burgeoning industries. It was not Southern racism but its Northern variant that prevented this outcome. This is worth emphasizing because it has become customary—part of America's liberal mythology on race—to place the blame for the nation's racist past wholly on the South. But it was not Southern segregationists and lynch mobs who excluded blacks from participating in the critical early phases of industrialization. Rather it was an invisible color line across *Northern* industry that barred blacks categorically from employment in the vast manufacturing sector, except for a few menial and low-paying jobs that white workers spurned. Nor can the blame be placed solely on the doorstep of greedy capitalists, those other villains of liberal iconography. Workers themselves and their unions were equally implicated in maintaining a system of occupational apartheid that reserved industrial jobs for whites, and that relegated blacks to the pre-industrial sector of the national economy. The longterm effects were incalculable since this closed off the only major channel of escape from racial oppression in the South. Indeed, had the industrial revolution not been "for whites only," it might have obviated the need for a civil rights revolution a century later.

The exclusion of blacks from the industrial sector was possible only because the North had access to an inexhaustible supply of immigrant labor. Some 24 million immigrants arrived between 1880 and 1930. A 1910 survey of twenty principal mining and manufacturing industries conducted by the United States Immigration Commission found that 58 percent of workers were foreign-born. When the Commission asked whether the new immigration resulted in "racial displacement," it did not have blacks in mind, but rather whites who were native-born or from old immigrant stock. Except for a cursory

examination of the competition between Italian and black agricultural workers in Louisiana, nothing in the forty-volume report so
much as hints at the possibility that mass immigration might have
deleterious consequences for blacks, even though black leaders had
long complained that immigrants were taking jobs that, they insisted,
rightfully belonged to blacks.[2]

If blacks were superfluous so far as Northern industry was concerned, the opposite was true in the South, where black labor was indispensable to the entire regional economy. Furthermore, given the
interdependence between the regional economies of the South and
the North, occupational apartheid had indirect advantages for the
North as well. Remember that the cotton fiber that Irish, Italian, and
Jewish immigrants worked with in mills and sweatshops throughout
the North was supplied by black workers in the South. In effect, a system of labor deployment had evolved whereby blacks provided the
necessary labor for Southern agriculture, and European immigrants
provided the necessary labor for Northern industry.

This regional and racial division of labor cast the mold for generations more of racial inequality and conflict. Not until the First
World War were blacks given significant access to Northern labor
markets. In a single year—1914—the volume of immigration plummeted from 1.2 million immigrant arrivals to only 327,000. The cutoff of immigration in the midst of an economic expansion triggered
the Great Migration, as it was called, of Southern blacks to the urban
North. Industries not only employed blacks in large numbers but
even sent labor agents to the South to recruit black workers. Between
1910 and 1920 there was a net migration of 454,000 Southern blacks
to the North, a figure that exceeded the volume of the previous forty
years combined. Here is historical proof that blacks were just as willing as Europe's peasants to uproot themselves and migrate to cities
that offered the opportunity for industrial employment. To suggest
that blacks "were not ready to compete with immigrants," as the author of a recent volume on immigration does, is a flagrant distortion
of history.[3] The simple truth is that Northern industry was open to

immigrants and closed to blacks. Whatever opprobrium was heaped upon these immigrants for their cultural and religious difference, they were still beneficiaries of racial preference.

It is generally assumed that the Second World War provided a similar demand for black labor, but initially this was not the case. Because the war came on the heels of the Depression, there was a surfeit of white labor and no compelling need to hire blacks.[4] Indeed, it was blacks' frustration with their exclusion from wartime industries that prompted A. Philip Randolph and his followers to threaten a march on Washington in 1941 until Roosevelt issued his executive order banning discrimination in federal employment and defense contracts. The opening up of Northern labor markets triggered another mass migration of Southern blacks—1.6 million migrated between 1940 and 1950; by the end of the war 1.5 million black workers were part of the war-production work force. This represented an unprecedented breach in the nation's system of occupational apartheid—one that set the stage for future change as well.

Still, as recently as 1950 two-thirds of the nation's blacks lived in the South, half of them in rural areas. It was not the Civil War, but the mechanization of agriculture a century later that finally liberated blacks from their historic role as agricultural laborers in the South's feudal economy. By the mid-fifties even the harvest of cotton became mechanized with the mass production of International Harvester's automatic cotton picking machine. The number of man-hours required to produce a bale of cotton was reduced from 438 in 1940, to 26 in 1960, to only 6 in 1980.[5] Agricultural technology had effectively rendered black labor obsolete, and with it the caste system whose underlying function had been to regulate and exploit black labor.[6] Thus it was that in one century white planters went all the way to Africa to import black laborers, and in the next century the descendants of Southern planters gave the descendants of African slaves one-way bus tickets to Chicago and New York.

When blacks finally arrived in Northern cities, they encountered a far less favorable structure of opportunity than had existed for immigrants decades earlier.[7] For one thing, these labor markets had been captured by immigrant groups who engaged in a combination of ethnic nepotism and unabashed racism. For another, the occupational structures were themselves changing. Not only were droves of manufacturing jobs being automated out of existence, but a reorganization of the global economy resulted in the export of millions of manufacturing jobs to less developed parts of the world.

Thus, the fact that the technological revolution in agriculture lagged nearly a half-century behind the technological revolution in industry had fateful consequences for blacks at both junctures. First blacks were restricted to the agricultural sector during the most expansive periods of the industrial revolution. Then they were evicted from rural America and arrived in Northern cities at a time when manufacturing was beginning a steep and irreversible decline. Yet, as I argued in Chapter 6, the fact that more blacks were not integrated into Northern labor markets cannot be explained only in terms of the operation of color-blind economic forces. At least as important was the pervasive racism that restricted the access of black workers not only to jobs in declining industries, but also to new jobs in the expanding service sector.

If, as is maintained here, occupational apartheid is the essence of racial oppression in America, one might think that it has also been at the center of liberal social science's writing on race. This is hardly the case. As we have seen, generations of social scientists treated discrimination as a by-product of racial prejudice, and therefore focused on rooting out prejudice rather than addressing the issue of employment discrimination directly. To be sure, countless studies by economists and demographers document the concentration of blacks in low-status and low-paying occupations. However, these studies generally downplay or sidestep the issue of discrimination on the part of employers and unions. Either they present an upbeat account of racial "progress" on the basis of trend comparisons; or they assume that blacks are deficient in "human capital," as though this is the main obstacle to their gaining access to better jobs.[8] Very few studies have sought to measure employment discrimination directly, or to examine racism in the workplace. As the authors of a recent study write:

"despite intense interest in the relation of race to employment, very few scholars have studied the matter at the level of the firm, much less queried employers directly about their views of black workers or how race might enter into their recruitment and hiring decisions."[9]

In telling contrast, employment discrimination has always been in the forefront of black thought and politics. In *An American Dilemma* Myrdal found that blacks in the South ranked employment discrimination at the top of the "rank order of discriminations"—that is, as the form of discrimination that they found most objectionable. "Negroes are in desperate need of jobs and bread," Myrdal wrote, "even more so than of justice in the courts, and of the vote."[10] Indeed, ever since Randolph's March on Washington Movement, job discrimination has always been at the center of the protest movement. The slogan of the 1964 March on Washington was "For Jobs and Freedom." Note how "jobs" has been elided from the collective memory. For all its carping about the work ethic, white society has consistently turned a deaf ear to the desperate pleas for jobs that emanate from the black community.

Nor is white indifference or acquiescence to employment discrimination limited to benighted groups in American society. Even leftists, despite their Marxist orientation—perhaps *because* of their Marxist orientation—have been loath to confront the brutal facts about working-class racism, particularly the implication of organized labor in maintaining the structure of occupational apartheid. This political bias has bedeviled the field of labor history, pioneered by Herbert Gutman, whose early work celebrated the United Mine Workers' success at building an integrated union. Gutman and the new labor history have been criticized by Herbert Hill and others for singling out those rare instances where unions lived up to the slogan, "Black and White, Unite and Fight," and for glossing over the far more pronounced pattern of blatant racial discrimination.[11] Historian Nell Painter put it succinctly: "The new labor history has a race problem."[12]

Nor did "the scholarship of confrontation" of the 1960s, despite its racial militancy and radical politics, give the issue of occupational segregation central focus. In *Racial Oppression in America* Robert Blauner showed how "the colonial labor principle" led to a racial dualism in labor markets that continues down to the present. However, like most theoretically oriented sociologists, Blauner did not explore the policy ramifications of his analysis. Scholars and activists during the 1960s did not hesitate to denounce the United States as "a racist society," and this reflected an unprecedented willingness to confront the magnitude of the nation's crimes against African Americans. Yet such a formulation lacks conceptual clarity about what aspects of the society need to be changed, what obstacles stand in the way of change, and how these obstacles might be surmounted. At its worst, the blanket condemnation of "the system" suffered from rhetorical overkill. If nothing less than the destruction of the entire system would suffice, then attempts to desegregate the work force were apt to be dismissed as mere "reforms" that left the larger structures intact. Blacks would have to "wait," not for the slow wheels of progress, but for a revolutionary upheaval that was never more than a political fantasy.

The Immigration Dilemma

The economic fortunes of African Americans have always been linked to immigration. Suppose that Europe's "huddled masses" had been flocking to the New World in the seventeenth century. Then Southern planters would not have been impelled to go all the way to Africa to find laborers, and the nation would have been spared the ignominy of slavery. Suppose, on the other hand, that the huddled masses of Europe had *not* flocked to America's cities during the century after slavery. Then Northern industrialists would have had to put aside their racist predilections and tapped the pool of black laborers in the South who were desperate to escape the yoke of Southern oppression. Indeed, this is precisely what happened during both World Wars when the cutoff of immigration led to the absorption of blacks into Northern labor markets. The two brief intervals in the twentieth century when immigration was at low ebb marked the two major periods of economic and social advancement for African Americans.

The post–civil rights era presented yet another opportunity to integrate blacks into the occupational mainstream, especially given the sharp decline of the white birth rate and the improved climate of tolerance toward blacks. But once again, African Americans have had to cope with an enormous influx of immigrants, this time from Asia, Latin America, and the Caribbean. Ironically, it was the civil rights movement that led to the passage of the 1965 Hart-Celler Act, which abolished the national origins quotas that had restricted immigration outside of Europe. In the two ensuing decades, there have been some 15 million immigrant arrivals, not to mention millions more who are undocumented.[13]

This massive volume of immigration amounts to a double whammy as far as African Americans are concerned: not only has there been an erosion of job structures in cities with high concentrations of blacks, but black workers must compete with increasing numbers of immigrants for scarce jobs. William Julius Wilson's whole emphasis is that the United States has been exporting millions of jobs to the Third World. However, the nation is also importing workers from these same countries at an even faster rate. The availability of large numbers of foreign workers allows employers to exercise their racial preferences when it comes to hiring new workers. As the last hired, blacks often find themselves in the hiring queue even behind recent immigrants.

The lesson of history is that blacks have overcome racist barriers in the occupational world only during periods when labor has been in tight supply. Given this well-established fact, the negative implications of such a massive volume of immigration would seem obvious. When it comes to African Americans, however, the capacity of social science for contriving ingenious explanations that deny the obvious should never be underestimated.

The standard cant among social scientists is that the new immigrants are not in competition with blacks since immigrants generally end up in jobs that native workers spurn. Sweatshop workers are commonly cited as a prime example of immigrants at work, followed by the claim that blacks and other native workers will not submit to this kind of super-exploitation. On closer examination, however, this position offers economic justice neither to immigrants nor to blacks. Instead of arguing for raising the minimum wage and extending health benefits to all workers, making these jobs attractive to native workers, these social scientists are in effect sanctioning the creation of a subminimum tier in the labor market occupied by immigrants. The social costs associated with this marginal class are either ignored or camouflaged behind mythologized accounts of immigrant success in pursuit of the American Dream.[14]

Of course, not all immigrants work in super-exploited jobs, and even those who do so typically regard these jobs only as a temporary expedient. In point of fact, large numbers of new immigrants have secured jobs in core sectors of the economy—in such areas as light manufacturing, construction, hospitals, hotels and restaurants, building management, and transportation. Many work sites and—in some cities—whole job sectors are populated almost entirely by immigrants.[15]

New York City provides an apt example. In the early 1980s the Department of City Planning undertook a study of the new immigration under the direction of Elizabeth Bogen. On the basis of census data, Bogen determined that there were 493,000 post-1965 immigrants employed in 1980, accounting for 17 percent of the total work force. While apparel manufacturing had the highest concentration of immigrants (some 42,000 workers), it accounted for less than 10 percent of post-1965 immigrant workers. Roughly the same number of new immigrants were employed in hospitals, and substantial numbers were employed in restaurants, banking, construction, and building management (as doormen, security personnel, and maintenance workers). The overall finding to emerge from Bogen's data is that immigrants are widely dispersed through the occupational structure, in both blue-collar and service sectors.[16]

Bogen acknowledges that the 1970s were "rocky economic times" in which the city sustained a net loss of nearly 250,000 jobs. Nor is she oblivious to the fact that New York City has a relatively high rate of unemployment, especially among minorities. This leads her to "the controversial question of whether immigrants take jobs away from native-born workers, especially native-born minorities."[17] Here Bogen invokes "the prevailing school of thought," which contends that immigrants do not displace native workers. Citing the work of a group of scholars based at Columbia University, she writes:

Freedman and her associates base their argument on the concept of the segmented labor market. In this view, there are several markets, not just one. The secondary market, in which many recent immigrants hold jobs, is characterized by loose administrative structure, low wages, and little job security. The preponderance of immigrants in the secondary market, Freedman holds, minimizes direct competition with native-born workers, most of whom are in the primary market.[18]

A moment's reflection reveals that this paragraph is riddled with illogical and unsubstantiated claims, contradicted by Bogen's own data. Specifically:

1. To say that "most" native workers are in the primary market, whereas "a preponderance" of immigrants are in the secondary market, begs the question altogether. Obviously, investment bankers, professionals, and electricians do not compete for the same jobs as garment workers, dishwashers, and orderlies. The question turns on what happens to blacks and other low-wage earners who compete with immigrants for jobs in the secondary market. The ultimate issue is whether blacks already on the fringes of the job market are being pushed outside the labor force altogether.[19]

2. Bogen's claim that immigrants and natives do not compete for the same jobs is contradicted by her own data. Many post-1965 immigrants work in job sectors that offer what native workers want: stable jobs, a living wage, and health benefits. Some of these jobs, furthermore, are precisely the ones that were traditionally relegated to blacks. This is not a new phenomenon. In the late nineteenth century, European immigrants displaced blacks from such jobs as longshoremen, barbers, waiters, and cooks. Today, as Bogen's data indicate, blacks compete with immigrants for service jobs in hospitals, hotels and restaurants, building maintenance, fast food outlets, and even as janitors. One study of the effect of undocumented workers on labor markets in California between 1977 and 1985 found that there

was not only a substantial decline in the number of black janitors, but that hourly wages had plummeted from an average of $13.00 an hour to just over the minimum wage.[20]

Having thus dispensed with the "unsettling question" of whether immigration has exacerbated problems for native workers, Bogen is free to trumpet the infinite benefits of immigration. As she wrote in an op-ed piece in *Newsday*:

Are more, and different, immigrants bad for New York? Our research shows that there has never been a time when immigrants hurt the city. They create new jobs, shore up flagging industries and move into those jobs that carry the label "immigrant." Their children will move to other, better-paying jobs, and the next wave of immigrants will step into our garment factories, greengroceries and newsstands.[21]

But what about the African-American youth, not to speak of Hispanic, Asian, and Caribbean youth—the children of these very immigrants—who often have no attachment to the job market whatsoever? Here was the blind spot in the Planning Commission's vision for New York City. During the 1980s the New York metropolitan area absorbed another 900,000 immigrants.[22] Because of a prolonged recession, between 1989 and 1992 the New York region lost nearly half a million jobs. The percentage of blacks living below the poverty line increased from 29.5 percent in 1979 to 33.1 percent in 1990; in the case of Hispanics, poverty increased from 35.7 percent to 43.1 percent. In June 1993 a front-page article in the *New York Times* reported that the unemployment rate for black teenagers in the city reached 40 percent, the worst in the twenty-five years that records have been kept.[23]

Yet the apostles of immigration not only defend present levels approaching one million immigrants a year, but advocate substantial increases in the level of immigration.[24] The major reason has to do with declining fertility rates and a projected decline in the number of new labor force entrants. Numerous other economic benefits are cited: immigrants keep labor costs down, they found new businesses; they pay taxes and help to subsidize the growing number of retirees; they boost consumption; they will even lower the deficit.[25] In all these ways immigration is assumed to generate economic activities that redound to the benefit of the economy *as a whole*. But what about the specific interests of African Americans and other marginal workers? This is not a problem, according to the apostles of immigration. In an article entitled "The Case for More Immigration," Ben Wattenberg and Karl Zinsmeister assert that "one finds little evidence of higher unemployment or of a serious depressive effect on wages even among the most vulnerable native groups—low-skill black workers or American-born Hispanics—when there is a rise in the proportion of immigrants in the local labor market."[26] Thomas Muller also writes: "Contrary to the position taken by some prominent figures in the African-American community, there is little evidence to show that immigrants are displacing blacks in the course of gaining employment in hotels, restaurants, and other low-wage services."[27] Similarly, Julian Simon writes: "A good-sized body of competent recent research shows that immigration does not exacerbate unemployment, even among directly competing groups; in California, for instance, immigrants have not increased unemployment among blacks and women."[28]

Let us examine this "good-sized body of competent research" showing that immigration does not have deleterious consequences for blacks. It consists of a dozen or so econometric studies that share a fatal methodological flaw: they ignore the effects of immigration that can be directly observed, and instead base their conclusion that immigration is not bad for blacks on hypotheticals—that is, on outcomes that would be expected if immigration were bad for blacks but that have not occurred.[29]

These studies, in other words, are notable less for what they do than for what they do *not* do. They do not examine trend data that would indicate whether blacks have lost ground in occupations that have experienced a large immigrant influx. Nor do they focus on specific job sites or job sectors to ascertain whether immigrants are given preference in hiring over blacks. Nor do they interrogate employers about their hiring practices. Nor do they document the labor-market experiences of blacks relative to immigrants. All these approaches, as we have seen, would have yielded results contradicting these authors' claim that immigration has no adverse consequences for blacks.

What these studies are based on is a macroscopic analysis that compares wages and levels of unemployment among blacks in cities with high and low immigrant populations. Generally they find that the rate of black unemployment is consistently high regardless of the size of the immigrant population. This is an indirect proof at best. It does not indicate what the rate of black unemployment would have been if it were not for immigration. Since immigrants are generally drawn to cities where there is economic growth, it is plausible that the rate of black unemployment in such cities would be *lower* than in cities that do not attract large numbers of immigrants. Equal levels of unemployment, in other words, may mask the displacement effects of immigration.[30]

To be sure, immigration may on balance be beneficial for the economy as a whole, as the apostles of immigration contend. There is obvious validity in the claim that immigrants do not just take jobs, but create them as well. This is especially evident when one examines the thriving ethnic economies in "gateway cities" like Los Angeles, New York, San Francisco, and Miami. On the other hand, as Jacqueline Jackson has pointed out, "too often the jobs created are not for domestic minorities but for the next wave of immigrants recruited through ethnic networks."[31] Besides, what is at issue here is not whether immigration is generally beneficial to the American economy, but whether it is specifically detrimental to the interests of African Americans and other marginal workers. In the prosaic language of one economist, these aggregate findings "can mask less benign redistributional effects upon the working class and native minorities."[32]

While demographers, economists, and sociologists debate the effects of immigration, a groundswell of resentment has built up within the black community itself. Public opinion polls indicate that a solid majority of blacks see immigrants as competitors for jobs and would favor lowering the ceiling on immigration.[33] Yet most black leaders have been reluctant to speak out against immigration policy. For one thing, many blacks sympathize with these struggling minorities, some of whom are also of African descent. For another, black leaders do not want to feed the forces of xenophobia and reaction that are behind the recent upsurge of nativism. Finally, black leaders have been wary about jeopardizing their coalition with Hispanics in Congress and elsewhere, even though public opinion polls indicate that most rank-and-file Hispanics also would support a lower ceiling on immigration.[34]

However, after the violence following the verdict in the Rodney King beating case, the issue could no longer be suppressed. Especially when Asian-owned businesses were singled out for attack, it was impossible to comprehend the events in South Central Los Angeles without reference to the influx of 750,000 immigrants into Los Angeles during the 1980s. Writing in *The Atlantic*, Jack Miles—a liberal editorial writer for the *Los Angeles Times*—showed how blacks had been largely closed out of the unskilled-labor market by Latinos. He added:

The immigration story becomes the riot story by becoming a part of the labor story. And by an irony that I find particularly cruel, unskilled Latino immigration may be doing to American blacks at the end of the twentieth century what the European immigration that brought my ancestors here did to them at the end of the nineteenth.[35]

Here we arrive at the critical question. If the rationale behind immigration has to do with declining fertility rates and an anticipated decline in new labor force entrants, then why is policy not directed at addressing the scandalously high rates of black unemployment? Why is there no crash program to provide job training for minority youth whose detachment from the job market has so many deleterious consequences for themselves as well as the rest of the society? Why is there no serious effort to enforce anti-discriminatory laws and to tear down racist barriers in major occupational structures, including the so-called "ethnic economy" where racial discrimination is virtually endemic? Why are there no incentives or mandates to induce employers to hire and train unemployed youth?

It is difficult to escape the conclusion that political and economic leaders have given up on black youth and opted to rely on immigrants to make up for any labor deficits. This position, furthermore, has found legitimation from certain social scientists who, not unlike employers who refuse to hire blacks, see black youth as undesirable employees. At least this is what is implied by statements like the following:

> Americans should not be concerned that immigration will limit advancement opportunities for native workers. More lenient immigration policies can provide native-born Americans, if properly prepared, with a greater array of new possibilities. *But too often, black and Hispanic young people lack the training, schooling, and good work habits essential for advancement. For young Americans not up to the challenge the importation of low-skilled workers could amount to a major setback.*[36]

← ed

Thus, if blacks are hurt by immigration, it is because they are "not up to the challenge." The answer to the projected labor deficit is to welcome the influx of foreign workers, who are then apotheosized for their determination and pluck, and used to make invidious comparisons with African Americans who are derided for having allowed opportunity to pass them by.[37]

To state the matter bluntly, immigration policy amounts to a form of disinvestment in native workers. In the case of low-wage jobs, there is clear preference for foreign workers who are more pliable and exploitable, especially if they are undocumented. There is also the belief, laced with racist assumptions, that American youth will not accept menial, low-paying jobs. To be sure, many youth will not submit to the debasing exploitation of the sweatshop. However, the stereotypical view that "young blacks don't want to start at the bottom" is belied by graphics that periodically appear in newspapers portraying droves of minority youth lined up for summer jobs programs. These are jobs that are not only menial and low-paying, but temporary and dead-end as well. Indeed, one of the pathetic ironies of the tragedy in South Central Los Angeles is that, according to the *New York Times*, "unemployed black men see the cleanup and rebuilding work as a rare job opportunity for them." However, hope turned to rage as Hispanic laborers were brought in for the cleanup operation. One black activist warned: "We don't always want to be in a position of confrontation, but we are not going to allow this community to be rebuilt without us."[38]

The disinvestment aspects of immigration policy are even more glaring when it comes to skilled workers. Instead of underwriting the costs of educating and training workers, in effect the nation imports workers already educated and trained at another nation's expense. A good example is nursing, which traditionally was a stepping stone of mobility for working-class women. Despite a dire shortage of nurses, the United States has cut back on the training of nurses, and imported tens of thousands of nurses from the Philippines and the Caribbean where nurses are virtually an export commodity. While there is obvious expediency in this practice, especially from the vantage point of hospitals that need to fill vacancies quickly, it should also be obvious that there are long-term costs as the nation puts off any reckoning with the "intractable" divisions of race and class.[39]

The idea of immigration as disinvestment is no mere abstraction: it is reflected in recent changes in immigration policy. According to provisions of the 1965 Hart-Cellar Act, family reunification was the primary basis for granting immigrant visas. The first wave of immigrants consisted disproportionately of professionals and other highly educated individuals who were seeking better opportunities than existed in their countries of origin. Since the early 1980s, however, immigration has consisted increasingly of people with little education and skill. Eventually Congress heeded the warnings of economists that the "quality" of immigrants was deteriorating, and that there was a need to move toward a "merit-based selection process" in the dispensation of immigrant visas. The Immigration Act of 1990 took a first step in this direction by lowering the ceiling on the number of people accepted under "family preferences," and reserving 140,000 visas for individuals with job skills and talent that are in demand. Instead of investing in education and job training of American youth, it has now become official policy to use immigration as an instant source of human capital. Leading economists not only advocate increasing the number of higher occupation-based quotas, but have even proposed auctioning immigrant visas to the highest bidders.[40]

The immigration of some 15 million documented immigrants over the past several decades represents another missed opportunity in American history. The nation could have taken advantage of a secular decline in its working-age population to integrate blacks and other marginal groups into the occupational mainstream. More is involved here than achieving parity and justice for blacks. This was the nation's chance to attack the structures of inequality that rend the society, undermining the stability of political institutions and compromising the quality of life.

Why was the opportunity missed? To have acted otherwise would have required a level of commitment to racial equality that was lacking. It would also have required programs and expenditures for which there was no political will. In the final analysis, the nation succumbed once again to its endemic racism, and to its collective indifference to the plight of its black citizens. Although immigration has produced a more racially diverse population, paradoxically this new diversity has reinforced the preexisting structure of occupational apartheid.[41]

The Myth of the Black Middle Class

At first blush the existence of a large black middle class would suggest that racist barriers in occupations are no longer insurmountable—in other words, that occupational apartheid is not the problem that it was in times past. To be sure, the existence of this middle class signifies a historic breakthrough. Never before have so many blacks been represented at the higher echelons of the occupational world—in the professions and in corporate management. Never before have so many blacks found employment in core industries, in both the white and blue-collar sectors. Nor can this new black middle class, given its size, be dismissed as "window dressing" or "tokenism." Yet there are other grounds for doubting that the existence of this large black middle class signifies the demise of occupational apartheid.

In the first place, insofar as this black middle class is an artifact of affirmative action policy, it cannot be said to be the result of the autonomous workings of market forces. In other words, the black middle class does not reflect a lowering of racist barriers in occupations so much as the opposite: racism is so entrenched that without government intervention there would be little "progress" to boast about.

Second, although a substantial segment of the new black middle class is found in corporate management, there is a pattern of racial segregation *within* these structures (similar to what happens in many "integrated" schools). Studies have found that many black managers work in personnel functions, often administering affirmative action programs. Others function as intermediaries between white corporations and the black community or the black consumer.[42] Cut off from the corporate mainstream, these black executives often find themselves in dead-end jobs with little job security. By outward appearances, they have "made it" in the white corporate world, but their positions and roles are still defined and circumscribed by race.

Much the same thing can be said about the black business sector. In an incisive analysis of "The Making of the Black Middle Class," Sharon Collins provides the following account:

Black entrepreneurs are concentrated in segregated rather than generalized services. In 1979, 68 percent of black-owned businesses were in retail and selected services that marketed their wares almost exclusively to black consumers. In 1979, 99 percent of all minority business was based on federal procurement or sales to the minority consumers.[43]

In her analysis of data on Chicago-based minority professional service firms, Collins found a similar pattern of racial segmentation, even with firms doing business with the government:

Personnel service firms provided workers for units with racial concerns, such as the Office of Manpower. Black law firms were hired for contract compliance and labor-management issues in segregated services such as Housing and Urban Development. Certified public accountant firms performed pre-grant and general audits for segregated sites such as Cook County Hospital. Management consulting firms provided technical assistance primarily to agencies such as Chicago's Department of Human Services or the Federal Office of Minority Business Development. Engineers provided professional services to predominantly black sites such as Chicago's Northshore Sanitary District.[44]

In short, the much ballyhooed growth of black-owned business has generally occurred within the framework of a racially segregated economy.[45]

Finally, there is the double-edged sword associated with public sector employment. On the one hand, the fact that government employment has opened up to blacks marks another change of historic dimensions. For two decades after the Second World War black representation in government was largely restricted to the Postal Service and to low-level clerical and service positions. As noted earlier, today some 1.6 million blacks, constituting one-fourth of the entire black labor force, are employed by government. Indeed, this is the source of much of the "progress" that we celebrate.

On the other hand, it shows once again that racial progress has depended on the intervention of government, in this instance as a direct employer. Furthermore, within the ranks of government there is a great deal of internal segregation. For the most part, blacks employed in government are social welfare providers in such areas as education, welfare, health, employment security, and public housing. Essentially, they function as intermediaries and as a buffer between white America and the black underclass. As Michael Brown and Steven Erie have argued, "the principal economic legacy of the Great Society for the black community has been the creation of a large-scale social welfare economy of publicly funded middle-income service providers and low-income service and cash transfer recipients."[46]

To conclude, as Collins does, that "the growth of a black middle class is *not* evidence of a decline in racial inequality in the United States" is perhaps an overstatement.[47] After all, the sheer existence of a large black middle class means that blacks are no longer a uniformly downtrodden people. On the other hand, it may signify not the dissolution so much as an artful reconfiguration of caste boundaries in the occupational world. To control the disorder emanating from the ghettos of America, a new class of "Negro jobs" has been created. They are not the dirty, menial, and backbreaking jobs of the past. On the contrary, they are coveted jobs that offer decent wages and job security. Nevertheless, they are jobs that are pegged for blacks and that function within the context of racial hierarchy and division.

Precisely because the new black middle class is largely a product of government policy, its future is subject to the vagaries of politics. Already it is apparent, as two economists have concluded, that "the epoch of rapid black relative economic advance ended sometime in the late 1970s and early 1980s and that some of the earlier gains eroded in the 1980s."[48] Court decisions restricting minority set-asides have already had a severe impact on black businesses.[49] The current attack on affirmative action will inevitably lead to a further erosion of black socioeconomic gains. Finally, just as blacks benefited disproportionately from the growth of government, they will certainly be severely affected by the current movement to cut the size of the government and the scope of government services. Black public-sector workers are especially vulnerable to layoffs because they are disproportionately found in positions that are heavily dependent on federal subsidies.[50]

The Job Crisis in Black America

If the new black middle class does not signify a fundamental decline in racial inequality, then what are we to conclude about the persistence and growth of the black underclass? In *Poor People's Movements*, written in 1979, Piven and Cloward provided an apt description of the current situation when they wrote: "In effect, the black poor progressed from slave labor to cheap labor to (for many) no labor at all."[51] Indeed, a job crisis of the magnitude that existed in the society at large during the Great Depression afflicts black America today. In the Depression, the crisis was defined as such, and extraordinary programs were developed to overhaul basic economic institutions and to create jobs for the unemployed. In the case of the black job crisis, however, social policy has been predicated on the assumption that black unemployment stems from the deficiencies of black workers, and social policy has rarely advanced beyond some meager job training programs.[52]

A few statistics will suffice to convey the dimensions of this job crisis. In 1994 the unemployment rate was 11.5 percent for blacks and

5.3 percent for whites.[53] According to one estimate, blacks would need 1.6 million jobs to achieve parity with whites. The job deficit for black men over 20 is 736,000 jobs; for black women over 20, it is 150,000 jobs; and for black teenagers it is 500,000 jobs.[54]

As is often pointed out, the government's measure of unemployment is only the tip of the iceberg, since it leaves out "discouraged workers" who have given up looking for work, as well as "involuntary part-time workers" who want full-time employment. The National Urban League has developed its own measure of "hidden unemployment" that includes these two groups. In 1992 the League's hidden unemployment rate was 13.3 percent for whites and 25.5 percent for blacks. Thus, one-quarter of the black population, involving roughly 3 million workers, are effectively jobless.[55] Even this figure does not sufficiently reflect the depth of the problem, since it leaves out the working poor—those who are employed full time, but whose wages leave them below the poverty line.

This job crisis is the single most important factor behind the familiar tangle of problems that beset black communities. Without jobs, nuclear families become unglued or are never formed. Without jobs, or husbands with jobs, women with young children are forced onto the welfare rolls. Without jobs, many ghetto youth resort to the drug trade or other illicit ways of making money. Ironically, those who end up in prison do find work—in prison shops that typically pay fifty cents or less an hour—only to find themselves jobless on the outside. Given this fact, the high rate of recidivism should come as no surprise. For different reasons, schools are generally ineffective in teaching children whose parents lack stable jobs and incomes. In short, there is no exit from the racial quagmire unless there is a national commitment to address the job crisis in black America.

Tragically, this nation does not have the political will to confront its legacy of slavery, even if this means nothing more than providing jobs at decent wages for blacks who continue to be relegated to the fringes of the job market. Instead, a mythology has been constructed that, in ways reminiscent of slavery itself, alleges that blacks are inefficient and unproductive workers, deficient in the work habits and moral qualities that delivered other groups from poverty. Nor is this cultural blaming of the victim any longer characteristic only of the political right. As Chapter 5 showed, many prominent liberals, inside and outside the academy, have resorted to gratuitous clucking about the cultural patterns of black families and black youth, utterly confusing cause and effect. One liberal journalist, Jim Sleeper, has written a book that preaches hard work and moral discipline to blacks in New York, a city where 101,000 people recently took the civil service exam for 2,000 expected openings in the Sanitation Department.[56] Still others on the left have declared that the problems confronting black America have less to do with race than with class, a strange message for the millions of tenth-generation African Americans still condemned to live out their lives in impoverished ghettos. By reifying "class" and shifting the focus away from "race," these theorists unwittingly undermine the anti-racist movement. They absolve the nation of moral and political responsibility for making restitution for its three-hundred-year crime, and play into the hands of those on the right who have already succeeded in removing issues of racial justice from the national agenda.

What would be involved in restoring racial justice to the national agenda? We must begin where the civil rights revolution ended—by attacking the deep-seated institutionalized inequalities that exist between the white and black citizens of this nation. The historic achievement of the civil rights revolution was to tear down the walls of segregation. The challenge today is to erect the structures of racial equality. If occupational apartheid is the essence of American racism, as has been argued here, then the keystone of remedial social policy must be a concerted attack on occupational apartheid.

To say this at the present time, given the political climate and the mounting attack on affirmative action, is bound to appear myopic, if not delusional. But the lesson of history, imbued in the folk wisdom of the civil rights movement itself, is that it is important to "keep your eyes on the prize," and not be deterred by the seemingly insuperable obstacles of the moment. Typically the seeds of political transformation are planted by visionaries, and must wait for a more propitious set of conditions before they germinate and come to fruition. For example, the agenda for change that A. Philip Randolph enunciated in the early 1940s became the blueprint for the civil rights movement in the late fifties. For this reason it is imperative to keep alive an emancipatory politics that is *not* tailored to "political reality." In a period of reaction like the current one, this serves pragmatic political ends as well, since it helps to hold the line against even further retrogression.

Any serious effort to resume the unfinished racial agenda must begin with the detailed policy agenda laid out by the Kerner Commission in 1968. At the top of this agenda was a series of proposals dealing with employment, consistent with the promise of the Employment Act of 1946 to provide "a useful job at a reasonable wage for all who wish to work." Specific proposals included beefing up the enforcement powers of the Equal Employment Opportunities Commission, creating new jobs in both the public and private sectors, providing subsidies to employers to hire and train the hard-core unemployed, and launching programs of economic development and social reconstruction targeted for poverty areas and racial ghettos.

Two other policy initiatives follow from the analysis in this chapter:

1. Immigration policy must take into account the legitimate interests of native workers, especially those on the economic margin. After all, the meaning of citizenship is diminished if it does not include the right to a job at decent wages.[57] For African Americans who have toiled on American soil for centuries, and whose sons and daughters have died in the nation's wars, the case for national action is especially urgent. Today we are confronted with the spectacle of these oldest of Americans again being passed over by new waves of immigrants. It is difficult to escape the conclusion that present immigration policy not only subverts the cause of racial justice, but, given the immense human and social costs of the racial status quo, is also antithetical to the national interest.

To be sure, other principles weigh on the formulation of immigrant policy. Many immigrants—especially Mexicans who are migrating to territory once possessed by Mexico—have historical and moral claim for access to American labor markets. Also to be consid-

ered is the proud liberal tradition of America as an asylum for the dis-
possessed. Like the immigrants of yore, the new immigrants contribute immeasurably to "the building of America," its culture as well as
its economy. These factors, however, must be balanced against the
deleterious effects that the continuing volume of immigration has on
groups on the economic margin—not only African Americans, but
immigrants themselves and their children.

The point about immigration is that it must be made part of a comprehensive human resource development policy that is committed to
the improvement of employment opportunities and wages of marginal workers. The 1990 Commission on the Skills of the American
Labor Force found that most other industrialized nations have comprehensive human resource development systems in place that include extensive job training, job placement, and income maintenance programs. As Vernon Briggs has commented: ". . . none of
these other industrialized countries saw immigration as a means of
bolstering the skill and educational levels of their respective work-
forces. Instead, they have decided to invest in their citizens through
these human resource development policies and have adopted or
strengthened restrictions on immigration."[58]

2. Human resource development policies, including more restrictive immigration, will not do much to alter the structure of occupational apartheid unless they are combined with policies that squarely
address this issue. We need a renewed national commitment to dealing with the job crisis that afflicts black America. This would begin
with vigorous enforcement of anti-discrimination laws. However,
the lesson of the post–civil rights era is that anti-discrimination laws
are minimally effective unless they are backed up with compliance
checks and other enforcement mechanisms—in short, affirmative
action. The significance of affirmative action is that it amounts to a
frontal assault on the racial division of labor. Whatever its limita-
tions, affirmative action has produced the most significant departure
from the occupational caste system that has existed since slavery. If racial progress is to continue, then affirmative action must be extended
to wider segments of the work force.

Again, it may seem gratuitous to say this at a time when racism and reaction are feeding upon one another, and there is a tidal wave of opposition against affirmative action. However, there is a maddening illogic to the current crusade against welfare, crime, out-of-wedlock births, and the other "pathologies" associated in the popular mind with the ghetto population. Unless jobs and opportunities are targeted for black youth and young adults, then punitive legislation and the withdrawal of public assistance will only produce more desperation and even greater disorder.

Even more maddening are the contradictory tendencies of federal policy. At the very time that one hand of the federal government attacks "welfare" and preaches the virtues of "work," the other hand sporadically engineers greater unemployment by increasing interest rates in order to "cool the economy" and keep inflation under control. This is an old story, of course. Whenever unemployment rates dip to the level where jobs might open up to the "last hired"—that is, to the ghetto population—this is construed as a sign of an overheated economy requiring the intervention of the Federal Reserve. The result is that the benefits of economic expansion never reach "the underclass" (which was precisely what Gunnar Myrdal meant when he coined the term).

The job crisis in black America is allowed to fester for one basic reason: because the power elites of this nation regard these black communities as politically and economically expendable. They can afford to do so as long as they are not under great countervailing pressure, either from a mobilized black protest movement or from spontaneous ghetto uprisings. This is a situation of politics-as-usual so long as poverty and joblessness manifest themselves as "quiet riots"—that is, as crime and violence that can be contained through a criminal justice system that currently has a prison population exceeding one million people.

On the other hand, when these communities do finally erupt in full-scale riots, as South Central Los Angeles did in the aftermath of the Rodney King episode, then suddenly race is back on the national agenda. Even the mainstream media resisted the temptation merely to resort to moral platitudes. *Newsweek* proclaimed that "This Was No Riot, It Was a Revolt," and described "the siege of L.A." as a "bloody wake-up call" to reverse the neglect of America's inner cities.[59] Coming as it did in the midst of the 1992 election, the Los Angeles uprising abruptly transformed the political discourse. As Leonard Silk observed in the business section of the *New York Times*: "a political campaign that started as a contest for the votes of the middle class has suddenly been transformed into a fight over the issues of poverty, urban neglect, jobs and race—and how to deal with them."[60] According to a nationwide poll conducted by the *New York Times*, 61 percent said that the federal government was not paying enough attention to the needs and problems of minorities and 78 percent said that more jobs and job training would help to reduce racial tensions and future riots.

Beneath this mobilization of opinion was a fear that like Watts thirty years earlier, the uprising might trigger a chain reaction in ghettos across the nation. This did not happen, however. In a matter of months the crisis had passed, the momentum for political action had dissipated, and once again race was off the national agenda. Aside from the rubble in South Central Los Angeles, we were left only with the naked truth: that our political system is incapable of addressing racial inequities unless the nation's ghettos erupt in violence.

10

America Again at the Crossroads

> In this unfolding conundrum of life and history there is such a thing as being too late. Procrastination is still the thief of time. Life often leaves us standing bare, naked and dejected with a lost opportunity.
>
> Martin Luther King, *Where Do We Go from Here?* 1967

When this nation's founding fathers betrayed the noble principles enshrined in the Declaration of Independence and the Constitution, and surrendered to temptation and greed by sanctioning the slave trade, they placed the nation on a calamitous path of racial division and conflict that continues down to the present. Yet the thirteen decades since the abolition of slavery are littered with lost opportunities—golden moments when the nation could have severed this historical chain, but either failed to do so or did not go far enough in eradicating the legacy of slavery.

The first lost opportunity, of course, was the failure of Reconstruction. The Thirteenth, Fourteenth, and Fifteenth Amendments to the Constitution elevated blacks to full citizenship, and ushered in a period of biracial democracy in which blacks voted, held office, and, despite a general pattern of social segregation, enjoyed a modicum of civil equality.[1] However, these gains were tenuous and short-lived. As W. E. B. Du Bois wrote in his 1935 study *Black Reconstruction in America*: "The slave went free; stood a brief moment in the sun; then moved back again toward slavery."[2]

Had the promise of Reconstruction been kept, then this would have obviated the need for a civil rights revolution a century later.

205

Nor can blame for the failure of Reconstruction be placed wholly on the South. As Neil McMillen writes in his history of Jim Crow in Mississippi: "Without the ready acquiescence of northern white sentiment, the national Republican party, and the three branches of the federal government, blacks could not have been driven from politics in any state."[3] Indeed, Northern acquiescence to black disfranchisement persisted until 1965, when Congress, under unrelenting pressure from the black protest movement, passed the Voting Rights Act. During the preceding century, however, even anti-lynching legislation was beyond the pale of political possibility.

The failure of Reconstruction goes beyond the subversion of the Reconstruction amendments. After two centuries of slavery, the bestowal of political rights on blacks scarcely began to address the needs of an expropriated people. Genuine reconstruction would have included a massive redistribution of land, as envisioned by a few "radical" Republicans. Not only would this have placed freedmen on a path toward self-sufficiency, but it also would have secured their newly won political rights as well. As Thaddeus Stevens commented when he submitted his proposal for a land redistribution to Congress in 1865: "How can republican institutions, free schools, free churches, free social intercourse exist in a mingled community of nabobs and serfs?"[4]

Indeed, "forty acres and a mule" epitomized the dream of blacks at the end of the Civil War. This was a dream unfulfilled, however. The legislation establishing the Freedmen's Bureau in March 1865 had provided for the distribution of land confiscated from Confederate soldiers and their supporters, but within months President Johnson ordered that the land be returned to its former owners. Most blacks ended up working as sharecroppers or tenant farmers, a system that amounted to a form of debt servitude that restricted the freedoms of workers and kept them tied to the land. As Myrdal lamented in *An American Dilemma*: "The story of the Negro in agriculture would have been a rather different one if the Negro farmer had greater opportunity to establish himself as an independent owner."[5]

The subjugation of the South's black population was so complete that we can only imagine how the course of race history might have been altered if white America had delivered on the promise of "forty acres and a mule." One historical example provides a glimpse into the future that never was: the so-called "exoduster movement." This involved a migration of tens of thousands of Southern blacks to Kansas in the spring of 1879. Kansas was only one of a number of emigration schemes that were explored by blacks desperate to escape the tightening noose of racial oppression. Emissaries had gone as far away as Haiti, Canada, and even Liberia. Kansas emerged as an option because it was in need of settlers, and the abolitionist Republicans who ruled the state accepted blacks on a parity with whites.[6] Word of "cheap land in Kansas" spread like wildfire throughout the South, with the help of blacks working on steamboats and railroads.

As the migration gained momentum, it assumed messianic overtones. Migrants, who were called "exodusters," saw themselves as fleeing Egypt for the Promised Land. The leader of the movement, "Pap" Singleton, was dubbed the Father of the Exodus and the Moses of the Colored People. In some respects the story parallels the one told by Leon Uris in *Exodus*. The land available for black settlement had been passed over during the westward migration because of the dearth of water. Lacking trees and shelter, settlers were forced to live in dugouts gouged out of the arid soil. Many gave up in frustration and resumed their northward migration. However, several "colonies" were established that eventually developed into flourishing agricultural communities, replete with churches, newspapers, hotels, businesses, and all of the other accouterments and amenities of a Midwestern town.

Like the rest of rural America, the black towns were hard hit by the Depression and the Dust Bowl, and most of the residents dispersed to cities in the North and West. However, one community, Nicodemus, still exists, a living symbol of "what might have been" if blacks had been masters of their own destiny.

I stumbled upon Nicodemus in 1975 while doing research on the impact of European immigration on African Americans. The re-

search began with the naive question: why did so few blacks migrate
to the Northern cities that offered opportunity to millions of immigrants at the turn of the century? The social science literature was of
little help. In *An American Dilemma*, for example, Gunnar Myrdal
puzzled about why so few blacks migrated to the North and West,
conceding that this was "a mystery."[7] Historians, for their part, are so
riveted on chronicling "what happened" that they tend to ignore non-
events—in this case, the *non*-migration of blacks to the North during
this period.[8] Nor in 1975 were there any major studies of the exoduster movement.[9] I found one nugget of information in the Kansas volume of the Federal Writer's Project that described Nicodemus as the
"last survivor of Kansas' three colonies settled by the exodusters." I decided to go see for myself.[10]

On my first field trip to Nicodemus I interviewed two women: Hat-
tie Burney and Ola Scruggs Wilson, both octogenarians who had
been schoolteachers to generations of Nicodemus's youth. They were
repositories of memory, and filled my notebook with stories about life
on the prairie where they battled droughts, dust storms, rattlesnakes,
and fierce winters; gave birth to children with the help of midwives;
and, despite the many privations, cultivated a singular grace and sophistication. Mrs. Burney's eyes filled with tears as she recalled what
breakfast was like, with her eight siblings encircling the breakfast
table, and the overpowering sense of gratitude that they felt for their
father who, despite hardships, had provided them with their daily
bread. She also loaned me a manuscript that her father had written
late in his life. It was a history of Nicodemus that traced its origins and
development, and celebrated its triumph over adversity.

Mrs. Wilson, who prided herself as Nicodemus's historian, re-
buffed some of my questions, accusing me of "stealing her thunder."
Like all historians, she jealously guarded her sources. But she did tell
me about the racism in the surrounding communities, and how Nicodemus was crippled when the decision was made to run the rail-
road through the neighboring town of Bogue. She also described her
mother's joy upon learning of her freedom. I was struck by the ease
with which Mrs. Wilson invoked the word "master." For me this word

had a cold abstract meaning. But here was a woman, only a generation removed from slavery, for whom the word was replete with deep
personal significance. And here I was, conversing with someone
whose *mother* had been a slave. It was a chilling reminder of how
proximate slavery is to the present.

I returned to Nicodemus a year later for the annual Homecoming.
Originally it was called "Emancipation Day," but the event was later
redefined as a homecoming. Between four and five hundred descendants return every August for a week of festivities. The community
boasts of a judge in Denver, an assistant attorney general in Colorado,
and a big-league football player, but aside from these success stories,
most of Nicodemus's progeny seem to have "made it" in various walks
of life. They returned to Nicodemus in late-model cars, with a sense
of pride, both of their shared origins and of their second lives in the
diaspora. To be sure, Nicodemus is a historical anomaly, but it signifies "what might have been"—if more blacks had been able to escape the yoke of Southern oppression, if they had been free to own
land and develop their own communities, if Reconstruction had not
wound up a broken promise.

A second lost opportunity spans the period between 1880 and
1924, the years of the last great wave of European immigration. With
the notable exception of Eastern European Jews, these immigrants—
like blacks—generally came from peasant origins and had high rates
of illiteracy. They were a surplus rural population drawn to America
primarily by the prospect of jobs in its burgeoning industries. Between 1880 and 1920 some 24 million immigrants arrived. At the beginning of this period—1880—the entire African American population totaled only 6.6 million, 90 percent of whom lived in the
South. Despite the "Great Migration" during the First World War, 85
percent of blacks still lived in the South in 1920. The chief reason so
few migrated North should have been obvious. A color line, maintained by employers and workers alike, barred blacks from virtually
the entire industrial sector. This simple truth may have eluded Myrdal, but it is clearly enunciated in a 1944 book by an obscure black
scholar, John G. Van Deusen, who wrote:

Regardless of qualifications, most Northern Negroes at this time found themselves forced into domestic and personal service or restricted to odd jobs at unskilled labor. History does not show many peoples who have migrated because of persecution alone. The Negro is not dissimilar to others, and where no economic base was assured, he preferred to endure those ills he had rather than fly to others he knew not of. [11]

In the categorical exclusion of blacks from the industrial work force, the nation missed a unique opportunity to incorporate blacks into the mainstream of the economy at a time when there was rapid growth and a dire shortage of labor. Needless to say, Europe's "wretched refuse" were hardly embraced as racial kin. They, too, were regarded as pariahs, feared and despised for their ethnic peculiarities, and ruthlessly exploited. Nativists of various stripes were determined to make Americans of them. But this is precisely the point: as whites they could be naturalized and assimilated into the body politic. In the final analysis immigration policy and employment practices were predicated on the racist assumption that even the most reprobate Europeans were preferable to African Americans.

A third lost opportunity came with the Second World War, when powerful forces for racial change were set into motion. On the level of ideology, the war against fascism served as a backlight on America's own racist and fascist tendencies. The contradiction of drafting blacks into a Jim Crow army to fight for American democracy could no longer be patched over, and A. Philip Randolph launched a "double-V campaign," standing for victory abroad *and* at home. Expectations ran high among blacks and whites alike that blacks would be rewarded for their patriotism. With characteristic optimism, Myrdal wrote: "There is bound to be a redefinition of the Negro's status in America as a result of this War." [12]

No less important were the economic and demographic changes wrought by the war. Rapid growth, combined with the mobilization of the armed forces, generated a need for black labor. A million and a half black workers were part of the war-production work force alone, and the income of black workers increased twice as fast as that of whites. The opening up of Northern labor markets to blacks stimulated the migration of Southern blacks. Between 1940 and 1950 net migration reached an all-time high of 1.6 million.

The ancillary effects of these changes were far-reaching. Blacks developed large and cohesive communities in major Northern cities. Membership in the NAACP mushroomed to 85,000.[13] Northern residence translated into greater political leverage, evident in the fact that black voters provided the margin of victory in the election of Truman in 1948. For the first time blacks consolidated the economic and institutional base from which they could mount resistance to white oppression.[14]

The momentum was quickly blunted, however. The Fair Employment Practices Commission that Roosevelt established during the war in order to forestall Randolph's march on Washington was a feeble organization with a skeletal staff and no enforcement powers. Even so, it was embroiled in controversy from the outset, and after a Southern filibuster in 1946 the agency was dismantled. Here was an early portent that the federal government would not be a champion of black rights during the postwar period. Black soldiers returning home had to accept the bitter fact that victory had been secured on one front only. For African Americans the return to normalcy—the hallmark of the 1950s—meant a return to second-class citizenship.

The fourth lost opportunity has been the focal point of this book: the failure to follow through on the momentous changes wrung out of white society by the civil rights movement. The passage of civil rights legislation in 1964 and 1965 was a monumental achievement. In securing civil rights for African Americans, they signified the end to official racism. Of paramount importance, the state of terror, so graphically documented in *An American Dilemma*, was brought to an end. Segregation in public accommodations, long the trademark of the Southern way of life, virtually disappeared. Eventually blacks derived benefits from the franchise, at least in municipalities with a black population majority.[15] After much foot-dragging and circumvention, school desegregation was implemented throughout the

South, even more successfully than in the North. By the standard of what preceded it, the post–civil rights era amounted to a great social metamorphosis.

On the other hand, to paraphrase James Baldwin, the crimes of the past cannot be used to gloss over the inequities of the present. The appropriate benchmark for assessing progress is not how much worse things were as we move closer to slavery, but rather, how much blacks continue to lag behind whites in terms of major social indicators. When these comparisons are made, a far less sanguine picture emerges—one of persistent and even widening gaps between blacks and whites in incomes and living standards.[16]

In their totality these four lost opportunities represent the greatest failure of American democracy: to come to terms with the legacy of slavery. Moreover, this failure occurred during the most expansive and prosperous period in its history, the century after slavery when the United States emerged as an industrial monolith, providing opportunity to tens of millions of immigrants, and boasting the highest standard of living in the world. Here, then, is the present conundrum: If the United States failed to come to terms with the legacy of slavery in an era of empire, what can we hope for in an era of decline?

That is to say, if the nation failed to incorporate African Americans into the economic mainstream during a century marked by overall growth and prosperity, what can we hope for at a time when real wages are declining and the nation's overall level of prosperity and standard of living are undergoing a secular decline? If white America turned a deaf ear to black demands in the halcyon days of "the affluent society," how will it respond in a time of national hand-wringing over "the end of the American dream" and "the fall of the middle class?"[17] What will the nation have to offer African Americans who were never included in the American dream and who never made it to the middle class?

The answers are becoming painfully obvious. In the first place, the number of blacks below the official poverty line (currently $14,763 for an urban family of four) has steadily *increased* over the past two decades—from 7.5 million in 1970 to 8.6 million in 1980, to 9.8 million in 1990, to 10.9 million in 1993. Today blacks, who are 12 percent of the population, account for 29 percent of the poor, the same proportion as in 1960.[18] Even these figures underestimate the extent to which poverty is concentrated among blacks. Nearly half of all black children under age eighteen are being raised in families below the poverty line, as compared to 16 percent of whites.[19] Poverty among blacks is also far more likely to be long-term. One study devised a measure of "persistent poverty," which applied to households that were below the official poverty level in at least eight of the ten years under examination. It found that persistent poverty was more than seven times as prevalent among urban blacks as among the rest of the urban population.[20] Another recent study found that blacks account for 58 percent of the "severely distressed" in ninety-five major cities.[21]

It was never easy to convince whites of the logic and justice of affirmative action. To make matters worse, affirmative action policy evolved during the 1970s, precisely the time that real wages began a secular decline. The erosion of wages has been especially pronounced among younger, less educated workers, precisely the group that constituted the traditional base for the Democratic Party. This group has also been the most vehement in its opposition to affirmative action and the most likely to defect to the Republican Party.

The 1994 election also marked the acme of an ominous new trend: to *blame* blacks for the ills that afflict American society, and to pretend that, if not for blacks, the economy would be restored to its erstwhile vigor. As early as 1986, Roger Wilkins wrote:

Anti-black racism is enormously useful to the right. As long as whites can be convinced of two things, they will readily accept the proposition dearest to the heart of the right. That is: as long as they believe that (1) poverty and joblessness are primarily black problems and (2) that black deficiencies account for those conditions, then you can easily reach the conclusion that there's nothing much wrong with American capitalism that a little tinkering by Paul Volcker can't fix.[22]

What is all the more remarkable is that racial issues have dominated recent elections with scarcely any mention of race in general or of

African Americans in particular. This was observed by Thomas and Mary Edsall in a 1991 cover story in *The Atlantic Monthly* entitled "When the Official Subject is Presidential Politics, Taxes, Welfare, Crime, Rights, or Values . . . the Real Subject Is RACE."[23] If race were given explicit mention, this would invite charges of "racism," which not only arouses opposition among sympathetic whites, but runs the risk of antagonizing blacks and setting off a race war. Through these code words it is possible to play on racial stereotypes, appeal to racial fears, and heap blame on blacks without naming them. Thus, in this cryptic vernacular we have a new and insidious form of racebaiting that is so well camouflaged that it does not carry the political liabilities that were evident, for example, in David Duke's abortive campaign for the United States Senate in 1990.[24]

The crowning irony is that white liberals who wish to augment government programs for blacks also invoke a race-neutral language. Terms such as "poverty," "the inner city," and "the truly disadvantaged" intentionally camouflage the real nature of their agenda. Thus we have the spectacle of a national debate over race that has been cleansed of any mention of race. This political discourse has given new life and meaning to James Baldwin's plaint that *Nobody Knows My Name*.

The tendency so manifest in recent elections to place the blame for all the ills of American society on African Americans amounts to scapegoating, pure and simple. It is instructive to consider the origins of this word. In biblical times ancient Hebrews would perform a ritual that symbolically transferred their sins to a goat. By then sacrificing the goat, they would purge themselves of sin. Perhaps, alas, this symbolic meaning lies behind the current agitation for capital punishment. It is as though by annihilating that sinner, which in the popular imagination is a young black male, the nation is purged of its myriad of ills. The ultimate irony, of course, is that blame for the demise of the American empire is placed on the group that has shared least in its bounty.

The nation's failure, even at propitious moments in its history, to come to terms with its legacy of slavery has always had regressive implications for race and politics alike. As Eric Foner wrote at the conclusion of *Reconstruction*:

If racism contributed to the undoing of Reconstruction, by the same token Reconstruction's demise and the emergence of blacks as a disenfranchised class of dependent laborers greatly facilitated racism's further spread, until by the twentieth century it had become more deeply embedded in the nation's culture and politics than at any time since the beginning of the antislavery crusade and perhaps in our entire history. The removal of a significant portion of the nation's laboring population from public life shifted the center of gravity of American politics to the right, complicating the tasks of reformers for generations to come. [25]

In much the same way, the failure of the Second Reconstruction, as the civil rights revolution has been called, to remedy the deep-seated inequalities between blacks and whites has engendered both racism and reaction, each feeding on the other.

This is the context for the recent recrudescence of scientific racism, in the form of Richard Herrnstein and Charles Murray's *The Bell Curve*. [26] This retrograde book represents the apogee of the backlash, the culmination of forces of retreat that have been building for three decades, fueled not only by the agents of racism and reaction, but also by white liberals and black conservatives who have made the fatal mistake of shifting the focus of blame away from societal institutions onto the individuals and groups who have been cast to the fringes of the social order. As Adolph Reed has written: "We can trace Murray's legitimacy directly to the spinelessness, opportunism and racial bad faith of the liberals in the social-policy establishment. . . . Many of those objecting to Herrnstein and Murray's racism embrace positions that are almost indistinguishable, except for the resort to biology." [27]

One would think from the extraordinary attention that has been showered on *The Bell Curve* that the book offered something new to the debate over inequality. Notwithstanding all the cybernetics that the authors bring to bear—a daunting array of statistics and graphs— the book's major tenets are only a rarefied version of arguments that began with the development of IQ testing early in this century: that there is a unitary thing called intelligence, that it exists independently of environmental influences and can be accurately measured by conventional IQ tests, that the source of intelligence is in the genes and is therefore a matter of biological inheritance, and that some groups—notably African Americans—have lower average intelligence and this genetic deficit explains why they occupy the lowest strata of society. Far from new, this timeworn model had long ago been relinquished to the trashbin of history, and perhaps would have remained there if not for the persistence and largess of the Pioneer Fund, an ultrarightist foundation that was founded by eugenicists in the 1930s and has subsidized much of the research that forms the basis for *The Bell Curve*.[28]

The question that needs to be addressed, therefore, is: Why now? What accounts for the book's publication by a major publishing house, and its extraordinary reception in the mass media? *The New York Times Magazine* christened the publication with a cover story under the title "Daring Research or 'Social Science Pornography'?" *Newsweek* and *Time* followed with feature stories. *The New Republic* printed a lengthy excerpt, along with an apologia from the editors explaining why such a reversion to scientific racism should appear on the pages of an ostensibly liberal journal.[29] Thanks to this media blitz, augmented with appearances by Charles Murray on numerous television programs, *The Bell Curve* rapidly climbed to second place on the *New York Times* Best Seller List. Against this background, it behooves us to ask: What is it about this book and the times that make them "right" for each other?

Biological determinism originally fell into disrepute not only because its knowledge-claims were debunked by the emerging social sciences, but also because the prevailing system of social relations was no longer conducive to maintaining a theory that defined social status as immutable and fixed. Notions of biological inferiority had been perfectly tailored to a caste-like society where, in the words of one anthropologist, "everyone is sentenced for life to a social cell shared by others of like birth, separated from and ranked relative to all other social cells."[30] In the twentieth century, however, the forces of industri-

alization, urbanization, and modernity transformed traditional society, and threw into question the ideological justifications of the old
order, including the pseudo-scientific theories that consigned whole
groups—racial minorities, women, and the poor—to permanent inferiority. Especially as these groups were elevated in status, it became
increasingly difficult to maintain the postulates of biological determinism. To state the obvious, if this nation had followed through on
the promise of the civil rights revolution, and enacted the changes
that would have established a basic parity between blacks and whites
in socioeconomic status and living standards, we would not today be
debating whether black subordination is a product of genes.

Clearly, it is the existence of a "permanent underclass" that is sus-
taining the recrudescence of scientific racism. *The Bell Curve* comes
on stream at a time when the American class system has become
more static, when poverty is on the increase, when the gap between
the haves and have-nots is growing wider, and when many of the middle rungs on the ladder of success have been eliminated, making it
more difficult than ever to escape poverty.[31] For the black poor in particular, who must cope with the impediments of race as well as the
disabilities of class, their situation is not far removed from one where
"everyone is sentenced for life to a social cell shared by others of like
birth." The significance of *The Bell Curve* is that it provides ideological justification for this rigidification of class lines. The book is
driven by the same ideological agenda as Murray's previous work,
Losing Ground, which argued that social programs to uplift the poor
are futile and even counterproductive, in that they foster a welfare dependency that keeps their beneficiaries trapped in poverty. Thanks to
his collaboration with Richard Herrnstein, Murray has added a biological twist to this argument. The underclass is destined by nature to
remain on the tail end of the socioeconomic curve. Ameliorative social policy is destined to failure. We can only resign ourselves to the
dictates of nature in the name of a perverse multiculturalism.

Yet it would be premature to conclude that *The Bell Curve* represents a decisive shift in the prevailing paradigm. For one thing, an av-
alanche of criticism was heaped on the book, even before it had been

reviewed in scholarly journals. As Adolph Reed has noted, "Even il-
liberals like Pat Buchanan, John McLaughlin and Rush Limbaugh
. . . are eloquently dissenting from Herrnstein and Murray's unsa-
vory racial messages."[32] The same is true of a number of conservatives
who participated in a symposium on *The Bell Curve* in *The National
Review*.[33] The reason these conservatives do not want "to play the IQ
card," as one put it, is not that they have seen the liberal light, but
rather that they prefer the neoconservative model that traces inequality to aberrant values rather than defective genes. As far as they
are concerned, Murray had it right the first time, and his fling into biology along with Herrnstein threatens to discredit the entire conservative paradigm. Besides, the idea that this is a nation where *everyone*
can rise to the top—where people are judged by the content of their
character—is the ideological linchpin of the American myth, irrec-
oncilable with Herrnstein and Murray's conception of a Brave New
World stratified by the content of one's germ plasm.

In the final analysis, *The Bell Curve* is flourishing on its notoriety,
on its petulant flouting of ideas long considered taboo. In this sense
the publication of the book, and the wide public discussion that has
ensued, represents the triumph of the anti-PC campaign. Nevertheless, there is good reason to think that, like the earlier publications
of William Shockley, Arthur Jensen, and Herrnstein himself, *The
Bell Curve* is destined to collect layers of merciful dust on our
bookshelves.

As Myrdal noted in *An American Dilemma*, periods of racial advance have typically been followed by periods of retreat, though "not
as much ground was lost as had been won."[34] Race history, one might
say, has observed the pattern of two steps forward and one step back.
The Bell Curve represents that metaphoric step back. It leaves "America Again at the Crossroads"—the title that Myrdal chose for the concluding chapter of *An American Dilemma*. Indeed, this is the tragedy
of history—that half a century later the nation finds itself again at the
crossroads, still uncertain whether to take the road back to the benighted past, or to forge a new path leading to a historical reconciliation between the black and white citizens of this nation.

What will it take to move history forward again? Clearly, there is no return to the civil rights movement: it was the product of forces unique to that time, and it fulfilled its chief purpose, which was the passage of civil rights legislation that brought an end to Jim Crow. Indeed, this has been the quandary that has stymied the liberation movement ever since: how to develop a theory and praxis for attacking the institutionalized inequalities that constitute the enduring legacy of slavery. Given the recent ascendancy of the political right, based in large part on its cynical use of race and racism to launch an attack on the welfare state, it is difficult even to imagine a political scenario leading to the fulfillment of Martin Luther King's celebrated dream.

Yet the lesson of history is that the flame of liberation cannot be extinguished. Racial oppression has always originated at the top echelons of society, but the irrepressible forces for black liberation have always sprung from the bottom. Not from the political establishment—its leaders, the political parties, or the vaunted institutions of American democracy. Not from white liberals who have too often equivocated and temporized, offering little more than a kinder and gentler version of the racial status quo. Certainly not from some armchair theorist or policy maven who has lit on some hitherto elusive truth. Not even from the civil rights establishment that, despite valiant efforts, must settle for meager concessions extracted from white power structures.

To be sure, democratic institutions, liberals, scholars, and civil rights organizations may again serve as constructive agents for change, as they have in the past. However, the paramount truth is that this nation has never had the political will to address the legacy of slavery until forced by events to do so. As in the past, the catalyst for change will be "the mounting pressure" that emanates from those segments of black society that have little reason to acquiesce in the racial status quo. It has yet to be seen exactly what form resistance and protest will take. However, we can take comfort from Lerone Bennett's astute observation: "There has been . . . a Negro revolt in every decade of this century. Each revolt failed, only to emerge in the next decade on a higher level of development."[35]

Our nation has chosen to canonize the Martin Luther King who, in his celebrated "I Have a Dream" oration, projected a racial nirvana in some indefinite future. But let us also remember the King who in the same speech said: "The whirlwinds of revolt will continue to shake the foundations of our nation until the bright day of justice emerges."[36]

Notes

Prologue

1. Thomas S. Kuhn, *The Structure of Scientific Revolutions* (Chicago: University of Chicago Press, 1985).

2. Stokely Carmichael and Charles V. Hamilton, *Black Power: The Politics of Liberation in America* (New York: Vintage Books, 1967), pp. 1–4.

3. Robert Blauner, *Racial Oppression in America* (New York: Harper & Row, 1972).

4. Nathan Glazer and Daniel Patrick Moynihan, *Beyond the Melting Pot*, 2d ed. (Cambridge, Mass.: M.I.T. Press, 1970; original edition 1963).

5. Daniel Patrick Moynihan, "The Negro Family: The Case for National Action," in *The Moynihan Report and the Politics of Controversy*, ed. Lee Rainwater and William L. Yancey (Cambridge, Mass.: M.I.T. Press, 1967), p. 47.

6. See Robert Merton, "Insiders and Outsiders: A Chapter in the Sociology of Knowledge," *American Journal of Sociology* 78 (1972): 9–47.

7. I single out Glazer in the discussion that follows because he wrote the chapters on blacks, Puerto Ricans, Italians, and Jews, while Moynihan wrote the chapter on the Irish; Glazer and Moynihan, *Beyond the Melting Pot*, 2d ed., p. vii.

8. Indeed, in an autobiographical essay Glazer reveals that his original conception for *Beyond the Melting Pot* was "to recruit a number of persons who had experience as members of an ethnic group and knew it from the inside"; "From Socialism to Sociology," in *Authors of Their Own Lives*,

ed. Bennett M. Berger (Berkeley: University of California Press, 1990), p. 204.

9. Nathan Glazer and Daniel Patrick Moynihan, *Beyond the Melting Pot*, 2d ed., p. 53. Actually, Glazer was expressing a viewpoint that was practically an article of faith in sociology for several decades. Robert Park and his followers at the Chicago School of Sociology embraced Franz Boas's theory about the absence of African survivals among blacks in America, and attributed the "backward" life-style of blacks to "cultural lag." In *The Myth of the Negro Past* (New York: Harper & Row, 1941), Melville Herskovitz argued that there were many survivals of African culture, and that these pervaded black social and cultural patterns. This conclusion, however, was aggressively challenged by E. Franklin Frazier and other Chicago sociologists. In *An American Dilemma* Gunnar Myrdal wrote that the Negro is "an exaggerated American" and that "in practically all its divergences, American Negro culture is not something independent of general American culture. It is a distorted development", or a pathological condition, of the general American culture"; Gunnar Myrdal, *An American Dilemma: The Negro Problem and Modern Democracy* (New York: Harper & Row, 1944), p. 928. For an analysis of the entire issue, see Robert Blauner, *Racial Oppression in America*, chapter 4.

10. "As the old culture fell away—and it did rapidly enough—a new one, shaped by the distinctive experiences of life in America, was formed and a new identity was created. Italian-Americans might share precious little with Italians in Italy, but in America they were a distinctive group that maintained itself, was identifiable, and gave something to those who were identified with it." *Beyond the Melting Pot*, p. xxxiii.

11. Ibid., pp. 88–89.

12. Oscar Handlin, "All Colors, All Creeds, All Nationalities, All New Yorkers," *New York Times Book Review*, September 22, 1963, p. 3.

13. Glazer and Moynihan, *Beyond the Melting Pot*, p. 33.

14. Ibid., pp. 33–34.

15. Ibid., p. 39.

16. Ibid., p. 53.

17. Ibid., pp. 49–50.

18. Ibid., p. 85. For a critique of the theory of Jewish mobility advanced by Glazer and others, see Stephen Steinberg, *The Ethnic Myth* (Boston: Beacon Press, 1989), chapter 3.

19. Richard Gambino, *Blood of My Blood* (Garden City, N.Y.: Anchor Books, 1975), p. 14.

20. Malcolm X, *The Autobiography of Malcolm X* (New York: Grove Press, 1964), p. 54.

Chapter 1. *An American Dilemma*

1. Gunnar Myrdal, *An American Dilemma: The Negro Problem and Modern Democracy* (New York: Harper & Row, 1944). The "monumental" designation was common even among contemporaneous writers. See, for example, Richard Wright in his introduction to *Black Metropolis,* by St. Clair Drake and Horace Cayton (New York: Harper & Row, 1945), p. xxix; W. E. B. Du Bois, "Review of *An American Dilemma,*" *Phylon* 5 (1944): 121–23; and Henry Steele Commager, "The Negro Problem in our Democracy," *The American Mercury* 60 (1945): 755. In an article in *Public Opinion Quarterly,* Leo P. Crespi begins on the following note: "There is no question but what the Swedish economist and sociologist, Gunnar Myrdal, has created a new landmark in social science with his monumental opus . . ." ("Is Gunnar Myrdal on the Right Track?" *Public Opinion Quarterly* 9 [Summer 1945]: 201).

As an example of the lavish praise that the book received upon publication, Robert Lynd called it "the most penetrating and important book on our contemporary American civilization that has been written" ("Prison for American Genius, *Saturday Review of Literature,* April 22, 1944, p. 5). Even Oliver Cox, Myrdal's harshest critic, conceded that "as a source of information and brilliant interpretation of information on race relations in the United States, it is probably unsurpassed"; *Caste, Class, and Race* (1948; reprint, New York: Monthly Review Press, 1959), p. 509.

2. David W. Southern, *Gunnar Myrdal and Black-White Relations* (Baton Rouge: University of Louisiana Press, 1987), pp. 14–15, and Walter Jackson, *Gunnar Myrdal and America's Conscience* (Chapel Hill, N.C.: University of North Carolina Press, 1990), p. 34. Southern's estimates are in 1986 dollars; my figures factor in subsequent inflation.

3. A year after its publication *An American Dilemma* had already gone through four printings; E. Franklin Frazier, review of *An American Dilemma, American Journal of Sociology* 50 (1945): 555. *An American Dilemma* ultimately went back to press thirty times in hardcover and paperback, including a twentieth-anniversary edition, and sold in the neighborhood of 100,000 copies; Victor S. Navasky, "In Cold Print: American Dilemmas," *New York Times Book Review,* May 18, 1975, p. 2.

4. Some indication of the book's enduring reputation can be gleaned from *The Social Sciences Citation Index* (Philadelphia: Institute for Scientific Information). The following results obtain: 1956–60: 212; 1961–65: 212; 1966–70: 300; 1971–75: 255; 1976–80: 216; 1981–85: 216; 1986–90: 215.

5. Jackson, *Gunnar Myrdal and America's Conscience,* p. xi.

6. John H. Stanfield, *Philanthropy and Jim Crow in American Social Science* (Westport, Conn.: Greenwood Press, 1985), p. 142.

7. Jackson, *Gunnar Myrdal and America's Conscience*, p. 35.

8. Ibid., p. 20.

9. Ibid., p. 17; emphasis added.

10. Quoted in ibid., p. 21.

11. Harvey Sitkoff, *A New Deal for Blacks* (New York: Oxford University Press, 1978), p. 37.

12. Quoted in ibid., p. 91.

13. Ibid., p. 208.

14. *New York Times*, "'Negro' with a Capital 'N'," March 7, 1930, p. 22.

15. Quoted in Jackson, *Gunnar Myrdal and America's Conscience*, p. 22. In the preface to *An American Dilemma*, Keppel gives Baker credit for proposing the study (p. xlviii).

16. Frederick Keppel, foreword to *An American Dilemma*, p. xlviii.

17. Thomas Kessner, *Fiorello H. La Guardia* (New York: McGraw-Hill, 1989), p. 371.

18. Anthony Platt, *E. Franklin Frazier Reconsidered* (New Brunswick, N.J.: Rutgers University Press), p. 104.

19. Ibid., p. 106.

20. E. Franklin Frazier, *The Negro in Harlem: A Report on Social and Economic Conditions Responsible for the Outbreak of March 19, 1935* (New York: Arno Press, 1968), p. 7.

21. Ibid., p. 122.

22. Ibid., pp. 122–23.

23. Ibid., p. 129.

24. Myrdal, *An American Dilemma*, p. 91.

25. Morton was no crackpot. When he died in 1851, the *New York Tribune* wrote that "probably no scientific man in America enjoyed a higher reputation among scholars throughout the world"; quoted in Stephen Jay Gould, *The Mismeasure of Man* (New York: W. W. Norton, 1981), p. 51.

26. Quoted in Gould, *The Mismeasure of Man*, p. 69.

27. Ibid., p. 74.

28. *Encyclopaedia Britannica* (1910), vol. 19, pp. 344–45.

29. Ibid., p. 345.

30. Thomas Kuhn, *The Structure of Scientific Revolutions* (Chicago: University of Chicago Press, 1985), p. 78.

31. Thomas F. Gossett, *Race: The History of an Idea in America* (New York: Schocken, 1965), p. 77.

32. George M. Fredrickson, *The Black Image in the White Mind* (New

York: Harper Torchbooks, 1971), p. 78. Nott, incidentally, referred to his field of study as "niggerology."

33. Gould, *The Mismeasure of Man*, pp. 98–99.

34. Ibid., p. 25.

35. Gossett, *Race: The History of an Idea in America*, p. 364.

36. Ibid., p. 368.

37. *Encyclopaedia of the Social Sciences*, Edwin R. A. Seligman, ed., 12 vols. (New York: Macmillan, 1933), 11:33.

38. Ibid.

39. Sitkoff, *A New Deal for Blacks*, pp. 194–95.

40. Stanfield, *Philanthropy and Jim Crow in American Social Science*, p. 139.

41. Jackson, *Gunnar Myrdal and America's Conscience*, p. 34. Myrdal's letter is dated October 7, 1937.

42. Alvin Ward Gouldner, *The Coming Crisis of Western Sociology* (New York: Basic Books, 1970), p. 28.

43. Edward Carr, *What Is History?* (New York: Vintage Books, 1961), p. 26.

44. The selection process is described in detail in Stanfield, *Philanthropy and Jim Crow in American Social Science*, pp. 139–52, and by Jackson, *Gunnar Myrdal and America's Conscience*, chapter 1.

45. Stanfield, *Philanthropy and Jim Crow in American Social Science*, p. 142.

46. Jackson, *Gunnar Myrdal and America's Conscience*, pp. 59–60.

47. Ibid., pp. 33–34.

48. Quoted in Jackson, *Gunnar Myrdal and America's Conscience*, p. 70.

49. Ibid., p. 69.

50. Stanfield, *Philanthropy and Jim Crow in American Social Science*, p. 150. Keppel expresses the same sentiment in his foreword to *An American Dilemma*. He notes that the "proper function" of the foundation is "to make the facts available and let them speak for themselves," adding that it is not the role of the foundation to "instruct the public as to what to do about them" (p. xlvii).

51. Stanfield, *Philanthropy and Jim Crow in American Social Science*, p. 151. In his review E. Franklin Frazier admits that he was initially skeptical about the decision to bring in a foreign scholar to direct the Carnegie study, and commends Myrdal for not ignoring the work of other scholars. "In fact," Frazier adds, "the success of the project was due to the fact that he could utilize the work of other scholars and secure their co-operation in the present study"; Frazier, review of *An American Dilemma*, p. 557.

52. Part of Myrdal's purpose in dispensing this academic patronage was to curry favor in American social science circles. According to David Southern, "he hired some collaborators primarily to soothe bruised egos or to increase the chances for a positive reception of his study"; *Gunnar Myrdal and Black-White Relations*, p. 16.

53. John Daniels, *In Freedom's Birthplace: A Study of the Boston Negroes* (1914; Reprint, New York: Negro Universities Press, 1968); p. 2.

54. Ibid., p. 412; emphasis added.

55. Myrdal, *An American Dilemma*, p. 75.

56. Myrdal, *An American Dilemma*, pp. 558–59.

57. Herbert Aptheker, *The Negro People in America: A Critique of Gunnar Myrdal's* An American Dilemma (New York: International Publishers, 1946), p. 19.

58. Myrdal, *An American Dilemma*, p. lxxi.

59. Ibid., p. lxxii.

60. Ibid., emphasis added.

61. Gerald W. Johnson, "Problem of the American Negro," *New York Herald Tribune Weekly Book Review*, August 13, 1944, p. 2.

62. Myrdal, *An American Dilemma*, p. 1021. Here Myrdal engages in the same teleological thinking that he criticized in the works of Sumner and Park (ibid., pp. 1048–50).

63. Ibid., p. 109; emphasis in original.

64. Ibid., p. 92.

65. Oliver Cox, "*An American Dilemma*: A Mystical Approach to the Study of Race Relations," in Cox, *Caste, Class, and Race*, p. 531.

66. Ibid., p. 535.

67. One study found that between 75 and 80 percent of the reviews on Cox's books referred to him as a Marxist. Elmer Martin, "The Sociology of Oliver C. Cox: A Systematic Inquiry" (Master's thesis, Atlanta University, 1971), cited in "The Life and Career of Oliver C. Cox," introduction to Herbert M. Hunter and Sameer Y. Abraham, eds., *Race, Class, and the World System* (New York: Monthly Review Press, 1987), p. xxxiii. Of course, Cox's "bias" stands in contrast to scholars like Myrdal whose unabashed anti-Marxism was construed, not as bias, but as proof of their commitment to objective social science.

68. Cox, "*An American Dilemma*: A Mystical Approach to the Study of Race Relations," in Cox, *Caste, Class, and Race*, p. 509.

69. Ibid., p. 510.

70. Myrdal's exact words are: "In this sense the Negro problem is not only America's greatest failure but also America's incomparably great opportunity for the future" (p. 1021).

71. Peter John Kellogg, *Northern Liberals and Black America: A History of White Attitudes, 1936–1952* (Ph.D. diss., Northwestern University; Ann Arbor: University Microfilms, 1971), p. 166.

72. Crespi, "Is Gunnar Myrdal on the Right Track?" *Public Opinion Quarterly* 9 (Summer 1945): 205.

73. Jackson, *Gunnar Myrdal and America's Conscience*, pp. 250–52; and Southern, *Gunnar Myrdal and Black-White Relations*, pp. 84–85 and 157–59.

74. Myrdal was not alone in his failure to confront the issue of civil rights, as Stanford M. Lyman shows in his incisive article "Race Relations as Social Process: Sociology's Resistance to a Civil Rights Orientation," in *Racism in America*, eds. Herbert Hill and James E. Jones (Madison, Wis.: University of Wisconsin Press, 1993), pp. 370–401.

75. See Robert L. Zangrando, *The NAACP Crusade Against Lynching, 1909–1950* (Philadelphia: Temple University Press, 1980).

76. Rayford W. Logan, ed., *What the Negro Wants* (1944; Reprint, New York: Agathon Press, 1969), pp. ii–iii.

77. Rayford W. Logan, "The Negro Wants First-Class Citizenship," in ibid., p. 16.

78. A. Philip Randolph, "March on Washington Movement Presents Program for the Negro," in ibid., pp. 133–62.

79. Langston Hughes, "My America," in ibid., p. 307.

80. Leslie Pinckney Hill, "What the Negro Wants and How to Get It: The Inward Power of the Masses," in ibid., p. 89.

81. Mary McLeod Bethune, "'Certain Unalienable Rights,'" in ibid., pp. 248–58.

82. Frederick D. Patterson, "The Negro Wants Full Participation in the American Democracy," in ibid., p. 265.

Chapter 2. Paradigm Crisis

1. Herbert Butterfield, *The Origins of Modern Science, 1300–1800,* quoted in Thomas S. Kuhn, *The Structure of Scientific Revolutions* (Chicago: University of Chicago Press, 1985), p. 85.

2. Kuhn, *The Structure of Scientific Revolutions*, p. 77.

3. W. E. B. Du Bois, *Dusk of Dawn* (New York: Schocken, 1968; originally published 1940), p. 131.

4. F. P. Keppel, foreword to Gunnar Myrdal, *An American Dilemma: The Negro Problem and Modern Democracy* (New York: Harper & Row, 1944), p. xlvii.

5. Henry Steele Commager, "The Negro Problem in Our Democracy," *American Mercury* (June 1945): 755; emphasis added.

6. Ibid.

7. Ibid., p. 756.

8. Frank Tannenbaum, *Slave and Citizen* (New York: Knopf, 1947).

9. Frank Tannenbaum, review of *An American Dilemma, Political Science Quarterly* 59 (September 1944): 334.

10. Ibid., p. 335.

11. Ibid., p. 338.

12. Ibid., p. 340.

13. Myrdal, *An American Dilemma*, p. 30.

14. Peter John Kellogg, *Northern Liberals and Black America: A History of White Attitudes, 1936–1952* (Ph.D. diss., Northwestern University; Ann Arbor: University Microfilms, 1971), p. 166.

15. Walter Jackson, *Gunnar Myrdal and America's Conscience* (Chapel Hill, N.C.: University of North Carolina Press, 1990), p. 122.

16. Ralph J. Bunche, "A Critical Analysis of the Tactics and Programs of Minority Groups," *Journal of Negro Education* 4 (1935): 314–15.

17. Ibid., p. 320.

18. C. L. R. James, "The Revolutionary Answer to the Negro Problem in the U.S.," (1948), reprinted in *The C. L. R. James Reader*, ed. Anna Grimshaw (New York: Blackwell, 1992), pp. 182–89.

19. See Mark Naison, *Communists in Harlem during the Depression* (Urbana: University of Illinois Press, 1983); and Robin D. G. Kelley, *Hammer and Hoe: Alabama Communists during the Great Depression* (Chapel Hill, N.C.: University of North Carolina Press, 1990).

20. See, for example, Ralph Ellison, *Invisible Man* (New York: Vintage Books, 1980; originally published 1952); and Harold Cruse, *The Crisis of the Negro Intellectual* (New York: Morrow, 1967). See also Julius Jacobson, "The Communist Past: Myth and Reality," *New Politics* 5 (Winter 1995): 125–67.

21. Kellogg, *Northern Liberals and Black America*, p. 9.

22. Ibid., p. 431.

23. Ibid., p. 436.

24. Stanford M. Lyman, "Race Relations as Social Process: Sociology's Resistance to a Civil Rights Orientation," in *Racism in America*, ed. Herbert Hill and James E. Jones (Madison, Wis.: University of Wisconsin Press, 1993), p. 394.

25. Ibid., p. 397.

26. James O. Young, *Black Writers of the Thirties* (Baton Rouge: Louisiana State University Press, 1973), pp. 37–38.

27. Paula F. Pfeffer, *A. Philip Randolph: Pioneer of the Civil Rights Movement* (Baton Rouge: University of Louisiana Press, 1990), p. 6.

28. Quoted in Young, *Black Writers of the Thirties*, p. 65.

29. Ibid., p. 71.

30. Pfeffer, A. *Philip Randolph*, p. 58.

31. Ibid., p. 66.

32. A. Philip Randolph, "March on Washington Movement Presents Program for the Negro," in *What the Negro Wants*, ed. Rayford Logan (New York: Agathon Press, 1969), p. 154.

33. Pfeffer, A. *Philip Randolph*, p. 57.

34. Randolph's account of this meeting and the ensuing negotiations leading up to the issuance of Roosevelt's executive order can be found in Jervis Anderson's biography, A. *Philip Randolph* (New York: Harcourt Brace Jovanovich, 1972), pp. 256–61.

35. Pfeffer, A. *Philip Randolph*, pp. 48–49.

36. Frances Fox Piven and Richard A. Cloward, *Poor People's Movements* (New York: Vintage Books, 1979), p. 205.

37. Harold M. Baron, "The Demand for Black Labor," *Radical America* (March–April 1971): 3.

38. Du Bois, *Dusk of Dawn*, p. 131.

39. Kuhn, *Structure of Scientific Revolutions*, p. 92.

40. Everett C. Hughes, "Race Relations and the Sociological Imagination," *American Sociological Review* 28 (December 1963): 879.

41. Ibid., p. 889.

42. For an analysis of "the politics of method" in the field of race relations, see John H. Stanfield II and Rutledge M. Dennis, eds., *Race and Ethnicity in Research Methods* (Newbury Park, Calif.: Sage Publications, 1993).

43. Hughes, "Race Relations and the Sociological Imagination," p. 889.

44. James, "The Revolutionary Answer to the Negro Problem in the U.S.," pp. 188–89.

45. Ernest Q. Campbell, "Moral Discomfort and Racial Segregation— An Examination of the Myrdal Hypothesis," *Social Forces* 39 (1961): 233.

46. Lewis M. Killian and Charles M. Grigg, "Rank Orders of Discrimination of Negroes and Whites in a Southern City," *Social Forces* 39 (1961): 235–39.

47. Nahum Z. Medalia, "Myrdal's Assumptions on Race Relations: A Conceptual Commentary," *Social Forces* (1962): 223.

48. Frank Westie, "The American Dilemma: An Empirical Test," *American Sociological Review* 30 (1965): 527–38.

49. Carl N. Degler, "The Negro in America: Where Myrdal Went Wrong," *New York Times Magazine*, December 7, 1959, pp. 64 ff.

50. Ibid., p. 152.

51. Ibid.

52. Langston Hughes, "Warning," in *The Collected Poems of Langston Hughes*, ed. Arnold Rampersad and David Roessel (New York: Knopf, 1994), p. 365.

53. Quoted in Degler, "The Negro in America: Where Myrdal Went Wrong," p. 153.

54. James, "The Revolutionary Answer to the Negro Problem in the U.S.," p. 187.

55. Degler, "The Negro in America: Where Myrdal Went Wrong," p. 153.

56. Ibid., pp. 158, 159.

57. Myrdal is quoted in "Liberalism and the Negro: A Round-Table Discussion," *Commentary* 37 (March 1964): p. 30; emphasis added.

58. For recent critiques of *An American Dilemma*, see Benjamin Ringer, *We the People and Others* (London: Tavistock, 1983); Stanford M. Lyman, *The Black American in Sociological Thought: A Failure of Perspective* (New York: Capricorn Books, 1972); and Michael W. Hughey, "Americanism and Its Discontents: Protestantism, Nativism, and Political Heresy in America," *Journal of Politics, Culture and Society* 5 (1992): 533–49.

Chapter 3. The 1960s and the Scholarship of Confrontation

1. The hiatus in racial protest during the decade following the Second World War was reflected in a similar lapse of interest in race in the academy. Thomas Pettigrew recounts that when he was a graduate student in Harvard's Social Relations Department in 1952, his interest in race relations was regarded with skepticism by his fellow doctoral students: "They advised me to choose another specialty, as there were few jobs, little status, and virtually no research funds in race relations." He adds that this all changed in 1954 after the Supreme Court issued its ruling in *Brown v. Board of Education of Topeka, Kansas*. Thomas F. Pettigrew, "How Events Shape Theoretical Frames: A Personal Statement," in *A History of Race Relations Research: First-Generation Recollections*, ed. John H. Stanfield II, (Newbury Park, Calif.: Sage Publications, 1993), p. 161.

2. Thomas F. Pettigrew, *The Sociology of Race Relations* (New York: Free Press, 1980), p. 133. The "exemplar" work representing this paradigm was Gordon Allport's *The Nature of Prejudice* (Reading, Mass.: Addison-Wesley, 1979; originally published 1954).

3. "Transcript of the American Academy Conference on the Negro American—May 14–15, 1965," in "The Negro American—2," *Daedalus* 95, no. 1 (Winter 1966): 312.

4. "Tips," *Publishers Weekly* 189 (January 24, 1966); and private corre-

spondence with Barney Rossett who signed *The Autobiography of Malcolm X* for Grove Press.

5. Mel Watkins, "The Black Revolution in Books," *New York Times Book Review*, August 10, 1969, pp. 8 ff.

6. John Tebbel, *A History of Book Publishing in the United States* (New York: R. R. Bowker, 1981), p. 730.

7. Ibid. Also see Morris Dickstein, *Gates of Eden: American Culture in the Sixties* (New York: Penguin Books, 1977), chapter 6.

8. Robert Conot, *Rivers of Blood, Years of Darkness* (Toronto: Bantam, 1967).

9. John Hersey, *The Algiers Motel Incident* (New York: Bantam, 1968).

10. Quoted in Charles E. Silberman, *Crisis in Black and White* (New York: Random House, 1964), p. 4.

11. Ibid., pp. 9–10.

12. Ibid., p. 10.

13. Ibid.

14. Ibid., p. 237.

15. The jacket of the paperback edition contained the following blurb from Malcolm X: "There can be no real progress in America's crucial race relations until the basic historic ingredients that created this explosive race problem are pointed out in blunt terms that both sides can see and understand. *Crisis in Black and White* goes straight to the historic roots of the problem. Mr. Silberman's swordlike pen scientifically vindicates the innocent, while indicting only the guilty who refuse to face up to the facts and atone while there is still time. If the 'WARNING' contained in this book goes unheeded . . . then America is indeed beyond hope, and all is lost."

16. Kenneth B. Clark, *Dark Ghetto* (New York: Harper & Row, 1965), p. 107.

17. Ibid., p. 131.

18. Jonathan Kozol, *Death at an Early Age* (Boston: Houghton Mifflin, 1967).

19. William H. Grier and Price M. Cobbs, *Black Rage* (New York: Bantam, 1968).

20. Watkins, "The Black Revolution in Books," p. 8.

21. Private correspondence with Charles Hamilton.

22. Stokely Carmichael and Charles V. Hamilton, *Black Power: The Politics of Liberation in America* (New York: Vintage Books, 1967), p. 4.

23. Ibid.

24. Malcolm X, *The Autobiography of Malcolm X* (New York: Grove Press, 1964), p. 362; emphasis in original.

25. Tom Wicker, introduction to the *Report of the National Advisory Commission on Civil Disorders* (Washington, D.C.: U.S. Government Printing Office, 1968), p. v. Another critic of the Commission complained that "President Johnson chose eleven members for his National Advisory Commission on Civil Disorders, a collection remarkable chiefly for its predictable moderation"; Andrew Kopkind, "White on Black: The Riot Commission and the Rhetoric of Reform," reprinted in *The Politics of Riot Commissions, 1917–1970*, ed. Anthony Platt (New York: Macmillan, 1971), p. 380.

26. Andrew Kopkind, "White on Black: The Riot Commission and the Rhetoric of Reform," p. 378.

27. Anthony Platt, "The Politics of Riot Commissions, 1917–1970: An Overview," in *The Politics of Riot Commissions, 1917–1970*, ed. Anthony Platt (New York: Macmillan, 1971), pp. 33–35.

28. *Report of the National Advisory Commission on Civil Disorders*, p. 110.

29. Ibid., p. 10.

30. The report was published only months before Nixon was elected to the presidency, on the basis of a "Southern strategy" that produced electoral majorities in ten of the eleven southern states. Partly for this reason, as Gary Orfield has pointed out, "no major new efforts . . . were launched after the report was published in the spring of 1968"; "Separate Societies: Have the Kerner Warnings Come True?" in *Quiet Riots*, ed. Fred R. Harris and Roger W. Wilkins (New York: Pantheon, 1988), p. 101.

31. Robert Blauner, *Racial Oppression in America* (New York: Harper & Row, 1972), p. 102. In another passage, however, Blauner concedes that compared to the McCone Commission that studied the Watts riot, the Kerner Report "is a more solid and better balanced work" (p. 214).

32. Kopkind, "White on Black: The Riot Commission and the Rhetoric of Reform," p. 380. A similar point was made by a group of student activists who collaborated on a study of institutional racism: "The recommendations are directed at ghetto conditions and *not* at the white structures and practices that are responsible for those conditions"; Louis L. Knowles and Kenneth Prewitt, eds., *Institutional Racism in America* (Englewood Cliffs, N.J.: Prentice-Hall, 1969), p. 3.

33. Gary T. Marx, "A Document with a Difference," *Trans-action* 6 (September 1968): 56–58; quoted in Platt, *The Politics of Riot Commissions*, p. 341.

34. Several of these seasoned radicals were quick to edit anthologies that sought to bring together the "new" critical writing on race. For example: Francis L. Broderick and August Meier, *Negro Protest Thought in the Twen-*

tieth Century (New York: Bobbs-Merrill, 1965); Arthur Max Ross and Herbert Hill, *Employment, Race and Poverty* (New York: Harcourt, Brace & World, 1967); Julius Jacobson, *The Negro and the American Labor Movement* (Garden City, N.Y.: Anchor Books, 1968).

35. One of the first was Gary Marx, an erstwhile activist in CORE and a graduate student in sociology at the University of California at Berkeley. In 1963 he published an article in the *American Sociological Review* entitled "Occupational Benefits to Whites from the Subordination of Negroes," followed by *Protest and Prejudice* (New York: Harper & Row, 1967), which contained some of the first systematic analysis of rank-and-file support of black militancy. It was not until 1969 and 1970, however, that the scholarship of confrontation began to gain momentum.

36. Among the noteworthy early studies of the Black Muslims are C. Eric Lincoln, *The Black Muslims in America* (Boston: Beacon Press, 1961); and E. U. Essien-Udom, *Black Nationalism: The Search for an Identity in America* (Chicago: University of Chicago Press, 1962); Theodore Draper, *The Rediscovery of Black Nationalism* (New York: Viking, 1970). Also August Meier and Elliott Rudwick, eds., *Black Nationalism in America* (Indianapolis and New York: Bobbs-Merrill, 1970).

37. The Moynihan Report and the ensuing controversy are reproduced in a useful volume, *The Moynihan Report and the Politics of Controversy*, ed. Lee Rainwater and William L. Yancey (Cambridge, Mass.: M.I.T. Press, 1967). Prominent among the subsequent studies of the black family are Herbert Gutman, *The Black Family in Slavery and Freedom* (New York: Pantheon, 1976); Elliot Liebow, *Tally's Corner* (Boston: Little, Brown, 1967); and Carol Stack, *All Our Kin* (New York: Harper & Row, 1974).

38. Carmichael and Hamilton, *Black Power: The Politics of Liberation in America*; Joyce Ladner, "What 'Black Power' Means to Negroes in Mississippi," *Trans-action* 5 (November 1967); Floyd B. Barbour, ed., *The Black Power Revolt: A Collection of Essays* (Boston: Porter Sargent Publishers, 1968); Julius Lester, *Look Out, Whitey, Black Power's Gon' Get Your Mama* (New York: Dial Press, 1968); Joel D. Aberback and Jack L. Walker, "The Meanings of Black Power: A Comparison of White and Black Interpretations of a Political Slogan," *American Political Science Review* 64 (June 1970).

39. *Report of the National Advisory Commission on Civil Disorders* (1968); Robert M. Fogelson and Robert B. Hill, "Who Riots? A Study of Participation in the 1967 Riots," in *Supplemental Studies for the National Advisory Commission on Civil Disorders* (New York: Praeger, 1968); Robert M. Fogelson, "From Resentment to Confrontation: The Police, the Negroes, and the Outbreak of the Nineteen-Sixties Riots," *Political Science Quarterly* 83 (June 1968); Robert Blauner, "Internal Colonialism and Ghetto Revolt,"

234   **Notes**

Social Problems 16 (Spring 1969); Jerome H. Skolnick, *The Politics of Protest*, Report of the Task Force on Violent Aspects of Protest and Confrontation of the National Commission on the Causes and Prevention of Violence (New York: Simon & Schuster, 1969). See also Robert Fogelson, *Violence as Protest* (Garden City, N.Y.: Doubleday, 1971).

40. For a critique of the literature on school desegregation, see Jennifer L. Hochschild, *The New American Dilemma: Liberal Democracy and School Desegregation* (New Haven: Yale University Press, 1984).

41. W. E. B. Du Bois, *Black Reconstruction* (New York: Harcourt, Brace, 1935), Chapter 17.

42. Stanley Elkins, *Slavery: A Problem in American Institutional and Intellectual Life* (Chicago: University of Chicago Press, 1959). As George Fredrickson points out, the book was published without fanfare, but Elkins's analogy between a slave plantation and a Nazi concentration camp in terms of their devastating psychological effects on their victims evoked furious controversy in the 1960s, especially after it was cited in support of Daniel Patrick Moynihan's thesis concerning the disintegration of the black family; see George M. Fredrickson, *The Arrogance of Race* (Hanover, N.H.: Wesleyan University Press, 1988), p. 113.

Also noteworthy is a 1950 study by Oscar and Mary Handlin, "Origins of the Southern Labor System," *William and Mary Quarterly* 7 (1950): 199–222; reprinted in Oscar Handlin, *Race and Nationality in American Life* (Boston: Atlantic Monthly Press, 1957), Chapter 1.

43. Winthrop D. Jordan, *White Over Black: American Attitudes Toward the Negro, 1550–1812* (Chapel Hill, N.C.: University of North Carolina Press, 1968).

44. Dan T. Carter, *Scottsboro: A Tragedy of the American South* (Baton Rouge: Louisiana State University Press, 1979); Carl N. Degler, *Neither Black Nor White: Slavery and Race Relations in Brazil* (Madison, Wis.: University of Wisconsin Press); Louis R. Harlan, *Booker T. Washington: The Making of a Black Leader, 1856–1901* (New York: Oxford University Press, 1972); Robert William Fogel and Stanley L. Engerman, *Time on the Cross: The Economics of American Negro Slavery* (Boston: Little, Brown, 1974); Eugene Genovese, *Roll, Jordan, Roll: The World the Slaves Made* (New York: Vintage, 1976); David Brion Davis, *The Problem of Slavery in the Age of Revolution, 1770–1823* (Ithaca, N.Y.: Cornell University Press, 1975); Barry W. Higman, *Slave Population and the Economy in Jamaica, 1807–1834* (Cambridge: Cambridge University Press, 1976).

45. Nathan I. Huggins, "The Deforming Mirror of Truth: Slavery and the Master Narrative of American History," *Radical History Review* 49 (1991): 29. George Fredrickson strikes a similar refrain: "Whatever else the

civil rights movement of the 1960s may have accomplished or failed to accomplish, it at least liberated Afro-Americans from historical invisibility"; *The Arrogance of Race,* p. 112.

46. Eric Foner, *Reconstruction: America's Unfinished Revolution, 1863–1877* (New York: Harper & Row, 1988), p. xxii.

47. Du Bois, *Black Reconstruction,* p. 727.

48. Irving Howe, "The Negro Revolution," *Dissent* (Summer 1963): 214. Howe continued: "Under these circumstances equality of opportunity (even if we had it!) can at best be a way of avoiding a *further* growth in the distance between white and Negro living conditions; but it will not remove that distance itself. For that, the Negro must be given special help, special privileges, if you will—in jobs, in the unions, in the universities. And these forms of help should remain in effect until the Negroes themselves declare the time has come when they are no longer needed."

49. Robert Blauner, "Race and Radicalism in My Life and Work," in *A History of Race Relations Research,* ed. John H. Stanfield II, p. 15.

50. Thomas S. Kuhn, *The Structure of Scientific Revolutions* (Chicago: University of Chicago Press, 1985), p. 157.

51. A crude indicator of a book's influence is how often it is cited in the social science literature. According to the *Social Sciences Citation Index* (Philadelphia: Institute for Scientific Information), *Racial Oppression in America* has been cited 228 times since its publication in 1972. The breakdown is as follows: 1971–75: 21; 1976–80: 66; 1981–85: 58; 1986–90: 55; 1991–93: 28. Published as a "college edition," the book sold between 50,000 and 60,000 copies. In addition, two of the book's key essays—"Colonized and Immigrant Minorities" and "Internal Colonialism and Ghetto Revolt"—have been reprinted in a number of popular anthologies.

52. Blauner, *Racial Oppression in America,* p. viii.

53. Blauner specifically mentions *The Autobiography of Malcolm X* and Harold Cruse's *The Crisis of the Negro Intellectual;* ibid., p. 5.

54. Blauner, "Race and Radicalism in My Life and Work," p. 10.

55. Ibid., p. 11.

56. Blauner, *Racial Oppression in America,* p. 2.

57. Ibid.

58. Ibid.

59. Ibid., p. 3.

60. Ibid., p. 7.

61. Ibid., p. 2.

62. Ibid.

63. Ibid., p. 9.

64. Ibid., p. 10.

65. Ibid., p. 2; emphasis in original.

66. Ibid., p. 62.

67. At the outset of his essay on "Internal Colonialism and Ghetto Revolt," Blauner writes that as early as 1962 Harold Cruse characterized race relations in this country as *domestic colonialism*, though his ideas were generally ignored until the 1967 publication of *The Crisis of the Negro Intellectual* (New York: Morrow, 1967). In *Black Power* Carmichael and Hamilton place the colonial analogy at the center of their analysis, and in *Black Awakening in Capitalist America* (Garden City, N.Y.: Doubleday, 1969), Robert Allen also interpreted ghetto revolts in terms of internal colonialism.

68. This adoption, in part, reflected the influence of Franz Fanon's *Wretched of the Earth*, originally published in 1961; the English translation first became available when it was published by Grove Press in 1963. Its impact reached front-line activists as well as intellectuals. Dan Watts of the black magazine *Liberator* told journalists during the hot summer of 1967: "You'd better get this book. Every brother on a rooftop can quote Fanon"; quoted in Allen J. Matusow, *The Unraveling of America: A History of Liberalism in the 1960s* (New York: Harper Torchbacks, 1986), p. 358. In a speech at Columbia University four days before his assassination in 1964, Malcolm X said: "It is incorrect to classify the revolt of the Negro as simply a racial conflict of black against white. Rather, we are seeing today a global rebellion of the oppressed against the oppressor."

69. For a more recent iteration of this position, see Barton Myers, "Minority Group: An Ideological Formation," *Social Problems* 32 (October 1984): 1–15.

70. Gans's original essay, "Escaping from Poverty: A Comparison of the Immigrant and Black Experience," is reprinted in Herbert Gans, *People, Plans, and Policies* (New York: Columbia University Press, 1991), Chapter 18.

71. Harold Cruse, *Plural But Equal* (New York: William Morrow, 1987).

72. Nathan Glazer, "Blacks and Ethnic Groups: The Difference and the Political Difference It Makes," originally published in 1981 and reprinted in Nathan Glazer, *Ethnic Dilemmas* (Cambridge, Mass.: Harvard University Press, 1983), pp. 75–76.

73. Ibid., p. 81.

74. Ibid., p. 80.

75. Ibid., p. 82.

76. See, for example, Douglas S. Massey, *American Apartheid* (Cambridge, Mass.: Harvard University Press, 1993).

77. Glazer, "Blacks and Ethnic Groups: The Difference and the Political Difference It Makes," pp. 83–88.

78. Ibid., p. 85; emphasis added.

79. Ibid., p. 86.

80. Ibid., p. 89.

81. Ibid.

82. Ibid., p. 90; emphasis added. It is worth noting that European theorists, no doubt reflecting their familiarity with European colonialism and the caste-like divisions that rend "plural societies," have been far less prone to economic reductionism and more favorably disposed to the colonial model. See, for example, John Rex, *Race Relations in Sociological Theory* (New York: Schocken, 1970).

83. Glazer, "Blacks and Ethnic Groups: The Difference and the Political Difference It Makes," pp. 92–93.

Chapter 4. Backlash Outside and Inside the University

1. Allen J. Matusow, *The Unraveling of America: A History of Liberalism in the 1960s* (New York: Harper Torchbacks, 1986), p. 139.

2. According to the Edsalls, the most important long-range effect of the Wallace phenomenon was on Republican strategy: "Wallace brought into mainstream presidential politics a new political symbol, a vilified Democratic establishment that replaced as an enemy of lower-income voters the Republican establishment of corporate America and the rich"; Thomas Byrne Edsall with Mary D. Edsall, "When the Official Subject Is Presidential Politics, Taxes, Welfare, Crime, Rights, or Values . . . the Real Subject Is RACE," *Atlantic Monthly* 269 (1991): 63. For an analysis of the consequences of the backlash for civil rights policy during this period, see Gary Orfield, "Race and the Liberal Agenda: The Loss of the Integrationist Dream, 1965–1974," in *The Politics of Social Policy in the United States*, ed. Margaret Weir, Ann Shola Orloff, and Theda Skocpol (Princeton: Princeton University Press, 1988), pp. 313–55.

3. To the Edsalls and others who blame blacks for the white backlash and the demise of the Democratic Party, Adolph Reed, Jr. and Julian Bond have a pithy rejoinder: "It is instructive . . . that the Edsalls identify race rather than racism as the pivotal issue"; "Equality: Why We Can't Wait," *The Nation* (December 9, 1991): 736. Insofar as the politics of confrontation are concerned, Piven and Cloward write: "The political truth is that blacks got what they got precisely because mass protest, by exacerbating divisions in the North/South and in big-city electoral coalitions, forced the Democratic Party to make voting-rights concessions intended to rebuild its strength in

the South and social-program concessions intended to moderate conflict in the cities"; Richard A. Cloward and Frances Fox Piven, "Race and the Democrats," *The Nation* (December 9, 1991): 740.

4. Matusow, *The Unraveling of America*, p. 458.

5. See Peter N. Carroll, *It Seemed Like Nothing Happened* (New York: Holt, Rinehart and Winston, 1982), Chapter 3.

6. Ibid., p. 40.

7. Ibid., pp. 49–55; Allen J. Matusow, *The Unraveling of America*, pp. 367–75.

8. Carroll, *It Seemed Like Nothing Happened*, p. 41. See also Richard Nixon, *The Memoirs of Richard Nixon* (New York: Grosset & Dunlap, 1978), p. 540.

9. See Nicholas Lemann, *The Promised Land* (New York: Vintage Books, 1991), pp. 202–18.

10. Quoted in Carroll, *It Seemed Like Nothing Happened*, p. 46.

11. Hugh Davis Graham, *The Civil Rights Era: Origin and Development of National Policy, 1970–1972* (New York: Oxford University Press, 1990), p. 448.

12. Herbert Roof Northrup and John Larson, *The Impact of the AT&T-EEO Consent Decree* (Philadelphia: Industrial Research Unit, Wharton School, University of Pennsylvania, 1979). p. 1.

13. Graham, *The Civil Rights Era*, p. 438.

14. Ibid., p. 438.

15. Ibid., pp. 438–39.

16. The Edsalls reach the same conclusion: "By the 1972 election Nixon was campaigning against the quota policies that his own Administration had largely engendered"; Edsall and Edsall, "When the Official Subject Is Presidential Politics, Taxes, Welfare, Crime, Rights, or Values . . . the Real Subject Is RACE," p. 66.

17. Graham, *The Civil Rights Era*, p. 447.

18. Robert R. Detlefson, *Civil Rights Under Reagan* (San Francisco: Institute for Contemporary Studies, 1991), p. 4.

19. This is grudgingly acknowledged by Robert Detlefson, who writes: "Contrary to conventional wisdom, contemporary federal affirmative action policy owes far more to the likes of John Mitchell, George Shultz (Nixon's secretary of labor) and Richard Nixon than to Lyndon Johnson, a fact that stands in sharp contrast to the typical caricatures of Johnson and Nixon one finds in contemporary political folklore"; ibid., p. 26.

20. In 1962–63 Glazer worked in the Housing and Home Finance Administration. By his own account, this experience was a major influence in his political transformation—from mild radical to mild conservative; "On

Being Deradicalized," *Commentary* 50 (October 1970): 75. Ironically, Glazer's de-radicalization was precipitated by the same event that accounted for Robert Blauner's re-radicalization: the crisis surrounding the Free Speech Movement at Berkeley that engendered schisms among its one-time liberal faculty. See Nathan Glazer, "What Happened at Berkeley," *Commentary* 39 (February 1965): 39–47; and "Berkeley," an exchange between Nathan Glazer and Philip Selznick, *Commentary* 39 (March 1965): 80–85.

21. Nathan Glazer, "Negroes and Jews: The New Challenge to Pluralism," *Commentary* (December 1964), reprinted in Nathan Glazer, *Ethnic Dilemmas* (Cambridge, Mass.: Harvard University Press, 1983), Chapter 5.

22. Daniel Patrick Moynihan, "The New Racialism," in Moynihan, *Coping: Essays on the Practice of Government* (New York: Random House, 1973), p. 205. This piece was originally a commencement address at the New School for Social Research, and was subsequently published in *The Atlantic Monthly* in August 1968. For a discussion of the defection of segments of the Jewish community on the issue of affirmative action, see Robert Weisbrot, *Freedom Bound: A History of America's Civil Rights Movement* (New York: W. W. Norton, 1989), p. 294.

23. Nathan Glazer, *Affirmative Discrimination: Ethnic Inequality and Public Policy* (New York: Basic Books, 1975).

24. Ibid., p. 221.

25. Nathan Glazer, *The Limits of Social Policy* (Cambridge, Mass.: Harvard University Press, 1988), p. 1. The book builds on an article by the same name that was published in *Commentary* in September 1971.

26. Ibid., p. 3. In a 1993 article on New York City, Glazer spelled out "the limits of social policy" even further: "The things a city can do include keeping its streets and bridges in repair, building new facilities to accommodate new needs and a shifting population, picking up the garbage, and policing the public environment. Among the things it can't do are redistributing income on a large scale and solving the social and personal problems of people who, for whatever reason, are engaged in self-destructive behavior—resisting school, taking to drugs and crime, indulging in self-gratification at the expense of their children, their families, their neighbors"; "The Fate of a World City," *City Journal* (Autumn 1993): 21.

27. Nathan Glazer and Daniel Patrick Moynihan, *Beyond the Melting Pot*, 2d ed. (Cambridge, Mass.: M.I.T. Press, 1970; original edition 1963), pp. 49–50.

28. Glenn Lowry was among the first to explicitly link Glazer's "limits of social policy" thesis to civil rights. In an address to the National Urban League in 1985, a version of which was subsequently published in *The New Republic* 193 (October 7, 1985), Lowry began: "My theme will be the limi-

tations of civil rights strategies for effectively promoting the economic and social progress of minorities." He then went on to flog the line that dominates his writing on race: "To win the equal regard of our fellows, black Americans cannot substitute judicial and legislative decree for what is to be won through the outstanding achievements of individual black persons"; "Beyond Civil Rights," in *State of Black America* (Washington, D.C.: National Urban League, 1986), pp. 163 and 172.

   29. Glazer, "On Being Deradicalized," pp. 74–80.

Chapter 5. The Liberal Retreat from Race during the Post–Civil Rights Era

   1. Murray Friedman, "The White Liberal's Retreat," *The Atlantic Monthly* 211 (January 1963): 43.

   2. Ibid., p. 44.

   3. Nathaniel Weyl, *The Negro in American Civilization* (Washington, D.C.: Public Affairs Press, 1960), p. 320.

   4. Quoted in Friedman, "The White Liberal's Retreat," p. 45. Other reviewers of *The Negro in American Civilization* were less charitable than Glazer: "Nathaniel Weyl has written a book to prove that the Negro is innately inferior to all the other human races"; John Davis, *Political Science Quarterly* 57 (March 1962): 150. "This pretentious book, in spite of glib claims to objectivity, is full of contradictions, blind race prejudice, confusion, fallacious reasoning, and superficial interpretations. The worst form of bias is that which masquerades as science and objective historical inquiry"; Samuel DuBois Cook, *Journal of Negro History* 46 (January 1961): 50.

   5. Quoted in Friedman, "The White Liberal's Retreat," p. 45.

   6. Ibid., p. 46.

   7. Martin Luther King, Jr., *Why We Can't Wait* (New York: Harper & Row, 1963), p. 147.

   8. Whitney M. Young, Jr., *To Be Equal* (New York: McGraw-Hill, 1963), p. 54. This was to become a common refrain among civil rights leaders. In 1964 Bayard Rustin wrote: "What is the value of winning access to public accommodations for those who lack money to use them?" That same year Hubert Humphrey commented in Congressional debate: "What good does it do a Negro to be able to eat in a fine restaurant if he cannot afford to pay the bill?" In 1968 Martin Luther King, Jr. wrote: "What good is it to be allowed to eat in a restaurant if you can't afford a hamburger?" Bayard Rustin, "From Protest to Politics: The Future of the Civil Rights Movement," *Commentary* 39 (February 1964): 25; Hubert Humphrey, quoted in Richard A. Epstein, *Forbidden Grounds* (Cambridge, Mass.: Harvard University Press, 1992), p. 400; Martin Luther King, Jr., quoted in "Showdown for Non-Violence," *Look* (April 16, 1968): 24.

9. Lee Rainwater and William L. Yancey, eds., *The Moynihan Report and the Politics of Controversy* (Cambridge, Mass.: M.I.T. Press, 1967), p. 11.

10. In October 1963, the issue of "compensation" was debated in no less public a forum than the *New York Times Magazine*: Whitney M. Young, Jr. and Kyle Haselden, "Should There Be 'Compensation' for Negroes?" *New York Times Magazine* (October 6, 1963), pp. 43 ff. Already on the defensive, Young wrote: "The Urban League is asking for a special effort, not for special privileges. This effort has been described as 'preferential treatment,' 'indemnification,' 'special consideration,' 'compensatory activity.' These are 'scare' phrases that obscure the meaning of the proposal and go against the grain of our native sense of fair play. . . . What we ask now is for a brief period there be a deliberate and massive effort to include the Negro citizen in the mainstream of American life." Kyle Haselden, who was an editor at *Christian Century* and author of a book entitled *The Racial Problems in Christian Perspective*, argued that "our goal should be parity, not preferment," and struck the chord that would pervade the anti-affirmative discourse: that "compensation for Negroes is a subtle but pernicious form of racism."

11. King, *Why We Can't Wait*, p. 147.

12. James Baldwin, Nathan Glazer, Sidney Hook, and Gunnar Myrdal took part in this discussion. The proceedings were published as "Liberalism and the Negro: A Round-Table Discussion," *Commentary* 37 (March 1964): 25–42. Also see the Letters from Readers in the August issue.

13. Ibid., p. 25.

14. Ibid., p. 26. Podhoretz's statement reiterated some of the ideas in an article by David Danzig, "The Meaning of Negro Strategy," *Commentary* 39 (February 1964): 41–46.

15. "Liberalism and the Negro: A Round-Table Discussion," p. 31.

16. Ibid.

17. Ibid., p. 39.

18. For a study of the white backlash and its relationship to the Democratic Party, see Jonathan Rieder, *Canarsie: The Jews and Italians of Brooklyn Against Liberalism* (Cambridge, Mass.: Harvard University Press, 1985). For another interpretation, see Stephen Steinberg, "The White Backlash in Social Context: A Critique of Jonathan Rieder's *Canarsie*," *Ethnic and Racial Studies* 11, no. 2 (April 1988): 218–24; and Adolph Reed, Jr., and Julian Bond, "Equality: Why We Can't Wait," *The Nation* (December 9, 1991): 733–37.

19. That the speech was written by Goodwin and Moynihan is indicated in Daniel Patrick Moynihan, *Family and Nation* (New York: Harcourt Brace Jovanovich, 1986), p. 30. At Johnson's direction the speech was read

to several prominent civil rights leaders. According to Moynihan, "each in turn was quite transported by propositions that a year later each, save one, would quite reject" (p. 30). The unnamed civil rights leaders who "cleared" the speech were Martin Luther King, Whitney Young, and Roy Wilkins; see Allen J. Matusow, *The Unraveling of America: A History of Liberalism in the 1960s* (New York: Harper Torchbacks, 1986), p. 196.

20. Johnson's Howard University address is reprinted in Rainwater and Yancey, *The Moynihan Report and the Politics of Controversy*, pp. 125–32; emphasis added. The speech was drafted by Richard Goodwin and Daniel Patrick Moynihan, but it would appear that Moynihan was the chief architect, judging from a paper that he delivered at a *Daedalus* conference only a month earlier. Moynihan began the paper by noting that the civil rights revolution was entering "a new phase," representing a shift from issues of liberty to issues of equality. He also predicted that this shift would result in an attenuation of liberal support. Finally, after a series of theoretical gyrations, he focused on the problems in the black family that, he held, were preventing lower-class blacks from taking advantage of expanding opportunities; "Employment, Income, and the Negro Family," *Daedalus* 94 (Fall 1965): 745–70.

21. Eli Ginzberg, *The Negro Potential* (New York: Columbia University Press, 1956), p. 7. Later Ginzberg writes: "The habits, the values, and the goals that the child acquires provide the basis for his later accomplishments in school and at work. Because of his history, the American Negro is not prepared in the same way as the white population to take full advantage of the economic opportunities that exist. The Negro must alter many of his values before he will be able to cope effectively with his new situation" (p. 93). Ginzberg also advanced the argument for universal as opposed to targeted social policy: "The best hope for the Negro's speedy and complete integration into American society lies in the continuation of a strong and virile economy in which his labor is needed and his skills and capabilities rewarded" (p. 117).

22. Tom Wicker, "Johnson Pledges to Help Negroes to Full Equality," *New York Times*, June 5, 1965.

23. Moynihan ascribes the term to "the world of diplomacy," and has used it in his political sparring over the years. See the *Wall Street Journal's* Notable and Quotable column, April 18, 1985; "'Loose Cannon' Moynihan on a Roll," *Buffalo News*, July 4, 1993; and *Firing Line*, January 15, 1994.

24. According to the *Washington Evening Star*, Johnson was interrupted eighteen times by applause; Orr Kelly, "President Calls Parley 'To Fulfill Civil Rights': 14,000 at Howard Give Him Ovation as Johnson Hails New

Era for Negro," *Washington Evening Star*, June 5, 1965. In his retrospective account, Moynihan makes a point of "the stunning ovation" that Johnson received at the conclusion of his speech, as if this placed a stamp of black approval on the speech; "The President and the Negro: The Moment Lost," *Commentary* 43 (February 1967): 34.

25. The conference transcript is published in a two-volume series of *Daedalus* in Fall 1965 and Winter 1966. The quoted excerpt is found in volume 2, pp. 288–89.

26. Review of the Week, *New York Times*, June 6, 1965, p. 10.

27. Quoted in Rainwater and Yancey, *The Moynihan Report and the Politics of Controversy*, p. 135.

28. Ibid., p. 59. It should have been obvious that the burgeoning welfare rolls were an artifact of two factors: the migration of young blacks to cities in the North and West, and the liberalization of eligibility as a response to rising black protest.

29. Daniel Patrick Moynihan, "The Negro Family: The Case for National Action," in Rainwater and Yancey, *The Moynihan Report and the Politics of Controversy*, p. 76.

30. Christopher Jencks, "The Moynihan Report," in Rainwater and Yancey, *The Moynihan Report and the Politics of Controversy*, p. 443 (emphasis added).

31. Herbert J. Gans, "The Negro Family: Reflections on the Moynihan Report," in Rainwater and Yancey, *The Moynihan Report and the Politics of Controversy*, p. 450.

32. As Rainwater and Yancey write: "The controversy was, then, a kind of lucky break for the administration since it served to distract from and conceal the fact that the Administration was not really ready to assume the independent role it had reached for at Howard University"; ibid., p. 294.

33. At the very outset of his study, Gutman writes: "This volume . . . was stimulated by the bitter public and academic controversy surrounding Daniel P. Moynihan's *The Negro Family in America: The Case for National Action* (1965)"; Herbert G. Gutman, *The Black Family in Slavery and Freedom, 1750–1925* (New York: Pantheon, 1976), p. xvii. The controversy also stimulated a plethora of studies in all of the social sciences on race, poverty, and the family.

34. Moynihan, "The President and the Negro: The Moment Lost," p. 31.

35. Ibid., p. 32; emphasis in original.

36. Ibid., p. 32.

37. Ibid., p. 34.

38. Michael B. Katz, *The Undeserving Poor* (New York: Pantheon,

1989), p. 24. Elsewhere Katz writes that "the furor over Moynihan's report, in fact, drove black families off the agenda of social science for nearly two decades. Similar attacks discredited the culture of poverty"; "The Urban 'Underclass' as a Metaphor of Social Transformation," *The "Underclass" Debate*, Michael B. Katz, ed. (Princeton: Princeton University Press, 1993), p. 13.

39. William Julius Wilson, *The Truly Disadvantaged* (Chicago: University of Chicago Press, 1987), p. 4.

40. Joyce A. Ladner, *The Death of White Sociology* (New York: Vintage Books, 1973).

41. Moynihan, *Family and Nation*, p. 42. Soon after the publication of *The Declining Significance of Race* (Chicago: University of Chicago Press, 1978), Nathan Glazer also commented: "These are not things that haven't been said before. It is the first time that a black social scientist has said them with such strength"; quoted in Hollie West, "Getting Ahead and the Man Behind the Class-Race Furor," *Washington Post*, January 1, 1979.

42. These ideas pervade Moynihan's writing, but are clearly articulated in "Employment, Income, and the Ordeal of the Negro Family," *Daedalus* 94 (Fall 1965): esp. 753–54.

43. For Wilson it is an article of faith that education translates into better jobs and higher earnings. However, he does not address the next order of questions concerning *who* gets schooling and the *conditions* under which schooling does or does not function as a channel of mobility.

44. Daniel Patrick Moynihan, transcript of the American Academy Conference on the Negro American, May 14–16, 1965, *Daedalus* 95 (Winter 1966): 288; emphasis in original.

45. This statement is based on the fact that in a chapter on "The Urban Underclass," published three years before *The Truly Disadvantaged*, Wilson indicated that "this chapter is based on a larger study, *The Hidden Agenda: Race, Social Dislocations, and Public Policy in America*, to be published by the University of Chicago Press"; in *Minority Report*, ed. Leslie Dunbar (New York: Pantheon, 1984), p. 75. The same notation is found in Wilson's chapter on "The Urban Underclass in Advanced Industrial Society," in *The New Urban Reality*, ed. Paul E. Peterson (Washington, D.C.: Brookings Institution, 1985), p. 129.

46. Wilson, *The Truly Disadvantaged*, p. 155.

47. William Julius Wilson, *New York Times*, March 24, 1990, p. I31, and March 17, 1992, p. A25. See also his article "Race-Neutral Programs and the Democratic Coalition," *The American Prospect*, no. 1 (Spring 1990): 74–81. See Kenneth Tollett's reply and Wilson's rejoinder in the subsequent issue.

48. This reference to Wilson was made by President Clinton in a speech to black ministers in Memphis on November 13, 1993, and cited in a profile on Wilson in *People* magazine (January 17, 1974, p. 81). According to one journalist: "Throughout the Presidential campaign, he [Clinton] quoted Wilson's work at every turn. '*The Truly Disadvantaged* made me see the problems of race and poverty and the inner city in a different light,' he said recently. 'It reinforced my conviction that we have to find broad-based economic solutions to a lot of our country's challenges'"; Gretchen Reynolds, "The Rising Significance of Race," *Chicago* 41 (December 1992): 82.

49. Reynolds, "The Rising Significance of Race," p. 81.

50. Alvin Ward Gouldner, *The Coming Crisis of Western Sociology* (New York: Basic Books, 1970), p. 29; emphasis in original.

51. In 1978 Wilson's *The Declining Significance of Race* was awarded the American Sociological Association's Sydney S. Spivak Award in intergroup relations. This evoked a protest from the Association of Black Sociologists, which passed a resolution stating that Wilson's book "obscures the problem of the persistent oppression of blacks" (quoted in Hollie West, "Getting Ahead and the Man Behind the Class-Race Furor"). Among Wilson's recent laurels was being named as a Member of the President's Committee for the National Medal of Science. He was also selected as the 1994 winner of the Frank E. Seidman Distinguished Award in Political Economy. Robert Solow, M.I.T. economist and former Nobel prize winner, who served on the selection committee, commented: "If anyone is a successor to Gunnar Myrdal in the study of black society in the U.S., it's Bill Wilson"; "W. J. Wilson Awarded Seidman Prize," *Footnotes*, American Sociological Association (October 1994): 5. Indeed, if *An American Dilemma* was the "exemplar study" of the pre-civil rights era, it is safe to say that *The Declining Significance of Race* and *The Truly Disadvantaged* are the exemplar works of the post–civil rights era.

52. Cornel West, *Race Matters* (Boston: Beacon Press, 1993).

53. These two articles were originally published in liberal/left journals: "Nihilism in Black America" in *Dissent* 38 in Spring 1991, and "Beyond Affirmative Action: Equality and Identity" in *The American Prospect* no. 9 in Spring 1992.

54. West, *Race Matters*, p. 1.

55. Ibid., p. 2.

56. Ibid., p. 12; emphasis in original.

57. Ibid., pp. 12–13.

58. Ibid., p. 15.

59. Ibid., p. 17.

60. Ibid., p. 36.

61. Ibid., p. 37.

62. Moynihan, "The Negro Family: The Case for National Action," p. 93.

63. West, *Race Matters*, p. 12.

64. Ibid., p. 18.

65. Ibid., p. 19.

66. Ibid.

67. Ibid., p. 20.

68. Ibid., p. 19.

69. Ibid., p. 20.

70. Ibid., p. 14.

71. Ibid., p. 46.

72. "Excerpts From Clinton's Speech to Black Ministers," *New York Times*, November 14, 1993. This speech also had the imprint of William Julius Wilson, who had dined at the White House the previous week. In an op-ed piece in the *Washington Post*, E. J. Dionne linked Wilson's ideas with Clinton's Memphis speech. To quote Dionne: "Clinton, as a good Wilson student, was thus insistent in his speech that if you couldn't address the plight of the African American poor without talking about moral values and personal responsibility, then neither could you expect worthy values to flourish in the absence of jobs"; "Clinton's Bully Pulpit," *Washington Post*, November 16, 1993.

73. Wilson's position is reported in Steven A. Holmes, "Mulling the Idea of Affirmative Action for Poor Whites," *New York Times*, August 18, 1991.

74. West, *Race Matters*, p. 64.

75. Ibid., p. 57.

76. W. E. B. Du Bois, "The Propaganda of History," in *Black Reconstruction* (New York: Harcourt, Brace, 1935), p. 714.

77. For another critique of *Race Matters*, see Eric Lott, "Culture and Politics in *Race Matters*," *Social Text* 40 (Fall 1994): 39–50.

78. Martin Luther King, Jr., "Letter from a Birmingham Jail," in *I Have a Dream: Writings and Speeches that Changed the World*, ed. James Melvin Washington (San Francisco: HarperSanFrancisco, 1992), p. 91.

79. Aldon Morris, *The Origins of the Civil Rights Movement* (New York: Free Press, 1984), p. 288.

Chapter 6. The Underclass

1. Richard McGahey, "Poverty's Voguish Stigma," Op-ed page, *New York Times*, March 12, 1982.

2. Walter Jackson, *Gunnar Myrdal and America's Conscience* (Chapel Hill, N.C.: University of North Carolina Press, 1990), p. 299.

3. Gunnar Myrdal, *Challenge to Affluence* (New York: Pantheon, 1962), p. 53.

4. Ken Auletta, *The Underclass* (New York: Random House, 1982).

5. Anonymous, "A Permanent Black Underclass?" *U.S. News and World Report* 100 (March 3, 1986): 21–22; Mortimer B. Zuckerman, "The Black Underclass," *U.S. News and World Report* 100 (April 19, 1986): 78; Nicholas Lemann, "The Origins of the Underclass," *The Atlantic* 257 (June 1986): 31–55; Myron Magnet, "America's Underclass: What to Do?" *Fortune* 115 (May 11, 1987): 130–50; Jonathan Alter, "Why We Can't Wait Any Longer," *Newsweek* 111 (March 7, 1988): 42–43; Pete Hammil, "America's Black Underclass: Can It Be Saved?" *Reader's Digest* 132 (June 1988): 105–10; Richard Stengel, "The Underclass: Breaking the Cycle," *Time* 132 (October 10, 1988): 41–42.

6. Martha A. Gephart and Robert W. Pearson, "Contemporary Research on the Urban Underclass," *Social Science Research Council Items* (June 1988): 4.

7. Erol R. Ricketts and Isabel V. Sawhill, "Defining and Measuring the Underclass," *Journal of Policy Analysis and Management* 7 (1988): 321–22.

8. Ibid., p. 317; emphasis added.

9. For a penetrating critique of the underclass discourse and the value assumptions that undergird it, see Adolph Reed, Jr., "The Underclass as Myth and Symbol," *Radical America* 24 (January 1992): 21–40.

10. See Herbert Gans, "The Dangers of the Underclass: Its Harmfulness as a Planning Concept," in Gans, *People, Plans, and Policies* (New York: Columbia University Press, 1991), pp. 238–43; Raymond S. Franklin, *Shadows of Race and Class* (Minneapolis: University of Minnesota Press, 1991), Chapter 5; and William Kornblum, "Social Breakdown: Who Is the Underclass?" *Dissent* 38 (Spring 1991): 201–11.

11. Thomas Sowell, *Ethnic America* (New York: Basic Books, 1981).

12. Stephen Steinberg, *The Ethnic Myth* (Boston: Beacon Press, 1989), pp. 267–80.

13. Douglas G. Glasgow, *The Black Underclass* (New York: Vintage Books, 1981), p. 25.

14. Myron Magnet, "America's Underclass: What to Do?" *Fortune* 115 (May 11, 1987), p. 130; emphasis added.

15. Elliot Liebow, *Tally's Corner* (Boston: Little, Brown, 1967).

16. William Julius Wilson, *The Declining Significance of Race* (Chicago: University of Chicago Press, 1978); and *The Truly Disadvantaged* (Chicago: University of Chicago Press, 1987).

17. Wilson, *The Truly Disadvantaged*, Chapter 7.

18. Wilson's advocacy of universal policies is forcefully defended by

Theda Skocpol in an article entitled "Targeting within Universalism: Politically Viable Policies to Combat Poverty in the United States"; for an opposing argument, see Robert Greenstein, "Universal and Targeted Approaches to Relieving Poverty: An Alternative View"; both articles are published in *The Urban Underclass*, ed. Christopher Jencks and Paul E. Peterson (Washington, D.C.: Brookings Institution, 1991).

19. Karen Gerard, "New York City's Economy: A Decade of Change," *New York Affairs*, 8, no. 2 (1984): 7.

20. Richard Levine, "New York Lost 34,000 Jobs over Summer," *New York Times*, October 19, 1990.

21. Norman Fainstein, "The Underclass/Mismatch Hypothesis as an Explanation for Black Economic Deprivation," *Politics and Society*, 15, no. 4 (1986–87): 439. According to data on New York City compiled by Roger Waldinger, in 1970 17 percent of whites were employed in manufacturing, as compared to 13 percent of blacks. By 1980 there were 38 percent fewer whites employed in manufacturing, whereas the decline for blacks was only 13 percent. In absolute numbers, 115,180 whites lost their jobs, as compared to 7,980 blacks; Roger Waldinger, "Ladders and Musical Chairs: Ethnicity and Opportunity in Post-Industrial New York," *Politics and Society* 15 (1986–87): 379–80. See also Walter W. Stafford, *Closed Labor Markets: Underrepresentation of Blacks, Hispanics and Women in New York City's Core Industries* (New York: Community Service Society of New York, 1985).

22. Kasarda's data show that blacks with more education fare better than those with less education. Equally revealing, however, are differences in rates of employment between blacks and whites with the same level of education. In 1982 black males with a college education had higher rates of unemployment than white males who had not completed high school. John Kasarda, "Urban Change and Minority Opportunities," in *The New Urban Reality*, ed. Paul Peterson (Washington, D.C.: Brookings Institution, 1985), p. 57.

23. Wilson, *The Truly Disadvantaged*, p. 41.

24. To quote Wilson: "One does not have to 'trot out' the concept of racism to demonstrate, for example, that blacks have been severely hurt by deindustrialization." Later he writes: "The problem, as I see it, is unraveling the effects of present-day discrimination, on the one hand, and of historic discrimination, on the other. My own view is that historic discrimination is far more important than contemporary discrimination in explaining the plight of the ghetto underclass, but that a full appreciation of the effects of historic discrimination is impossible without taking into account other historical and contemporary forces that have also shaped the experiences and

behavior of impoverished urban minorities"; *The Truly Disadvantaged*, p. 12 and pp. 32–33.

25. Steven Holmes, "Jobless Data Show Blacks Joining Recovery," *New York Times*, January 12, 1995, p. A12. The same article reported that the December unemployment rate for blacks dipped below 10 percent for the first time in more than two decades (9.8 percent as compared to 4.8 percent for whites). As Andrew Brimmer cautioned, however, this could be a temporary aberration, easily reversed with a slowdown in the economy. A spokesman from the NAACP also noted that the government figures leave out the large numbers of blacks who have given up looking for a job.

26. Sheldon H. Danziger and Daniel H. Weinberg, "The Historical Record: Trends in Family Income, Inequality, and Poverty," in *Confronting Poverty*, ed. Sheldon H. Danziger, Gary D. Sandefur, and Daniel H. Weinberg (Cambridge, Mass.: Harvard University Press, 1994), pp. 33–34; emphasis added. Their data showed that between 1980 and 1990 poverty increased from 10.2 percent to 10.7 percent among whites, and decreased from 32.5 percent to 31.9 percent among blacks.

27. William Julius Wilson, "The New Urban Poverty and the Problem of Race," *Michigan Quarterly Review* 33 (Spring 1994): 266.

28. Roger Wilkins, "Progress and Policy: A Response to William Julius Wilson," in ibid., pp. 282 and 287. Nor can this be dismissed as political hyperbole. As Hugh Heclo writes: "The Model Cities proposal, the Great Society's *only* concentrated attack on ghetto poverty, was administratively fragmented and quickly broadened by Congress to include most congressional districts"; "Poverty Politics," in *Confronting Poverty*, ed. Danziger, Sandefur, and Weinberg, p. 408. Heclo's assertion is based on a study by Charles Haar, *Between the Idea and the Reality: A Study in the Origin, Fate, and Legacy of the Model Cities Program* (Boston: Little, Brown, 1975).

29. Gary Orfield and Carole Ashkinaze, *The Closing Door* (Chicago: University of Chicago Press, 1991), p. 4.

30. Ibid., p. 15.

31. Ibid., p. 115. William Julius Wilson amplified his reservations about affirmative action in a subsequent article entitled "Race-Neutral Policies and the Democratic Coalition," *The American Prospect*, no. 1 (Spring 1990).

32. William L. Taylor, "*Brown*, Equal Protection, and the Isolation of the Poor," *Yale Law Journal* 95 (1986): 1714. Wilson, in fact, quotes this very passage, but still goes on to portray affirmative action as a "creaming" process that primarily helps "those with the greatest economic, educational, and social resources" (*The Truly Disadvantaged*, p. 115). Clearly, affirmative action does not reach those worst off, but those who are reached can hardly

be characterized as the "cream" of black society: they are socially and economically marginal, and have few alternative channels of mobility. Besides, given the caste system in occupations, it is imperative that racist barriers be eliminated at *all* occupational strata.

33. Wilson, *The Truly Disadvantaged*, p. 126.

34. U.S. Department of Labor, Bureau of Labor Statistics Bulletin no. 2402, May 1992.

35. For example, John Kasarda, "Urban Change and Minority Opportunities," p. 57.

36. Neil McMillen, *Dark Journey* (Urbana: University of Illinois Press, 1990), p. 117.

37. Gerald David Jaynes and Robin M. Williams, Jr., *A Common Destiny* (Washington, D.C.: National Academy Press, 1989), p. 146. "Consequently," they add, "the extent of employment discrimination must be inferred from less direct evidence."

38. Margery Austin Turner, Michael Fix, and Raymond J. Struyk, "Opportunities Denied, Opportunities Diminished: Discrimination in Hiring" (The Urban Institute, 1991), p. 1.

39. Leonard Buder, "Employment Agency Accused of Bias," *New York Times*, February 21, 1990. Two years later the agency settled a lawsuit brought by the State Attorney General's office by paying more than $1.75 million dollars to the aggrieved parties. However, the counsel for the employment agency "denied the company ever used code words on applications and said that it plans to continue using the placement practices instituted before the lawsuits were filed"; Calvin Sims, "Job Discrimination Case Settled for $1.7 Million," *New York Times*, December 26, 1991, p. B5.

40. Reported in Turner, Fix, and Struyk, "Opportunities Denied, Opportunities Diminished: Discrimination in Hiring."

41. Gretchen Reynolds, "The Rising Significance of Race," *Chicago* 41 (December 1992): 81 ff.

42. These findings are reported in Kirschenman and Neckerman, "'We'd Love to Hire Them, But . . . ': The Meaning of Race for Employers," *passim*.

43. Ibid., p. 128.

44. Ibid.

45. Wilson's position is also spelled out in a 1992 paper, "The Plight of the Inner-City Black Male," *Proceedings of the American Philosophical Society* 136 (September 1992): 320–25. He begins with the observation that employers in Chicago's neighborhoods regard black men as poor and unreliable workers. Wilson then asserts that "the deterioration of the socioeco-

nomic status of black men may be associated with increases in these negative perceptions" (p. 322). He then asks: "Are these perceptions merely stereotypical or do they have any basis in fact?" Even though his survey data showed that black men were willing to work for even less than Mexican jobless fathers, he insists, on the basis of his ethnographic studies, that their "underlying attitudes and values" were different, and that black men exhibited greater hostility and resistance than their Mexican counterparts. On this basis he concludes that "the issue of race cannot simply be reduced to discrimination" (p. 324).

A similar line of reasoning is found in the work of Christopher Jencks, who was one of the early critics of the Moynihan Report and the culture-of-poverty school. However, in *Rethinking Social Policy* (New York: Harper-Collins, 1993), Jencks states that "our inability to maintain a tight labor market deserves most of the blame for increased idleness among young blacks." He adds, however: "It is not the only culprit" (p. 125). Jencks goes on to argue that black youth are not willing to work at low-wage jobs, and that aspects of their culture are off-putting to prospective employers. Because "moral ideas and norms of behavior have a life of their own," Jencks reasons, "institutional reforms must be complemented by a self-conscious effort at cultural change" (p. 142). This theoretical construction is identical to Oscar Lewis's position that "the elimination of physical poverty *per se* may not be enough to eliminate the culture of poverty which is a whole way of life" (*La Vida* [New York: Vintage Books, 1965], p. lii). To effect cultural change, Jencks advocates a moral crusade within the black community that would "reinforce poor urban blacks' sense of obligation to one another, to their unborn children, or to the society from which they must derive their livelihood" (p. 142). "Wilson's greatest contribution," he writes in conclusion, "may be his discussion of how liberals' reluctance to blame blacks for anything happening in their communities has clouded both black and white thinking about how we can improve those communities" (p. 142). For a critique of Jencks's essays in the *New York Review of Books*, see David Wellman, "The New Political Linguistics of Race," *Socialist Review* 16 (May–August 1986): 43–79.

46. Reynolds, "The Rising Significance of Race," p. 128.

47. In her profile of Wilson in *Chicago* magazine, Gretchen Reynolds observed: "In the five years since the publication of his most famous book, *The Truly Disadvantaged*, Wilson has become the darling of centrist politicians for one reason: because he declared, in effect, that the best way to deal with racial issues was not to" (p. 82). Later she adds: "Wilson's prescriptions were of the grand-scale, society-wide variety. They began with a call for full

employment. But what endeared Wilson to many national politicians—
what turned Bill Clinton into an acolyte—was his de-emphasis of affirmative action" (p. 127).

Chapter 7. The Politics of Memory

1. Joseph Epstein, "The Joys of Victimhood," *New York Times Magazine*, July 2, 1989, p. 21.
2. Ibid.
3. Ibid., p. 41.
4. Martin Luther King, Jr., *Why We Can't Wait* (New York: Harper &
Row, 1963), p. 148.
5. Malcolm X, *The Autobiography of Malcolm X* (New York: Grove
Press, 1964), p. 204.
6. George Orwell, "A Hanging," in *Shooting an Elephant and Other Essays* (New York: Harcourt Brace Jovanovich, 1950).
7. Alfred Holt Stone, "Is Race Friction Between Blacks and Whites in the
United States Growing and Inevitable?" *American Journal of Sociology*
(1908), p. 692.
8. Shelby Steele, "A Negative Vote on Affirmative Action," *New York
Times Magazine*, May 13, 1990, 46 ff.
9. Shelby Steele, "The Memory of Enemies," *Dissent* 37 (Summer
1990): 326–32; reprinted in Steele, *The Content of Our Character* (New
York: St. Martin's Press, 1990), pp. 149–65.
10. Ibid., pp. 326–27.
11. Alexander Stille, "What the Holocaust Meant in the Thinking of
Primo Levi and Jean Améry," *Dissent* 37 (Summer 1990): 361–66.
12. Jean Améry, *At the Mind's Limits: Contemplations by a Survivor on
Auschwitz and Its Realities* (New York: Pantheon, 1990).
13. Jean Améry, *At the Mind's Limits: Contemplations by a Survivor on
Auschwitz and Its Realities* (Bloomington: Indiana University Press, 1980),
p. xi.
14. Stille, "What the Holocaust Meant in the Thinking of Primo Levi
and Jean Améry," p. 365.
15. Améry, *At the Mind's Limits*, p. vii.
16. Isaac Deutscher, *The Non-Jewish Jew* (London: Oxford University
Press, 1968), p. 41.
17. Steele, "The Memory of Enemies," p. 327.
18. Ibid.
19. James Baldwin, *Notes of a Native Son* (Boston: Beacon Press, 1955),
pp. 113–14.

Chapter 8. Affirmative Action and Liberal Capitulation

1. Herbert R. Northrup and John A. Larson, *The Impact of the AT&T-EEO Consent Decree*, Labor Relations and Public Policy Series, no. 20 (Philadelphia: University of Pennsylvania, 1979), pp. 41–44.

2. Bernard E. Anderson, "Equal Opportunity and Black Employment in the Telephone Industry," in *Equal Employment Opportunity and the AT&T Case*, ed. Phyllis A. Wallace (Cambridge, Mass.: M.I.T. Press, 1976), p. 189.

3. Northrup and Larson, *The Impact of the AT&T-EEO Consent Decree*, p. 12.

4. Robert Pear, "Dispute on Policy on Jobs Continues," *New York Times*, January 30, 1986.

5. See Sharon M. Collins, "The Making of the Black Middle Class," *Social Problems* 30 (April 1983): 369–81; Jonathan S. Leonard, "The Impact of Affirmative Action on Employment," *Journal of Labor Economics* 2 (October 1984): 439–63; and John F. Zipp, "Government Employment and Black-White Earnings Inequality, 1980–1990," *Social Problems* 41 (August 1994): 363–82.

6. There is a curious illogic to Wilson's position, as Kenneth Tollett has noted: "I take umbrage at Wilson's repeated criticism of affirmative action for benefiting primarily the middle-class or those who need help least and not helping the underclass. . . . It is as if one were to criticize penicillin for not curing or anticipating and preventing AIDS or cancer"; "Racism and Race-Conscious Remedies," *The American Prospect* no. 5 (Summer 1990): 92.

7. Michael K. Brown and Steven P. Erie, "Blacks and the Legacy of the Great Society: The Economic and Political Impact of Federal Social Policy," *Public Policy* 29 (Summer 1981): 299.

8. Andrew Hacker, *Two Nations* (New York: Macmillan, 1992), p. 121.

9. Thomas Sowell, "A Black 'Conservative' Dissents," *New York Times Magazine*, Aug. 8, 1976, p. 15.

10. Shelby Steele, "A Negative Vote on Affirmative Action," *New York Times Magazine*, May 13, 1990; reprinted in Steele, *The Content of Our Character* (New York: St. Martin's Press, 1990), p. 120.

11. Stephen Carter, *Reflections of an Affirmative Action Baby* (New York: Basic Books, 1991).

12. Ibid., p. 85.

13. Jonathan S. Leonard, "The Impact of Affirmative Action Regulation and Equal Employment Law on Black Employment," *Journal of Economic Perspectives* 4 (Fall 1990): 47–63.

14. Carter, *Reflections of an Affirmative Action Baby*, p. 234.

15. Derrick Bell, *And We Are Not Saved* (New York: Basic Books, 1987), p. 14.

16. Paul Starr, "Civic Reconstruction: What to Do Without Affirmative Action," *The American Prospect* no. 8 (Winter 1992): 7–14. For another example of liberal back-pedaling on affirmative action, see Christopher Jencks, "Affirmative Action," in *Rethinking Social Policy* (New York: HarperCollins, 1993), Chapter 1 (revision of articles published in the *New York Review of Books* on March 3 and 17, 1983).

17. Starr, "Civic Reconstruction: What to Do Without Affirmative Action," p. 8.

18. Ibid., p. 10.

19. Ibid., p. 14.

20. Ibid., p. 8.

21. William Julius Wilson, "Race-Neutral Policies and the Democratic Coalition," *The American Prospect* no. 1 (Spring 1990): 74–81.

22. Starr, "Civic Reconstruction: What to Do Without Affirmative Action," p. 9.

23. Ibid.

24. Ibid., p. 11.

25. Ibid., p. 14.

26. Joe Klein, "The End of Affirmative Action," *Newsweek* (February 13, 1995): 36.

27. For example: Howard Glickman and Tim Smart, "Race in the Workplace: Is Affirmative Action Working?" cover story, *Business Week*, issue 3221 (July 8, 1991): 50; Jerry Madkins, "Affirmative Action Is Necessary and Ethical," *Personnel Journal* 68 (August 1989): 29–30; Alan Farnham, "Holding Firm on Affirmative Action," *Fortune* 119 (March 13, 1989): 87–88.

Chapter 9. Occupational Apartheid and the Myth of the Black Middle Class

1. For an excellent analysis of the historical relationship between race and occupational structures, see Harold M. Baron, "The Demand for Black Labor," *Radical America* 5 (March–April 1971); and idem, "The Web of Urban Racism," in *Institutional Racism in America*, ed. Louis L. Knowles and Kenneth Prewitt (Englewood Cliffs, N.J.: Prentice-Hall, 1969), pp. 134–76.

2. See Lawrence H. Fuchs, "The Reactions of Black Americans to Immigration," in *Immigration Reconsidered*, ed. Virginia Yans-McLaughlin (New York: Oxford University Press, 1990), especially pp. 295–97, and

David J. Hellwig, "Patterns of Black Nativism," *American Studies* 23 (Spring 1982).

3. Thomas Muller, *Immigrants and the American City* (New York: New York University Press, 1993), p. 91.

4. Gunnar Myrdal, *An American Dilemma: The Negro Problem and Modern Democracy* (New York: Harper & Row, 1994), p. 1005.

5. *Historical Statistics of the United States* (Washington, D.C.: Government Printing Office, 1975), p. 500. Gerald David Jaynes and Robin M. Williams, Jr., *A Common Destiny* (Washington, D.C.: National Academy Press, 1989), p. 273.

6. See Frances Fox Piven and Richard A. Cloward, *Poor People's Movements* (New York: Vintage Books, 1979), Chapter 4.

7. In a paper written for the National Advisory Commission on Civil Disorders in 1968, Herbert Gans debunked the notion that blacks arriving in Northern cities were following in the footsteps of earlier immigrants, and could therefore anticipate the same beneficial outcomes; "Escaping from Poverty: A Comparison of the Immigrant and Black Experience," in *People, Plans, and Policies* (New York: Columbia University Press, 1991), Chapter 18.

8. See William Darity, Jr., "What's Left of the Economic Theory of Discrimination?" in *The Question of Discrimination*, ed. Steven Shulman and William Darity, Jr. (Middletown, Conn.: Wesleyan University Press, 1989), pp. 335–74, and Stephen Steinberg, "Human Capital: A Critique," *Review of Black Political Economy*, 14, no. 1 (Summer 1985): 67–74.

9. Joleen Kirschenman and Kathryn M. Neckerman, "'We'd Love to Hire Them, But . . .': The Meaning of Race for Employers," in *The Urban Underclass*, ed. Christopher Jencks and Paul E. Peterson (Washington, D.C.: Brookings Institution, 1991), p. 104.

10. Myrdal, *An American Dilemma*, p. 61.

11. Herbert Hill, "Myth-Making as Labor History: Herbert Gutman and the United Mine Workers of America," *Politics, Culture, and Society* 2 (Winter 1988): 132–95. Hill's piece unleashed a spirited debate in the Spring 1989 issue (pp. 361–99). David Roediger comments that, notwithstanding his penchant for sentimentalism, Gutman "did better than most labor historians, who generally ignore issues of race and racism. . . . Clearly, most left and anti-racist scholars will want to devote sympathetic attention to past advocates of class unity across racial lines. They should do so. But, and here is where Gutman's essay on the UMW founders, there is a political obligation to discuss not only Black-white unity *but also the limits of that unity*" ("History Making and Politics," p. 371; emphasis in original). Steven Shul-

man writes: "Only by recognizing and not denying the role of race in the making of the American working class can new possibilities be introduced for the future. Gutman may have had the best of intentions, but his efforts to promote working class unity have only convinced a new generation of activists to reiterate the same useless slogans" ("Racism and the Making of the American Working Class," p. 365). On the other hand, see Stephen Brier, "In Defense of Gutman: The Union's Case," pp. 382–95.

12. Nell Irvin Painter, "The New Labor History and the Historical Moment," *Politics, Culture, and Society* 2 (Spring1989): 369.

A number of labor historians have made race and racism central to their intellectual project; chief among them are Herbert Hill and David Roediger. See Herbert Hill, "Race, Ethnicity and Organized Labor: The Opposition to Affirmative Action," *New Politics* 1 (Winter 1987): 31–82; and idem, "Black Workers, Organized Labor, and Title VII of the 1964 Civil Rights Act: Legislative History and Litigation Record," in *Race in America*, ed. Herbert Hill and James E. Jones, Jr. (Madison, Wis.: University of Wisconsin Press, 1993), pp. 263–341; David Roediger, "Notes on Working Class Racism," *New Politics* 2 (Summer 1989): 61–66; idem, *The Wages of Whiteness* (New York: Verso, 1991); and idem, *Toward the Abolition of Whiteness: Essays on Race, Politics, and Working-Class History* (New York: Verso, 1994). See also Barry Goldberg, "'Wage Slaves' and 'White Niggers,'" *New Politics* 3 (Summer 1991): 49–63, and idem, "Theory, History and Politics of Race and Class," *New Politics* 4 (Winter 1993): 50–68.

13. For a recent demographic analysis of the new immigration, see Reubén G. Rumbaut, "Origins and Destinies: Immigration to the United States Since World War II," *Sociological Forum* 9 (December 1994): 583–621.

14. The counter-argument, of course, is that higher labor costs would drive these low-wage industries out of business or out of the country. Others have argued, however, that the economic benefits of retaining these low-wage industries do not justify the human and social costs of creating and maintaining a tier of workers far below the wages and conditions that prevail in the rest of the work force. See "The New Immigration: An Exchange" in *Dissent* (Summer 1980), which includes articles by Otis L. Graham, Jr., on "Illegal Immigration and the Left" and Michael Piore, "Another View on Migrant Workers." For more recent statements, see Peter H. Schuck, "The Great Immigration Debate," *The American Prospect* no. 2 (Fall 1990): 100–118, and Vernon M. Briggs, Jr., *Mass Immigration and the National Interest* (Armonk, N.Y.: M. E. Sharpe, 1992), Chapter 8.

15. There is much spurious discussion in the literature about "network hiring" that suggests that employers are not actively discriminating against blacks so much as they are opting to recruit new workers through immigrant

networks. Needless to say, the end result is the same: a pattern of black exclusion. As Philip Martin points out: "Network recruitment and ethnic supervision explain how illegal aliens gain a foothold with certain businesses and then exclude unemployed English-speaking workers from job vacancies"; "Network Recruitment and Labor Displacement," in U.S. *Immigration in the 1980s: Reappraisal and Reform*, ed. David E. Simcox (Boulder: Westview Press, 1988), p. 74.

16. Elizabeth Bogen, *Immigration in New York* (New York: Praeger, 1989), esp. Chapter 7.

17. Ibid., p. 83.

18. Ibid., p. 91.

19. Even at McDonald's, which has come to represent the bottom of the service economy, immigrants have made inroads in recent years, sharply reducing the number of blacks in the company's work force; Jennifer Parker, "The Globalization of Fast Food: Third World Immigrants in New York City Franchises," dissertation in progress, Ph.D. Program in Sociology, City University of New York.

20. Richard Mines, "Undocumented Immigrants and California Industries: Reflections on Research," paper for Hearings of the Intergovernmental Relations Committee, November 15, 1985; reported in Jacquelyne Johnson Jackson, "Seeking Common Ground for Blacks and Immigrants," in U.S. *Immigration in the 1980s: Reappraisal and Reform*, ed. David E. Simcox, p. 94. The influx of Asians and Hispanics into Los Angeles County has triggered an exodus of blacks. According to surveys conducted by the census, between 1985 and 1990 61,773 blacks have moved out of Los Angeles County. Some have moved to outlying areas, but many others have left for other states, particularly in the South; Kenneth B. Noble, "Blacks Say Life in Los Angeles Is Losing Its Allure," *New York Times*, January 8, 1995.

21. Elizabeth Bogen, "A Renewable Resource," in *New York Newsday*, March 9, 1990, p. 72.

22. Muller, *Immigrants and the American City*, p. 284. These figures are partly inflated by the Immigration Reform and Control Act, which granted legal status to formerly undocumented persons living in New York prior to 1982.

23. Thomas J. Lueck, "Youth Joblessness Is at Record High in New York City," *New York Times*, June 4, 1993.

24. Two notable examples are Julian L. Simon, "The Case for Greatly Increased Immigration," *Public Interest* no. 102 (Winter 1991): 89–103; and Ben J. Wattenberg and Karl Zinsmeister, "The Case for More Immigration," *Commentary* 89 (April 1990): 19–25.

25. On this last point, see Julian L. Simon, "More Immigration Can Cut the Deficit," op-ed page, *New York Times*, May 10, 1990.

26. Wattenberg and Zinsmeister, "The Case for More Immigration," pp. 20–21.

27. Muller, *Immigrants and the American City*, p. 171.

28. Simon, "The Case for Greatly Increased Immigration," p. 96. Groups that oppose immigration out of economic fear are guilty, Simon says, of putting their particular interests ahead of "the welfare of the country as a whole" (p. 90).

29. See Julian L. Simon, *The Economic Consequences of Immigration* (Cambridge: Basil Blackwell, 1989), Chapter 12; and George J. Borjas, *Friends or Strangers* (New York: Basic Books, 1990), Chapter 5.

30. Other methodological criticisms of these studies are found in Jackson, "Seeking Common Ground for Blacks and Immigrants," pp. 93–95; Briggs, *Mass Immigration and the National Interest*, Chapter 1; and Randall K. Filer, "The Effect of Immigrant Arrivals on Migratory Patterns of Native Workers," in *Immigration and the Work Force*, ed. George J. Borjas and Richard B. Freeman (Chicago: University of Chicago Press, 1992), pp. 245–69. This last study reviews research showing that immigration retards internal migration, concluding that "the effect of immigrant arrivals on native workers was so large that natives' migratory responses more than totally offset any arrival of immigrants" (p. 267).

31. Jackson, "Seeking Common Ground for Blacks and Immigrants," p. 95.

32. Muller, *Immigrants and the American City*, p. 160.

33. For example, a 1983 national poll found that 69 percent of black respondents agreed that "illegal immigrants are a major harm to U.S. jobless," and 73 percent said that "the U.S. should admit fewer or a lot fewer legal immigrants"; Jackson, "Seeking Common Ground for Blacks and Immigrants," p. 96. For a comprehensive review of poll findings on the immigration issue, see Muller, *Immigrants and the American City*, pp. 161–66. A recent New York Times/CBS News Poll found that the percentage of Americans who favored a decrease in immigration had risen to 61 percent, up from 49 percent when the question was last asked in 1986. Compared to whites, black Americans were nine percentage points more likely to see immigrants taking jobs away, but nine percentage points less likely to prefer a decrease in immigration; Seth Mydans, "Poll Finds Tide of Immigration Brings Hostility," *New York Times*, June 27, 1993.

34. For an informative discussion of the role that black organizations and the Congressional Black Caucus played in the debate over the Simpson-

Mazzoli bill in 1983 and 1984, see Muller, *Immigrants and the American City*, pp. 52–67.

35. Jack Miles, "Blacks vs. Browns: The Struggle for the Bottom Rung," *The Atlantic* 270 (October 1992): 59–60. See also Wanda Coleman, "Blacks, Immigrants and America," *The Nation* (February 15, 1993): 189.

36. Muller, *Immigration and the American City*, p. 275, emphasis added. In "The Case for More Immigration," Wattenberg and Zinsmeister also write: "A future of more jobs may sound like a happy circumstance, but it reflects imbalances for which there can also be penalties. One such penalty is deteriorating service, and an increase in underqualified, rude, and weakly committed employees" (p. 22).

37. For example, Myron Magnet, an editor at *Fortune* magazine, opines that immigration "highlights economic realities that have been obfuscated," and points up the deficiencies of the underclass since "immigrants who are succeeding by means of low-skill jobs face similar barriers and overcome them"; *The Dream and the Nightmare* (New York: William Morrow, 1993), pp. 49 and 50. Lawrence Mead also writes: "The immigration experience disproves the contention that the U.S. economy systematically creates fewer jobs than there are workers to fill them"; *The New Politics of Poverty* (New York: Basic Books, 1992), p. 93.

38. *New York Times*, June 10, 1992, p. A16.

39. According to Representative Bruce Morrison, chairman of the House Subcommittee on Immigration, Refugees and International Law, "the nursing crisis is a test case for how we deal with a labor force emergency without inducing hospitals to look at immigration as the easy answer to their problems and without letting them give up efforts to draw Americans into those jobs"; *New York Times*, July 16, 1989, p. E5. If nursing is a test case, then it is clear that the nation has failed. In New York City alone, there were already 14,000 foreign-born registered nurses in the labor force in 1980; Bogen, *Immigration in New York*, p. 83. Other data indicate that enrollment in nursing schools hovered around 250,000 between 1974 and 1983, and then declined sharply to about 180,000. After 1987 the number increased to about 230,000; Tamar Lewin, "Big Gain in Nursing Students Lifts Hopes Amid a Shortage," *New York Times*, December 28, 1990, p. A18.

The importation of foreign nurses also relieved pressures to improve wages and working conditions for nurses. According to Gordon Lafer, who worked for the Office of Economic Development in New York: "At least in New York during the 1980s, even while hospitals were experiencing a severe shortage of RN's, there were many thousands of RN's living in the city who chose not to work in their profession due to low wages, high stress, and sense of disrespect which they experienced at work. The importation of cheap Filipino nurses was used both to avoid training local labor and to avoid fixing the institutional failures which caused mass numbers of trained RN's to drop out of the labor market"; private correspondence (October 26, 1993).

40. This proposal was originally put forward by Nobel laureate Gary Becker in an unpublished paper entitled "A Radical Proposal to Improve Immigration Policy." It is endorsed by Julian Simon in *The Economic Consequences of Immigration*, pp. 329–35. Becker's proposal has been implemented in part. The 1990 Immigration Act created a category of "investor immigrants." This includes 7,000 visas for investors of $1 million or more in urban areas and 3,000 visas for investors of $500,000 or more in rural areas.

41. A note on the politics of immigration. As Otis L. Graham, Jr., suggests, it is a mistake to equate immigration restriction with xenophobia or reaction; "Illegal Immigration and the Left," *Dissent* 29 (Summer 1980). Historically, elements of organized labor, including unions made up largely of immigrants, have favored restrictive immigration policies because they feared that unlimited immigration depressed wages and standards, created a bottom tier of immigrant workers, and prevented changes in the structure of the secondary labor market. For Graham's more recent statements on this issue, see "Immigration and the National Interest," in *U.S. Immigration in the 1980s: Reappraisal and Reform*, ed. David Simcox, pp. 124–36; and "Uses and Misuses of History in the Debate Over Immigration Reform," *The Public Historian*, 8, no. 2 (Spring 1986): 41–64.

Although working-class opposition to immigration often stemmed from xenophobia and racism, other legitimate interests were also involved. This has been acknowledged by John Higham, author of *Strangers in the Land*—the classic history of nativism—in the preface to the book's second edition. In the revised edition of *Send These to Me: Immigrants in Urban America* (Baltimore: Johns Hopkins University Press, 1984), Higham writes sympathetically of the Simpson-Mazzoli bill, which included sanctions on employers who hired undocumented workers. The commission that led to the passage of this legislation was headed by a prominent liberal, Father Theodore Hesburgh.

On the other hand, free-market economists and business interests have championed the cause of expanded immigration. See, for example: M. S. Forbes, Jr., "We Need More People," *Forbes* (February 9, 1987); "The Rekindled Flame," Editorial, *Wall Street Journal*, July 3, 1989; Michael J. Mandel and Christopher Farrell, "The Immigrant: How They're Helping to Revitalize the U.S. Economy," *Business Week* (July 13, 1992); Wattenberg and Zinsmeister, "The Case for More Immigration," pp. 19–25; and Simon, "The Case for Greatly Increased Immigration," pp. 89–103.

42. Heidrick and Stuggles, Inc., "Chief Personnel Executives Look at Blacks in Business," cited in Sharon M. Collins, "The Making of the Black Middle Class," *Social Problems* 30 (April 1983): 379. See also Sharon M. Collins, "The Marginalization of Black Executives," *Social Problems* 36 (October 1989): 317–29; and idem, "Blacks on the Bubble: The Vulnerability of Black Executives in White Corporations," *Sociological Quarterly* 34 (August 1993): 429–47.

43. Collins, "The Making of the Black Middle Class," p. 377.

44. Ibid. p. 379.

45. Also to be considered are the many and subtle ways in which old-fashioned racism afflicts even the black middle class. For two recent works, see Joe E. Feagin and Melvin P. Sikes, *Living with Racism* (Boston: Beacon Press, 1994); and David Wellman, *Portraits of White Racism* (Cambridge: Cambridge University Press, 1993).

46. Michael K. Brown and Steven P. Erie, "Blacks and the Legacy of the Great Society: The Economic and Political Impact of Federal Social Policy," *Public Policy* 29 (Summer 1981): 301.

47. Collins, "The Making of the Black Middle Class," p. 379.

48. John Bound and Richard B. Freeman, "Black Economic Progress: Erosion of the Post-1965 Gains in the 1980s," in *The Question of Discrimination*, ed. Shulman and Darity, p. 47.

49. Michael de Courcy Hinds, "Minority Business Set Back Sharply by Courts' Rulings," *New York Times*, December 23, 1991.

50. For example, when the Reagan administration reduced social spending between 1980 and 1981, 76 percent of the 400 employees laid off in Chicago's Department of Human Services were black, as were 40 percent of the 186 workers laid off in the Department of Health. In contrast, the federal cutbacks barely affected the predominantly white work force in Chicago's Streets and Sanitation Department, which is funded with local revenues; Collins, "The Making of the Black Middle Class," p. 377.

51. Piven and Cloward, *Poor People's Movements*, p. 184.

52. As Margaret Weir points out with respect to the 1960s: "This decade of intellectual ferment and policy experimentation left a surprisingly meager legacy for employment policy. Labor market policy became subsumed into the poverty program, offering job preparation to those on the fringes on the labor market, and to the black poor in particular"; *Politics and Jobs* (Princeton, N.J.: Princeton University Press, 1992). For an incisive analysis of the political functions of job training programs, see Gordon Lafer, "Minority Unemployment, Labor Market Segmentation, and the Failure of Job Training Policy in New York City," *Urban Affairs Quarterly* 28 (December 1992).

53. *Employment and Earnings, January 1995*, U.S. Department of La-

bor, Bureau of Labor Statistics (Washington, D.C.: Government Printing Office).

54. David H. Swinton, "The Economic Status of African Americans: 'Permanent' Poverty and Inequality," in *The State of Black America* (Washington, D.C.: National Urban League, 1991), p. 53. Swinton states that the remainder of the overall shortage is due to demographic factors.

55. "Quarterly Economic Report on the African American Worker," National Urban League, Report No. 32 (September 1992): 1.

56. Jim Sleeper writes: ". . . . what kinds of hard work and moral discipline may people who envision a democratic and just society demand even of the poorest and most oppressed; what, indeed, would it be condescending and worse not to demand of 'the least among us'?" *The Closest of Strangers* (New York: W. W. Norton, 1990), p. 37. Regarding the scarcity of jobs, see George James, "The Job Is Picking Up Garbage; 100,000 Want It," *New York Times*, September 21, 1990.

57. At least in principle, this has been government policy over the past half-century. With the passage of the Employment Act of 1946, a large bipartisan majority in Congress endorsed the principle that "it is the continuing policy and responsibility of the Federal government" to bring about "conditions under which there will be afforded useful employment opportunities . . . for those able, willing, and seeking work." This principle was affirmed in the 1978 Humphrey-Hawkins Act. Except for a few sporadic attempts at government job creation programs, however, the mechanisms to achieve full employment have never been put into place. On the contrary, government fiscal policy is commonly used to engineer unemployment in order to contain inflation. For an astute analysis of "the political collapse of full employment," see Weir, *Politics and Jobs*, Chapter 5.

58. Briggs, *Mass Immigration and the National Interest*, p. 219.

59. David H. Hackworth, "This Was No Riot, It Was a Revolt," *Newsweek* (May 11, 1992): 30; and ibid., (May 25, 1992): 33.

60. Leonard Silk, "Riots Put Focus on Economic Ills," *New York Times*, May 8, 1992.

Chapter 10. America Again at the Crossroads

1. Eric Foner, *Reconstruction: America's Unfinished Revolution, 1863–1877* (New York: Harper & Row, 1988).

2. W. E. B. Du Bois, *Black Reconstruction* (New York: Harcourt, Brace, 1935), p. 30.

3. Neil R. McMillen, *Dark Journey: Black Mississippians in the Age of Jim Crow* (Urbana and Chicago: University of Illinois Press, 1989), p. 38.

4. Foner, *Reconstruction: America's Unfinished Revolution, 1863–1877*, p. 236.

5. Gunnar Myrdal, *An American Dilemma: The Negro Problem and Modern Democracy* (New York: Harper & Row, 1944), p. 237.

6. Nell Irvin Painter, *Exodusters* (New York: Knopf, 1977), p. 159.

7. Myrdal, *An American Dilemma*, pp. 189–90.

8. An exception is Peter Uhlenberg, "Noneconomic Determinants of Nonmigration: Sociological Considerations for Migration Theory," *Rural Sociology* 38 (Fall 1973): 296.

9. Nell Irvin Painter's excellent study, *Exodusters*, was published in 1977.

10. A second field trip involved oral histories and the production of a film under a grant from the Ethnic Heritage Studies Program of the Office of Education.

11. John G. Van Deusen, *The Black Man in White America* (Washington, D.C.: Associated Publishers, 1944), p. 30. See also Stephen Steinberg, *The Ethnic Myth* (Boston: Beacon Press, 1989), Chapter 7.

12. Myrdal, *An American Dilemma*, p. 997.

13. Ibid., p. 821.

14. Francis Fox Piven and Richard A. Cloward, *Poor People's Movements* (New York: Vintage Books, 1979), p. 205.

15. For an assessment of the impact of the civil rights movement on Southern blacks, see James Button, *Blacks and Social Change* (Princeton, N.J.: Princeton University Press, 1989).

16. For detailed analyses of income trends and related issues, see Gerald David Jaynes and Robin M. Williams, Jr., *A Common Destiny* (Washington, D.C.: National Academy Press, 1989), especially Chapter 6. See also Gerald David Jaynes, "The Labor Market Status of Black Americans: 1939–1985," *Journal of Economic Perspectives* (Fall 1990); 9–24; James P. Smith and Finis R. Welch, "Black Economic Progress After Myrdal," *Journal of Economic Literature* 27 (June 1989): 119–164; and Reynolds Farley, *Blacks and Whites: Narrowing the Gap?* (Cambridge, Mass.: Harvard University Press, 1984).

17. These themes are at the center of a number of recent works: Katherine S. Newman, *Falling from Grace: The Experience of Downward Mobility in the American Middle Class* (New York: Free Press, 1988); Michael W. Haga, *Is the American Dream Dying?* (Denver: Acclaim Publishing, 1994); Lillian B. Rubin, *Families in the Front Line* (New York: HarperCollins, 1994).

18. *Statistical Abstracts of the United States*, 1994 (Washington, D.C.:

Government Printing Office, 1994), p. 475; *Income, Poverty, and Valuation of Non-Cash Benefits*, Current Population Reports, series P-60, no. 188 (Washington, D.C.: Government Printing Office, 1993).

19. *Statistical Abstracts of the United States, 1994* (Washington, D.C.: Government Printing Office, 1994), p. 475.

20. The time period under examination was 1974–1983. Terry K. Adams, Greg J. Duncan, and Willard L. Rodgers, "The Persistence of Urban Poverty," in *Quiet Riots*, ed. Fred R. Harris and Roger W. Wilkins (New York: Pantheon, 1988), pp. 83–85. Another study reports that while 63 percent of whites who are in poverty are there for only one year, the figure for blacks is 48 percent. The percentage of those in poverty for seven years or more is 4 percent for whites, but 15 percent for blacks; Peter Gottschalk, Sara McLanahan, and Gary D. Sandefur, "The Dynamics and Intergenerational Transmission of Poverty and Welfare Participation," in *Confronting Poverty*, ed. Sheldon H. Danziger, Gary D. Sandefur, and Daniel H. Weinberg (Cambridge, Mass.: Harvard University Press, 1994), p. 94.

21. "The severely distressed" is a composite measure consisting of five factors: low education; single parenthood; poor work history; public assistance recipiency; and poverty. John D. Kasarda, "The Severely Distressed in Economically Transforming Cities," in *Drugs, Crime, and Social Isolation*, ed. Adele V. Harrell and George E. Peterson (Washington, D.C.: The Urban Institute Press, 1992), pp. 49–54.

22. Roger Wilkins, "The New Political Linguistics of Race: A Debate," *Socialist Review* 16 (May–August, 1986): 65–66.

23. Thomas Byrne Edsall with Mary D. Edsall, "When the Official Subject Is Presidential Politics, Taxes, Welfare, Crime, Rights, or Values . . . the Real Subject Is RACE," *Atlantic Monthly* 269 (1991): 53–86; this theme is further developed in their book *Chain Reaction* (New York: W. W. Norton, 1991), especially Chapters 10 and 11.

24. Tyler Bridges has observed that the Republican National Committee worked toward Duke's defeat because "defeating Duke would help diminish charges that the party was racist, a charge most recently provoked by the Willie Horton television ad during the 1988 presidential campaign"; *The Rise of David Duke* (Jackson: University Press of Mississippi, 1994), p. 151.

25. Eric Foner, *Reconstruction: America's Unfinished Revolution, 1863–1877*, p. 604.

26. Richard J. Herrnstein and Charles Murray, *The Bell Curve: Intelligence and Class Structure in American Life* (New York: Free Press, 1994).

27. Adolph Reed, Jr., "Looking Backward," *The Nation* (November 28, 1994): 661–62.

28. According to Charles Lane, Herrnstein and Murray cite thirteen

scholars who were beneficiaries of grants over the last two decades totalling over $4 million. Seventeen researchers cited in the bibliography have contributed to *Mankind Quarterly*, a neo-fascist journal that espouses the genetic superiority of the white race; "The Tainted Sources of 'The Bell Curve,'" *New York Review of Books* (December 1, 1994), p. 15. The role of the Pioneer Fund in underwriting research on race and IQ was also the subject of a report on ABC news with Peter Jennings, November 22, 1994.

29. Jason DeParle, "Daring Research or 'Social Science Pornography'?" *New York Times Magazine* (October 9, 1994): p. 48; "IQ: Is It Destiny?" *Newsweek* (October 24, 1994); Richard Lacayo, "For Whom the Bell Curves: A New Book Raises a Ruckus by Linking Intelligence to Genetics and Race," *Time* (October 24, 1994). Charles Murray and Richard J. Herrnstein, "Race, Genes and I.Q.—An Apologia," *The New Republic* (October 31, 1994): 27–37; the issue included responses from an array of critics.

30. Gerald D. Berryman, "Race, Caste, and Other Invidious Distinctions in Social Stratification," reprinted in *Majority and Minority*, ed. Norman R. Yetman (Boston: Allyn & Bacon, 1991), p. 22.

31. For recent documentation of the increase in the absolute and relative rates of poverty, and the growing gap between those at the top and those at the bottom of the income distribution, see Sheldon H. Danziger and Daniel H. Weinberg, "The Historical Record: Trends in Family Income, Inequality, and Poverty," in *Confronting Poverty*, ed. Sheldon H. Danziger, Gary D. Sandefur, and Daniel H. Weinberg, pp. 18–50.

32. Reed, "Looking Backward," p. 661.

33. "*The Bell Curve*: A Symposium," *The National Review* (December 5, 1994): 32–61.

34. Myrdal, *An American Dilemma*, p. 997.

35. Lerone Bennett, "Tea and Sympathy: Liberals and Other White Hopes," in Bennett, *The Negro Mood and Other Essays* (Chicago: Johnson Publications, 1963), p. 22.

36. Martin Luther King, Jr., *I Have a Dream: Writing and Speeches that Changed the World*, ed. James Melvin Washington (New York: HarperCollins, 1992), p. 103.

Index

Clark, Kenneth, 74, 112, 137
Class: concepts of race and, 52–55, 85–86,
    123–124, 137, 139–140, 149–155, 217,
    245n.51; and culture, 13, 15–16, 85,
    139–142. *See also* Underclass
Cleaver, Eldridge, 70
Clinton, Bill, 125, 245n.48, 246n.72,
    251n.47; and Cornel West, 132; and Wil-
    liam Julius Wilson, 125, 245n.48
Cloward, Richard A., 198, 237n.3
Cobbs, Price, 74–79
Collins, Sharon, 196–197
Colonial analogy, 2–3, 88–89, 185,
    236n.67, 237n.82; arguments against,
    89–93
Color-blindness, and racism, 85–86, 104,
    124–125, 135–136, 140, 174
Color line, in industrial jobs, 180, 209
Commager, Henry Steele, 52–53
Commentary roundtable, 110–112
Commissions, riot. *See* "Riots"
Communists, 41, 55, 63
Compensatory programs for blacks: need for,
    67, 72, 73, 109–110; opposition to, 116–
    119, 168–175; as reverse racism, 147–
    148, 168–171, 173, 241n.10; success of,
    166–168
Conot, Robert, 71
Consent Decree, AT&T-EEO, 101–102, 166,
    238n.12
Conservatives: black, 123–134; white, 98–
    100, 119–123, 218
Corporations, affirmative action in, 147–
    148, 166–167, 174, 196
Couch, W. T., 47–48
Cox, Oliver C., 21, 44–45, 223n.1,
    226n.67
Craniology, 29–31, 32–33
Crespi, Leo, 46
Crisis in Black and White (Silberman), 68,
    71–74, 231n.15
Cruse, Harold, 89, 235n.53, 236n.67
Culture: and class, 141–142, 200; deviant
    subculture, 5, 8–10, 91, 119–120, 128–
    132, 139, 141–142; ghetto, 128–132,
    139–140, 154, 199–200; of "hyphenated"
    American groups, 9, 14–15; material
    sources and functions of, 13–14
Culture of poverty, 5–6, 8–10, 119–120,
    128–132, 139–142, 154, 243n.38,
    246n.72, 250n.45, 264n.20. *See also*
    Underclass

Daniels, John, 38–39
Darity, William, Jr., 255n.8

Dark Ghetto (Clark), 74
Davis, Angela, 70
The Declining Significance of Race (Wilson),
    123–124, 125–126, 142–143,
    244nn.41,43, 245n.51
Degler, Carl, 65–67
Deindustrialization, 143–149, 183, 248n.21
Democratic Party: and black voters, 25; lib-
    eral Southern coalition, 53, 60, 98; in the
    1960s, 82–83, 97–98; race-neutral poli-
    cies of, 117–118, 124–125, 249n.31; and
    white backlash, 98, 237n.3, 241n.18
Dennis, Rutledge M., 229n.42
Depression, the Great, 24, 35, 198
Detlefson, Robert, 103, 238n.19
Deutscher, Isaac, 162
Dionne, E. J., 246n.72
Discrimination: employment, 27–28, 144,
    147, 182–185, 250n.37, 256n.15; em-
    ployment agency, 152, 250n.39; occupa-
    tional apartheid, 46, 179–195; patterns of,
    27–28, 39–40, 147, 149, 196–198; pres-
    ent-day and historic, 160–162, 248n.24,
    254n.1. *See also* Institutionalized racism;
    Unemployment
Dixiecrats, Democratic Party, 53, 60, 98
Du Bois, W. E. B., 51, 61, 81, 82, 133, 169,
    205
Duke, David, 214, 264n.24
Duncan, Otis Dudley, 137

Edsall, Thomas B. and Mary D., 214,
    237nn.2–3, 264n.23
Education: and black unemployment, 145,
    148, 199, 248n.22; as a remedy for pov-
    erty, 123–124, 148, 151; as a remedy for
    racism, 66, 69, 74, 118, 151; and social
    mobility, 105, 123–124, 148, 244n.41
Elections, national: racial issues in, 97–98,
    138, 204, 213–214
Elkins, Stanley, 81, 234n.42
Employment. *See* Jobs; Labor markets;
    Unemployment
Employment Act of 1946, 201, 262n.57
Employment discrimination. *See*
    Discrimination
Epstein, Joseph, 157–158
Equal Employment Opportunity Commis-
    sion (EEOC), 101–102, 167, 201
Equality: and identity, 131, 133, 169; and
    liberty, 109, 114, 118, 164–165, 242n.20
Equality of opportunity, 78, 113–114,
    235n.48
The Ethnic Myth (Steinberg), 15
European immigration. *See* Immigration